T0354942

TEACHING
BABY**GANGSTERS**

REFORM SCHOOL OR EDUCATIONAL REFORM?

MARILYN K. GIFFORD

iUniverse, Inc.
Bloomington

iUniverse books may be ordered through booksellers or by contacting:

iUniverse
1663 Liberty Drive
Bloomington, IN 47403
www.iuniverse.com
1-800-Authors (1-800-288-4677)

ISBN: 978-1-4502-7925-3 (sc)
ISBN: 978-1-4502-7926-0 (hc)
ISBN: 978-1-4502-7927-7 (ebook)

Printed in the United States of America

iUniverse rev. date: 01/13/2011

To my granddaughter Kailey who has encouraged me to write this book. For all of my former middle school students who taught me as much as I taught them. For all the public school teachers, administrators and staff who dedicate their time and talents to teach our nation's youth.

To parents, I would say, you are my real heroes when you manage to raise beautiful, healthy children in our inner city neighborhoods while surrounded with drug use, gangs and violence.

My thoughts and prayers are with you all.

"Children are a heritage of the Lord"

Psalms 127: 3

King James Version Holy Bible

Table of Contents

1. Setting the Scene

Our alternative school was located at a crossroads of a major highway and a belt line around the inner-part of the city which made it easy for students throughout the district to reach our location by rail or bus. The location was especially convenient for low-income families who lived in public housing or moderate priced apartment complexes nearby the school. The structure was a simple one story concrete building hardly distinguishable between a maintenance facility and a school, except the words learning center were on the building and a flag pole was in the yard. The name was hardly noticeable from the street but could be seen from the parking lot that encircled the building. District school buses were parked in a fenced area behind our building and this vehicle storage area may have added to our school's satellite facility appearance.

The school housed alternative education programs for grades from the first through the twelfth. One hallway of the building contained middle school classrooms which were designated according to core class subjects: science, math, English, and social studies. The special education room, foreign language room, and the ISS (in school suspension) rooms were on our same hall. The school contained both a library and a computer lab which were used by all grade levels. Due to the nature of the student population we served, our classrooms were small and designed to hold no more than twelve students at one time but the capacity was exceeded frequently at the beginning of my employment. Therefore, classrooms were often overcrowded and students were difficult to supervise in the small confined areas. The threat of student violence was always escalated when overcrowding occurred because students were never an arm's length away from each other.

Our immediate surrounding neighborhood was a combination of business strip malls and residential dwellings. The city police department building was no more than ten city blocks away and was located on our same street. Along the highway-frontage road that ran directly behind our school were restaurants and office buildings in an area often referred to as the technology corridor. Most apartment complexes in the area were either totally unsafe or they were moderate to high-end, expensive, gated communities. Therefore, I did not live in a neighborhood close to the school. Originally, since I was new to the area, I had placed a down payment on an apartment around the corner from my school thinking I could walk to work. However, when I went for a final inspection of the reserved apartment, I happened upon a drug deal going down in the parking lot and I was greeted by a garbage sack hanging off a tree next to the complex's dumping container. It appeared as if someone had simply opened their patio door, aimed for the dumpster and missed while hanging their trash up in a tree. Needless to say, I forfeited my deposit and found an affordable and safe apartment complex in the district which was only a fifteen minute driving distance away. For the first three years, I lived in the school district until my apartment complex started experiencing daylight break-ins then I purchased a small home in the suburbs which turned out to be less expensive than living in an apartment in my district.

Our school's neighborhood location inspired safety concerns for staff and during my first two years of employment, teachers were told not to stay after students departed the building or keep students after regular school hours for discipline. Although this severely limited some of the consequences we could give students, our principal's concern for staff's safety was appreciated. Our building continued to receive security upgrades throughout my employment and teachers were eventually able to provide after school discipline and tutoring services for students.

Most of my students were suspended from their home schools due to conduct punishable as a felony on school property, a few wore ankle monitors, and others were using our school to transition from the juvenile justice system back to a traditional classroom. Many of these students had committed offenses equal to adult felonies. My middle school students were a challenge to motivate because they had too much drama going on in their daily lives. These youth were often functioning like adults outside of school and due to this, many resented adult authority. Yet, they were emotionally delayed, vulnerable, and at some level, wanted an adult to be in charge. These students evidenced they were life-stressed and some demonstrated extreme anxiety disorders. These middle school youth often made poor choices regarding their own welfare and they could have been categorized as risk takers.

Some were parents at thirteen or fourteen years old, were well on their way to developing addiction problems, and many were heavily involved in gang initiated crime. Students were members of well known gangs like the Bloods, Cripps, Latin Kings or others. Gang membership was more a rule than an exception among my students. It was not unusual to have rival gang members present in the same classroom but I found negotiating a truce between these two factions was possible. I had 'Chunked the Duce' on more than one occasion when things looked like they were getting out of hand and reminded my students that school was neutral territory for them. Once I informed these middle school children that I was in charge of the classroom and they were not students honored me with the title OG, "Original Gangster." They added a Miss to the title and I became Miss OG. Although I had encouraged students to call me Mrs. Gifford or allowed them to use Mrs. G, students continued to call me Miss OG which indicated they were giving respect to the authority in the classroom.

After a while, I became accepting of the title because it brought with it compliance to my classroom rules and I realized that my honorary OG title increased my students feelings of safety. I surmised students wanted to know the turf assignment in school since they were territorial in their home neighborhoods. I believe that when I verbally told the students the classroom belonged to me it may have relieved some of their anxiety about rival challenges. However, students became curious and started quizzing me about my gang affiliation and I informed them my gang members were students who were interested in getting an education and no other type of gang activity would be allowed in my classroom. I know I gained the students' respect and I gained compliance to my classroom rules when I acknowledged the nickname students chose for me and allowed them to use it.

In the beginning, I was more than a little concerned what the administrator at our school might think about my new nickname but it never became an issue. So, I developed a personification to match the title just to relate to the kids and before I knew it, stories were circulating about me among the middle school students with reference to a life I had never lived. Then,

I became really worried what my supervisor might think if he heard the middle school rumors! Regardless of my apprehensions, baby gangsters relinquished all claims to my classroom territory as long as I played the part of an old-school thug so I continued to personify Miss OG throughout my employment at the alternative school.

Some of our students were gang members and they were special education students. Up to one half of our student population could be receiving special education services and many could have been classified as (EBD) emotionally behavior disordered. These students could be particularly challenging because they were prescribed psychotropic drugs and used illegal drugs or drank alcohol in combination with their prescription medications. Their behaviors were pretty much unpredictable and could become suddenly unmanageable or even dangerous. Many of these students had individual aids assigned to them at their home schools who sat next to them in every class so their classroom teachers could present a lesson. Our alternative school teachers did not have that same support of individual aids and we could have more than one behavioral disordered student assigned to our class that needed one. Our school schedule compounded our problematic EBD population assignments because all special education students had to be placed in the same class section. There was a seventh grade special education section and an eighth grade special education section. Due to our scheduling restrictions, I could have more special education students assigned to me, without an aid to help, than what the special education teacher had in her classroom.

The special education placement rule for traditional teachers is one special needs student per ten traditional students. That rule did not apply at the alternative school and when my class sections became both filled exclusively with special education students and the classroom population exceeded the physical capacity of the room, I had to make drastic changes in my teaching style to maintain order and ensure student safety. Our special education population spent more than one year in the same grade which allowed them extra time to learn the curriculum but placed them chronologically up to four years older than most their classmates. When this happened, special education students often resented or blamed teachers for their failure and could cause severe disruptions in the classroom. Many of these students were repeat placements at our alternative school and entered and exited our program through a revolving door. Once these special education students chose to join gangs, the threat of danger was often intensified toward educators because part of their initiation could be "Go to school and beat up a teacher." All the middle school staff was warned of this possibility during teachers' meetings.

The summation of our school's student profile was pretty much what anyone would expect in a large inner-city district. Students served were: Hispanic, African American, Caucasian, Asian, and a small percentage were from Middle Eastern countries. A high proportion of all these came from low-income families. However, these students had one thing in common; they were being raised in a homogenous culture of the inner city where illegal activities and drug use create the economy of neighborhoods and through violent acts, gangs maintain the status quo. Due to this, the students were familiar with each other, had developed ways of communicating to confound the staff, and continued to use drugs and carry drugs to school. The school staff was always on high alert regarding the safety of our students and ourselves but we were never totally effective in eliminating the toxic influences of drugs and gangs from our classrooms.

Teaching children who are under the influence or distracted by their need to obtain, use or deal drugs during the school day posed unique challenges to our staff. These distractions and resulting safety issues which accompany drug use, evidence why unique educational reforms are needed to help inner city students focus on their education. However, the problems our alternative education staff encountered with our student population were not unique in our school district. Teachers who taught in traditional classrooms faced the same problems because our students were returned to their home schools after spending a few short weeks in our alternative education setting.

Students were assigned attendance at our school based on levels of offense. Most students had to earn thirty good days, equal to six weeks of school, in order to process back to their traditional classrooms. When a student was awarded a good day it meant that a student was in compliance with our program rules. Initially, teachers were tempted to give students good days when they did not deserve them because some challenging students were not a good match for our program and we just wanted them gone. After all, alternative teachers could not refer students to a different school or program when they misbehaved. The only way students left our program was to either successfully complete it or get arrested and sent to another education program in juvenile detention. We could get stuck with students who were not in compliance to our program and who were not earning good days. The staff relied heavily upon our special education director's expertise and her ability to complete referrals for these troubled youth who obviously needed more specialized services than what our program could provide. Many of these students who caused the majority of discipline problems at our alternative school had both started using drugs and were classified as learning disabled. Their limited academic abilities were hindered further by their drug use and their behavior problems intensified when illegal drug consumption was added to their prescribed medications.

Since the teachers at the alternative school had a very small window of time to work with our students, we could not fix these kids; we could only initiate change, if we were lucky. We had to gain the students' acquiescence to our program quickly, evaluate the student's learning gaps, and provide academic interventions to help these students regain their education momentum. The students who did not do well in our program were often students who posed extreme threats to the safety of their classmates and teachers. It became necessary to identify students quickly who might be disposed to violence or who would constantly disrupt class. Any evidence of program non-compliance had to be met with swift discipline or teachers would lose the ability to teach. Classroom structure and school rules could not be negotiated with students and students had to accept responsibility for their actions.

My job had some unique challenges since forty percent of the time my students were supposed to be involved in lab activities. Some of my students had been sent to our school for their irresponsible behaviors in science lab, they could not be trusted with anything that could start a fire, and all labs involving glass and other hazardous material had to be closely supervised. It was particularly difficult to provide clinical activities because I did not have an aide assigned to help me with special education students and the special education teacher did not always have time to provide assistance. My last year of teaching, I received the help of an elementary special education aide which made lab activities much easier to manage.

Many of my students had could not read or do math above a third grade level. Teaching chemistry and physics without students being able to comprehend written assignments or do homework without assistance caused me to spend extra long hours planning. I had to break down the required concepts into manageable bites of learning. Many students who could not read were also very slow at copying notes in their science journals so I had to give simplified, printed class notes and furnish highlighters for those students so they could identify their vocabulary words. Other students could not understand lab instructions so often clinical labs had to be demonstrated the day before, reviewed prior to doing the labs, and extra time had to be allowed for the students to complete labs on their own. The process was laborious and there never was enough time in the scope and sequence to fully teach the required concepts to these students who were delayed. It frustrated me to see these students who had documented disabilities struggle to learn something they would never use or need to know as an adult. The material covered was often not relevant to their abilities or their future education and career goals. It was not pragmatic for them and they were smart enough to know it was a waste of their time and many said so.

However, the thing that frustrated me most was that many of my students did not remember what had been taught the day before and it was almost impossible to build upon concepts supposedly learned without extensive daily reviews. My students were engaged in learning but they just did not retain. I always received the highest marks on my teacher evaluation for student engagement because all my students participated in class, they said they liked science, and they were all engaged in learning when I was observed. However, many of my students just could not remember and my additional time spent tutoring these children did not always improve their outcomes. Their short term memories could have been damaged from either prenatal drug use by their parents or their own use of marijuana, inhalants, or other drugs. Something was just off with these students because many of them, regardless of their lack of interest, really tried hard to please me and acquire the information.

In addition to teaching core courses at two grade levels, seventh and eighth grades, middle school staff had two elective classes to teach which were named Personal and Social Responsibilities and Learning Power. The learning Power Classes were often extensions of core courses and helped prepare students to take the end of the year state test which measured student academic growth. Our PSR (Personal and Social Responsibility) class did not have a specific curriculum so additional researching and planning was required to prepare for this job assignment. I used my prior experience as a substance abuse educator and made the focus of my PSR class alcohol and substance abuse prevention. I encouraged open dialogue about issues the students wanted to discuss and gave them correct information based on research. Often, I had the students use the computer lab to research for themselves the effects of alcohol and drug use on their bodies and minds. I felt the PSR class was the one element of our program which allowed me to develop a relationship with my students and the relationship building afforded by this one class, may have prevented some discipline problems in my classroom. Students expressed trust in me, in regards to giving them straight answers about substance abuse and other teen issues and many times students would ask questions which related directly to their own personal drug use or life decisions openly in class.

I do want my readers to understand the student's problems did not go away just because they were sent to an alternative school nor was I an expert at dealing with the children's unique and individualized behaviors. Quite the contrary, sometimes the problems were magnified because the students reinforced each others' negative actions and I often flew by the seat of my pants when confronted with unexpected situations needing a discipline intervention. However, educators gain expertise in managing students' behaviors and covering the curriculum, in a sink or swim fashion regardless of the teaching assignment so I learned and used what worked with this population.

The purpose for writing this book is to put the readers in touch with the realities teachers face in today's large city school district classrooms and to inspire an open dialogue about educational reforms. I believe my goals are best served by sharing my students' stories. In these stories, I have changed the names of the children, staff and other entities to protect their privacy and I have consciously made an effort to change any details of communication exchanged where a person could identify anyone involved. These stories are not in chronological order and the incidents told are from different teaching assignments in two different states. Although most of the stories recorded here come from my alternative school assignment there are some incidents recorded which relate back to a previous teaching experience or back to my social work career. Therefore, no one should assume the stories portrayed here happened at one particular school or during one time period and no one should imagine a character or event relates to them.

In order to make the stories flow, for literary purposes only, I have inserted dialogue which may not be exact though it portrays the veracity of the situation. This book, Teaching Baby Gangsters, is about my middle school students' lives and how they overcame difficulties to succeed in school or how they gave into their environmental influences and failed to get an education. At the end of each story, I have inserted research and recommended education reforms based on my experiences with these students. I would ask that my readers be gentle as they glimpse into the lives of my middle school students for they are just children and who they are or who they will become, has not yet been determined! Since students should be considered partners in their own education, let's try to identify their needs when considering education reforms; I hope some of the stories recorded here will prove useful for this purpose.

Why should someone in rural America care about the stories of my students? Take a good look and listen to teen culture. The dress, the music, and the language of the inner city have already spread to Midwest farmland communities. Teen culture born in large cities makes its way into the hearts and minds of all young people through expressions of music, dress, and speech. Inner city kids are setting the standard for what is cool, sweet, and fly. Drug use is not limited to students attending inner city schools and certainly there are pockets of rural and suburban use which parallels the inner city student population.

Lost human potential is another reason why we should all care. The children I taught were creative and evidenced problem solving by surviving in a hostile living environment. These students were smart and they had potential. However, many of my inner city students are currently teetering on a tightrope strung between a life of drug addiction and crime on one side, to obtaining an education and being a good citizen on the other side. After teaching in a large city school district, I am concerned about the academic failure of our upcoming citizens and how it might affect our country's ability to remain a free nation. Other educators and politicians might be concerned more about our future citizens not being able to read or do math at an acceptable level but a few of us, who acknowledge student drug use as a primary issue, dread a future generation of people entrusted with our country who may not care what direction our nation takes as long as they have access to their drugs of choice. We are losing young people every day to the streets because drugs and gangs have established a strong hold in our inner city neighborhoods. Youth growing up in perverted, drug-economy based neighborhoods may not know there are other ways to live. Some of these young people have special abilities and talents they will never recognize and their uniqueness may be needed by the rest of us, in a national time of trouble.

I want everyone to know the school districts I have worked for accomplished amazing things with the populations they served. One of the districts received state and national recognition for their achievements educating at-risk students. It was an honor to work with such dedicated individuals who put the welfare and education of their students first and who sacrificed their own family time to encourage and educate some of the neediest inner city children in the United States. For the most part, I believe educators' efforts are still unrecognized because public school teachers are being maligned as incompetent when their students fail to achieve. However, good educators are handicapped by an archaic education model which promotes failure and spawns student dropout rates. At the same time, students are destroying their bodies and minds with drug and alcohol use while limiting their own abilities to learn. Both of these things, our archaic education system and student drug use, should become topics of academic reform.

Teacher incompetency should not be the main focus of reform. Regardless of teacher unions and contracts, federal employment laws allow for termination of incompetent employees with proper documentation. In addition, teachers are the most evaluated employees on the face of the Earth and there are ample opportunities to fire incompetent teachers. Today, most teachers have to post their lesson plans and maintain a web page for students and parents. Teaching supervisors can access these sites to determine if educators are following the scope and sequence of the assigned curriculum and they can evaluate some of their teachers' interactions with parents via the net. In addition, principals can listen into classrooms, in real time, through communication systems used to make school announcements and without specific prior notice, supervising principals, department chairs or even regional directors of education can walk in to a teachers' classroom for the purposes of observation and evaluation. Finally, in some instances there are cameras in schools that document teacher-student interactions on film that can be replayed. Minute by minute, teachers can be observed and transparency has been steadily increasing with technological advancements. It should be literally impossible for an incompetent teacher to escape notice and their terminations should be executed swiftly with the level of scrutiny now in place. It is illogical to assume that incompetent teachers bare sole responsibility for failing students or teacher unions and contracts are more powerful or binding than federal employment laws applied to other professionals.

The level of current educator accountability should cause us to look beyond teacher incompetency as the primary reason for student failures. Therefore, this book will try to identify other factors which might be overlooked by an ordinary citizen without a complete knowledge of our failing education system. For this reason, there are documented articles at the end of each student story that address reforms which are needed to help students, like the ones in the stories, succeed in school. There are also processing questions at the end of each story with suggestions for things readers can do to become more informed or help students combat some of the negative events in their lives. I have not shied away from difficult topics like: drug testing, sexual harassment, bullying or other things because these are real life issues teachers' face in middle school classrooms today.

Education reform will not be a one size fits all solution and every school district will have to decide priorities when attacking such important issues as the ones recorded here. I just pray that districts will first look at improving classroom environments by identifying student drug use and limit the influence of both drugs and gangs in our inner city schools. Schools have tried in the past but have failed to do this. Certainly, there are strategies in this book which may encourage new attempts at limiting our growing problem with drug affected students in our classrooms. Next, let's change our model to one that acknowledges students' ability levels and career interest. Our ever increasing learning disabled student population should motivate us to do this. It possible to accomplish individual instruction for all students with varied models; I have extolled some models here that show promise.

In closing, if this book enlightens parents, politicians, and educators or causes one school district to initiate a reform that makes a difference in the lives of young people then I will think the writing was well worth the effort. This book has been quickly put together due to the urgency of our nation's education reform interest and may not always be grammatically correct for that reason. I apologize to my readers in advance and hope you can look beyond the obvious errors to hear the message.

2. Street Lies

My students believed "Street Lies" which are basically denial statements which allow people to use drugs and alcohol or participate in high-risk behaviors. All of the statements exposed here evidence why young people may do some things which seem obviously destructive to the rest of us. In some instances, adults who are abusing substances may swear these same statements are true. I frequently read information published by NIDA, National Institute on Drug Abuse, and SAMHSA, Substance Abuse and Mental Health Services, U.S. Department of Health and Human Services. Both of these sources can be found on the internet by typing in the acronyms, NIDA.gov or SAMHSA.gov. I highly recommend interested individuals read these sources to update their knowledge base.

1. There is a cure for AIDS.
Students swore there was a cure for AIDS and listed famous people who had the disease and were still alive.

Truth: There is better medicine. At one time people infected by the HIV virus who contracted AIDS had to take a lot of pills each day in an effort to stay alive. Now, medicine has been developed which may keep the HIV infected person from ever developing the disease, AIDS, and one pill a day may be a reality. However, people who escape developing the disease still have the virus in their bodies and can pass the virus to someone else. If the virus could be entirely eliminated from an infected person and it did not come back after a certain amount of time, then that person would truly be cured. This has not happened to my knowledge. An official United States Health Department announcement has not been issued which states there is a cure for AIDS.

Outcomes: According to a NBC news announcement in January 2010, teen pregnancy rates increased by 3% in 2009. My local news channel announced that the fastest growing group of individuals contracting the HIV virus was young adults between the ages of thirteen and twenty-four. If teens believe there is a cure for AIDS they no longer have to protect themselves from this killer. Although the evening news program did not mention this as a cause of the pregnancy rate increase, teens at my school said they did not worry about using protection because there is a cure for AIDS. Also, teens acknowledged they lacked information about other STD's and resulting health problems like cervical cancer.

2. You can clean out your system and clean up your drug test by drinking bleach.
When asked how much bleach to drink the students offered a variety of answers about the amount and the ratio of bleach to water a person should drink. All of the mixing directions purposed would have damaged the human body. In addition, some students said drinking vinegar could do the same thing. Once again, students had a variety of mixing directions or amounts and some were very unhealthy.

Truth: Time is the only variable which can change the outcome of a drug test. Alcohol and drugs are processed by our internal organs and are broken down at different rates. Each toxin or poison takes a specific time for the body to process. Some pills can be purchased which aid with this process but they leave metabolites behind which identify an attempt to throw off the drug test. If someone drank bleach or vinegar and their test came back negative then it was probably due to the human error of the person performing the test.

Outcomes: Teens who are addicted to certain drugs and are in trouble with the justice system may routinely experiment ingesting substances while trying to beat their drug test. Drinking bleach is especially dangerous because it eats away skin cells and eats through blood vessels and could result in hemorrhages in the throat and stomach. Bleach contains chlorine, a dangerous poison.

3. Marijuana is natural because it comes from a plant and it is good for you.
Marijuana is a plant and it does have some medical uses. However, students could only list one benefit for healthy people; they said marijuana was good for stress relief or relaxation.

Truth: It is not the plant that causes problems; it is what humans do with the plant! Whenever something is burned (smoked) chemical changes occur. The chemicals produced vary in toxicity. One joint of marijuana may have toxins equal to smoking between five – fifty tobacco cigarettes. This is due to the development of marijuana hybrid plants which have increased toxicity from the original weed. In addition, seldom is marijuana the only drug in a joint. Drug dealers competing for customers cook up weird and sometimes dangerous concoctions. They lace the marijuana with: cocaine, PCP, LSD, Meth, and sometimes embalming fluid (wet weed). In addition, <u>doctors don't want humans to smoke anything</u>. Smoking damages the lungs and coats each individual air sac in the lungs with sticky substances which inhibit the exchanges of oxygen and carbon dioxide from our atmosphere. Eating marijuana which is cooked up in brownies or other foods may be more dangerous still because it travels through the digestive system and an overdose may occur. The latest research states that marijuana is addictive and does not only cause a psychological dependency as once thought. I asked my students, "If marijuana is safe to use because it comes from a plant then is cocaine safe to use because it comes from a plant? What about heroine; it comes from a plant too?"

Outcomes: If students believe Marijuana is safe because it comes from a natural plant then they will not hesitate to use the drug. This naturalization approach to drug use may be softening the public opinion about the acceptance of marijuana. In addition, most people who use marijuana smoke it. So, the same consequences can be expected for marijuana used by this method as smoking cigarettes. Increased lung cancer and other health concerns could result. Opposite to what teens believe, they actually may experience additional stress when smoking marijuana because they have to worry about being caught and receiving legal consequences.

4. Marijuana is good for the eyes and it cures cancer.
Many of my students were convinced by adults smoking marijuana that it was a remedy for cataracts and marijuana could prevent cancer.

Truth: Marijuana is <u>not</u> good for healthy eyes and the evidence of Marijuana's effects can be seen in the broken eye blood vessels of the user. It has no documented positive effect on cataracts by either preventing the development or halting the progress of that condition. There is one type of glaucoma, just one type out of many, which may be delayed by smoking marijuana. This type of glaucoma is the result of constricting blood vessels and Marijuana might act to enlarge those vessels. However, the person is not cured from this type of glaucoma by smoking Marijuana and the disease is probably only delayed. <u>There are other medications which work the same or better which do not require the patient to smoke and coat their lungs with chemical toxins which we know cause cancer.</u>

Continuing, Marijuana pills are available and are prescribed for cancer patients who are undergoing chemotherapy treatments. These pills alleviate nausea, increase appetite and may allow the patients to gain some weight thereby improving their all over health outcomes. It is possible that the use of marijuana pills may increase survival rates after treatment. However, marijuana does not cure cancer; it only helps patients develop an appetite while combating nausea. Again, Marijuana in the pill form is a better choice for these patients because someone who already has cancer does not need to expose their lungs to cancer causing toxins. In the future, there may be other uses found for this plant because most of our medicines come from plants.

Outcomes: This excuse is used by people who are in denial about the health risk associated with smoking Marijuana. They believe that the medical use of marijuana somehow legitimizes the recreational use of the drug. <u>Disease prevention is not a valid medical use of Marijuana.</u> Naturalization of marijuana use may inspire more young people to try the drug. <u>My students who were non users of marijuana said they would probably try the drug if it was legalized.</u> Here is another concern. Students who said they would not smoke tobacco cigarettes because they cause cancer and other health problems would smoke marijuana. If this drug is legalized then there should be extensive education about the health hazards of using marijuana. Education efforts have worked regarding the use of tobacco and prevention education focusing on this drug will be needed if Marijuana is legalized.

5. Boys can't get girls pregnant when they smoke Marijuana.
This has been added to the long wish list for males and serves as a persuasion when girls say no! Other excuses to which the reader might relate are: The mumps went down on me and I can't make babies or Girls can't get pregnant if they have sex standing up.

Truth: Marijuana affects the reproductive system of both males and females. Marijuana does influence the amount and the health of a male's sex gamete, the sperm. The male may not produce as much sperm or the sperm may become deformed. However, males manufacture sperm as it is needed and old sperm not used is discarded through body functions. The amount and frequency of Marijuana used are variables and not all males would be effected the same depending on their using patterns. Smoking Marijuana might have less affect on sperm production than soaking in a hot tub or wearing too tight of underwear; both of which can be short duration causes of infertility. However, females may face a greater risk of contributing to birth defects when they smoke weed because females are born with all the sex gametes they will ever have and do not manufacture eggs as needed. Scientific knowledge has,not identified an egg repairing mechanism in the female body so once an egg has been damaged through drug use it appears the egg would remain damaged and a resulting pregnancy which used that damaged egg, could result in a person born with genetic defects.

Outcomes: If teens believe this street lie every young male has a reason to both smoke Marijuana and engage in unprotected sex. Of course, the outcomes could be: teen pregnancy, venereal diseases, AIDS, and children born with birth defects.

6. All teens have sex and only some get pregnant. Having a baby proves womanhood. My parents will raise my baby and I can go on to live my life. These three things are grouped together because they were equally frequent comments made by my middle school female students. Most girls saw no shame nor feared any family consequences associated with getting pregnant.

Truth: <u>Parents do not talk to their children about the personal and family consequences of becoming a teen parent.</u> For my students, most of the time pregnancy was related directly to the girl using alcohol or drugs. Some girls said their parents had not talked to them about the possibility of being victimized at parties where alcohol and drugs were being used. They were not warned or educated about this danger or other health risks teen mothers may experience like: giving birth to premature sickly babies, babies born with birth defects like Downs Syndrome, life threatening complications because the mother is too small for delivery, injury to the reproductive system which prevents future pregnancy and other risks. However, the teenage mothers at my school regretted having babies early when they were thrust into the adult world and their parents made them responsible for the care of the infant. When their parents no longer allowed the girls to date and the girls had to seek part time employment to provide for their infants, the realty of their decision to have unprotected sex materialized. These girls lost their own childhoods and missed out on adolescent milestones like prom and athletic competitions. In addition, their bodies changed, they were uncomfortable with their own appearance, and often complained they were ashamed of their scars. Also, these girls stated that the boys who wanted to date them were not looking for long lasting relationships. My students were young teens twelve to fifteen years old.

Outcomes: Teen girls place their health and the lives of both the infant and themselves at risk when they become pregnant. Some try to hide their pregnancy by not eating or gaining weight, wearing clothes that bind their bodies, and some tried home remedies to terminate the pregnancy. I had many thirteen and fourteen year old girls in my classes who were so very tiny that I could imagine they would need a cesarean section to deliver their child. Once a young girl has a baby she faces emotional and psychological challenges due to chemical and physical changes in her body. She may not finish her education because of lack of space in programs for teen mothers and loss of her family's support. She may have to work part time, take care of a baby, and try to keep up with her studies. One additional consequence a teen mother-to-be shared with me was, if the girl is of the Hispanic culture then she may be sent back to live with relatives outside the United States where an education above the sixth grade is not required and she would lose her opportunity to receive an education in the United States.

7. If I quit drinking, smoking, and using drugs by the time I am eighteen I will not become addicted.
My students often said that they would quit using and abusing substances when they turned eighteen. Part of their reasoning had to do with their fear of receiving adult consequences at eighteen. However, the students believed that addiction was an adult problem and as long as they stopped before becoming a legal adult then they would never become an addict.

Truth: Scientific studies have been completed which prove that adolescences are at a higher risk than adult populations for becoming addicts. Children who begin using alcohol and drugs at twelve or thirteen have a fifty percent chance of becoming addicted. Hormonal changes in the body enhance the likelihood the bodies of these children will be fooled into believing that alcohol or illicit drugs which are present, need to be there for the body changes to be completed. The same study shows the risk percentage for addiction goes all the way down to ten percent if individuals would wait for the first use of these substances until they are eighteen years old. The research is plain; delaying the first use is the best way to prevent addiction to anything.

Outcomes: Some students are trying every type of drug currently used and drinking as many types of alcohol as they can find, in an effort to do it all before they become eighteen. These students are diluting themselves into believing they will be able to walk away from a six year binge unscathed. After poisoning their own bodies for years they believe they can go on to achieve their mental and physical potentials. Their life outcomes are the same as adult addicts and include: periods of abuse and then required treatment, lost income, legal problems, family problems, and health consequences. The most disturbing outcome for these students is they missed their chance at getting an education. They were high or drunk so much of the time their bodies had to use all their energy to clean and heal itself. The brain function was affected so these students could not reach their full academic potentials.

8. My criminal record will be forgiven when I become eighteen years old and will not follow me into adulthood.

Students who deal drugs and or belong to gangs believe whatever legal consequences they have faced for criminal activity goes away like magic when they turn eighteen.

Truth: Police officers can access the juvenile records of an adult they may suspect of committing a crime. Due to this, the crimes people commit when they are under legal age never really go away. Juvenile offenders build a reputation and memories of dealing with their antisocial behaviors aren't automatically cleansed from the minds of arresting police officers or judges when the offenders turn eighteen. In addition, police may watch for the chronic juvenile offender to turn legal age so they can send them away for a longer time period and get them off the street. Some adult false arrest and convictions could result from this memory residue of juvenile crimes committed. The only protection an adult has from their juvenile record being made public is the protection from potential employers finding out their youthful transgressions.

Outcomes: The teens I taught were not motivated to change or deterred by juvenile consequences received through the courts. Multiple arrest and convictions were common for juvenile offenders at our alternative school. The students would comply with programs and court orders to get free of their ankle monitors then go back to commit more crimes. These students were determined to make as much money as possible, through illegal activities, before facing possible adult consequences. The outcomes for these students were a life of crime and adult convictions.

9. Everybody drinks alcohol and everyone smokes Marijuana

My students believed that everyone uses drugs and drinks alcohol. This belief is rooted in their experience and their inner city culture. Their family, friends and neighborhood confirm this narrow belief system.

Truth: The truth is there are adult people who have never smoked Marijuana or tobacco and there are adult people who have never and currently do not drink alcohol. It is true many students do <u>not</u> know anyone who does not use alcohol and drugs. This lack of exposure to living without these substances, cause students to believe it is alright for them to indulge and that using these substances is normal and expected. When family members initiate the student's first use they may be both giving approval and simultaneously encouraging the student to use.

Outcomes: Students believe that alcohol and drug use are part of their ritual into adulthood and they are obligated to try these substances. Currently, childhood addiction may be on the rise and some children who are still in elementary school may be establishing a pattern of use that will develop into early teen addiction. Lifelong health problems, limited mental and educational potential and legal consequences await these children.

10. I make my own decisions about using drugs, alcohol or having sex and nobody is influencing me.
My students often said they were making their own choices and no one could make them do anything. They emphasized they did not believe in peer pressure and they could not be led into behaving a certain way because they were leaders.

Truth: A TV commercial may only last thirty seconds and it is still effective to produce the desired results. The truth is our inner city students' neighborhoods and sometimes their families, advertize drug and alcohol use twenty-four seven. Students may be exposed to drug and alcohol use by seeing people use these substances and by hearing people talk about using these substances. The constant advertisements for substance abuse young people receive may promote generational abuse of drugs and alcohol.

Outcomes: Students are making mindless choices to use drugs and alcohol, join gangs, or participate in sex at a young age because of a saturation factor. When students see people use drugs, hear people talk about drugs, and are involved in drug use, even indirectly, they are programmed to do what others are doing around them. Children are jeopardizing their health and limiting their ability to get an education by not being aware of the choices they have. Students are choosing a life of addiction and legal or family problems by not choosing to live differently than their role models and examples set before them. My students often said they wanted to be drug dealers or pimps when they grew up.

Discussion: After being exposed to my middle school students' belief systems it is easy to understand their life choices. **Do children exposed to drug use from early ages who live in neighborhoods where drug manufacturing and dealing rule the economy, really have choices?**

3. The Gentleman Killer and Redbone

Robert was tall, muscular, and possessed a Neanderthal looking forehead. His heavy brow gave him a foreboding look that could have caused someone to read an imaginary message "Don't mess with me" across the protruding expanse of skin just above his eyes. He came into the room like a bull charging into a china shop and began looking around the room like he was trying to determine what he could destroy first. He set his sights on a choice seat and motioned his thumb backwards while flaring his nostrils at the unfortunate boy sitting there. Needless to say, the other student moved quickly while giving me a pleading look. I was really surprised when James looked up doggedly at me like a pup that had just messed on the floor and when he tucked his tail between his legs while moving quickly to another seat. James had not made a show of teeth but he had not whimpered a retreat either. His inaction made me realize the matter was clearly not settled and I knew James was looking at me to make things right. James had a reputation for not backing down and the knowledge of his character was my first indication that I needed to proceed with caution around Robert. As I looked at James I knew that I needed to do something quickly to regain the homeostasis in my classroom because James would shortly loose his ability to remain calm.

I concluded the two young men were rivals since I had heard James use "CUZ" on an occasion and Robert had said, "Wuz up, BRO" as he walked into my room. These phrases were identifying expressions from two well known gangs in our area. I looked again at Robert who was larger than all the other students in class, James included, outweighing the next biggest I guessed by thirty or forty pounds. His physical appearance may have initially intimidated James but now it appeared James might be regaining some of his courage. When I crossed the room to retrieve the attendance book off my desk, James was sitting tall in his seat and throwing dagger looks in Robert's direction. Robert must have felt the pricks from James' blades because he twisted around in his seat to face him. I quickly intervened and got Robert's attention by telling him he would need to move because we had assigned seats in science class. I knew I would lose face with my other students if Robert wasn't moved but now I had set the scene for a confrontation between Robert and me with my order.

I began to formulate an intervention in my mind and began to think of a retreat path should I need one. Although I usually did not place new students at the back, when I called Robert's name, I assigned him a seat to the rear left corner of my classroom because that position was farthest away from my desk and gave me the advantage of being closer to the hallway door than Robert. Reluctantly, Robert moved without conflict and I breathed a little easier. Once James was returned to his former seat my authority was reestablished in the classroom and all was soon forgotten as Robert tried to engage students around him in conversation.

I watched Robert closely and listened intently while I silently assessed his propensity for violence. I was listening to the students' muted dialogues as I passed out our work for the day. Robert wanted to talk about gang affiliation to the student seated next to him but one of my older students warned him, "You don't want to talk in front of the OG. She's into what we are saying."

Robert glared at me to find I was starring back and he muttered, "She ain't nothn' about nothn'. Why you call her OG?"

The other student replied, "Miss O.G., Dawg. Give respect! She is fly with us but she's got our 214."

Robert eyed me suspiciously as I introduced myself to the new students and finished passing out assignment sheets to the class. Next, I gave a brief review of classroom expectations and pointed at the rewards and discipline posters on my classroom walls. I informed my new eighth grade students that they would not be sleeping in my class and I would keep them after school minute for minute of any time they caused to be wasted on discipline. I ended by saying, "I'm not playing with any of you. My discipline will be swift, you will be leaving here and you may find yourself back in the juvenile justice system if that's how you want it to play out. On the other hand, if you want to make up your missed school work and you are interested in getting an education, I will work really hard to help you accomplish that goal. Don't worry about any failures you have had in the past at school. I guarantee you that your grades will improve as long as you are here in my class every day because you are going to do your work."

We began our lesson and all the students focused except for Robert. When I called on him to pay attention to his work he responded, "Are you talk'n to me? Don't talk to me. You ain't got nothn' to do with me."

In my calmest manner I informed Robert I had everything to do with him, this was my classroom and I would run it, not him. I admit this was a bold move on my part but I could not give into this kid's intimidation on his first day. However, I kept my distance; he was sitting down across the room from me when I spoke boldly. I maintained my composure as he narrowed his eyes and began clenching and unclenching his fists in an intimidating manner.

A male student sitting next to him said, "Man, don't do this. She's O.K. Science class is good. Everybody likes Miss OG. She's gangsta!"

Almost immediately, Robert's face softened like a little child's and he became almost radiant. He began speaking in very proper English and his body posture relaxed. Now he acted like a complete gentleman, apologized and called me Miss OG. I thought, "That's a switch up if I ever saw one. Could this kid have DPD (Dissociative Personality Disorder) and could the protector personality be the nasty one I first met when he walked into my classroom?" It would not be unusual for a student attending our alternative education program to have serious psychological concerns. Although, an instant diagnosis of DPD should not have been in my repertoire and most teachers probably would not have even thought of it. However, after providing play therapy to abused children in foster care, under the supervision of a licensed clinical therapist, the diagnosis jumped out at me. The personality switch with the physical posturing change Robert demonstrated was just too stark to ignore.

I would need to be very careful in my approach to this new student and I would need to warn my co-teachers of the danger. Some of the methods we used with the other youth like proximity control to gain compliance could result in violence if we tried to use them with Robert. I had seen many unpredictable children at our school, most of whom were bi-polar disordered and on psychotropic medications, pose safety risks to all the staff. I knew how quickly a situation could turn dangerous if a child had mental health issues. I was sure Robert was more than a troubled kid and I saw elements of serious psychological problems during my classroom interactions with him on that very first day.

In addition to the quick and drastic personality change I had witnessed, there was something else that bothered me about this student. His eyes were depthless and flat, without any sparkle, and they were zombie like in appearance. Even the glaring florescent lights in our classroom did not reflect off their surface. Without his eyes cluing me to his mood, I knew I would have trouble anticipating Robert's actions and I would need to closely watch this student for other physical signs of stress, like the fists clenching I had noted earlier. The dead eyes phenomenon was a disturbing trait and it indicated to me that Robert was not fully in touch with all his emotions. Now sitting docile in his seat, I realized Robert's sorrowful corpse animated emotions only when he switched to other personalities. Each of his normal human emotions seemed tied to independent characters of himself.

Over the course of my next few days with Robert, I thought I saw at least three other personalities switch up, each with their own distinct posture and voice. The strangest personality was a cartoon character. He wasn't just mimicking the voice and movements of the character, he was the character! Robert acted extremely happy and he was friendly when he was in this personality. He would do things like try to sit on the desk top instead of in his chair, which was strange to see because of his large size, and he would try to walk backwards down the hall. When he was disciplined for this behavior he would apologize with a huge smile on his face and state, "I'm sorry. I didn't know. I've never been to this school before." When he was in this personality, he would readily comply with my wishes. His face glowed around his deep-set, dark eyes while looking at me with child like adoration. It was too weird!

I'm sure other staff members thought Robert might have been under the influence of some type of drug when he displayed this personality and he could have been. However, he was referred to our school police officer for suspected drug use by another middle school teacher and he was sent back to class with the officer's opinion, "The kid is just acting goofy." Since Robert's goofy character was less threatening than the dark person I had met on the first day of his attendance, I should have relaxed a little when he was present. However, I knew the other person I first met was hiding inside Robert and his reappearance could be unannounced and sudden.

After seeing Robert switch up, I could not help but draw a parallel in my own mind between him and another child by the name of Reba who had been a play therapy client of mine years ago. The foster parents had complained to me that this very unusual seven-year old girl would climb on the furniture and growl angrily while playing with their children. She would make ugly, scary faces which made their kids not want to play with her and she would act territorially challenged when approached about sharing her toys. During therapy, I discovered Reba's protector personality was an ape. She would stop talking and start moving like an ape by jumping around on the furniture and by dragging her arms across the floor. She would growl and charge at me with angry looking eyes. Reba would spin me in my office chair, stop me when she had enough, and sniff me to see if she could smell fear. Her role play was so real that Reba truly frightened a mental health intern I was supervising. I understood the foster parents' concerns after witnessing Reba switch to her protector personality and I was afraid this child might be moved due to her threatening behaviors.

I learned to sit very still in my office chair, avert my gaze from Reba's face and wait for her to finish acting like an ape. Once the intense anger displays and intimidation tactics ceased, Reba would draw me a picture, without talking, on the child size white board in my office. She would always draw the same picture of a person standing outside a door and two other people sleeping in a bed. When the picture was completed, Reba would come to me and ask me to hold her and she would request a lullaby be sung to her. It appeared that Reba needed emotional reassurance that she was safe after exposing the vulnerable side of her psyche. When her body completely relaxed in my arms I ventured, in a very soft voice, an inquiry about her drawing.

Reba explained that only one person could be awake at one time. There was a mother who stood guard at the door and two people were sleeping behind the door. One personality was a male, Reba called him brother; and he never was awake. Reba insisted we had to be quiet so we would not wake him. When asked how old her brother was, Reba reported he was two or three and he could not talk yet. Only the girl and the mother were allowed to be awake and when one was up, the other had to sleep. Since Reba did not have a brother and the male personality was the same age of Reba at the time of her abuse, I surmised he was her secret keeper. I discovered that females often reasoned if they had been a male the abuse would not have happened. The male personality represented denial and allowed Reba not to acknowledge the abuse. Working with children like Reba was exhausting and some days when Reba had enough probing and she did not want me poking around in her little tender soul, she would demonstrate bizarre behaviors and the ape would come out.

The strange behaviors I witnessed from clients like this young girl led me to believe that I could expect unusual actions from Robert and that his protector personality could spontaneously erupt and pose a threat to everyone's safety. I tried to avoid confronting that personality by establishing a safe classroom environment where Robert felt valued and protected. I knew the key to all of our safety concerns rested in Robert feeling safe and accepted. I thought his bonding ritual in my classroom was complete when the cartoon character went away and that Robert no longer felt it was necessary to act cute to be accepted. When I began to see a middle school student personality emerge I became cautiously optimistic about this student's progress. This happened the fourth week in our program.

However, it appeared the other students in my room were still not at ease with Robert's presence and they seemed to be in tune with my character evaluation of their classmate because they acted like they expected Robert to become violent at any given moment. They walked out of their way to avoid Robert and many chose not to work in groups with him. In fact, the entire learning environment became dependent upon Robert's moods some days. The classroom could be extremely uncomfortable for my other students when Robert was present. This opened up my mind to the possibility my principal was correct when he had told me, "Put all that stuff you learned about education on the shelf. This is a different ball game and you will need to adjust to the students." His motto of supervise, supervise, and supervise was beginning to make more sense to me every day. Safety had to take priority over education when Robert was present in my class room and I adjusted my lesson plans based on Robert's moods.

Going back to that first day with Robert, I had wanted to make sure my co-workers understood the danger he presented so I had located the other teachers as soon as I could and I explained to them this student's characteristics which gave me cause for worry and I issued a strong warning. "I know our principal tells us to stand up to the kids and not let the students disrespect us. Please be careful when interacting with this young man and don't get up in his face. Things we use with other students like proximity control could lead to violence with this student. We need to talk after school about how we will manage his behavior. I believe he is extremely dangerous so please don't physically challenge him." All I could do was sound an alarm because I really didn't have any hard facts that this young man was as dangerous as I thought.

We had our meeting at the end of that first day after all the other teachers had an opportunity to observe Robert and we came to the conclusion that we would ask for the police officer to intervene the very first time Robert showed aggressive behavior of any type. We were not going to wait until he became physical with a teacher or another student. We all felt our safety depended on us having a zero tolerance for any hostility that was demonstrated. Also, we decided to watch Robert closely to make sure he was not throwing up gang signs or issuing rival gang members a challenge.

The very next day after our meeting, Robert's second day in class, he came into my classroom and tried to grab someone else's assigned seat. Both he and the other student fell on the floor. No one was really hurt, but before Robert could even get off the floor, I rang the call-button to summon the police officer. He was taken out of the class and to the officer's credit he brought the young man back to apologize to me and the class. The officer said, "I have spoken to this young man and he knows he cannot enter your classroom the way he did this morning. I have told him that I will issue a five-hundred dollar ticket for classroom disruption if he causes any more trouble." I thanked the officer and thought, yes! This is how it is supposed to work. We will need a team effort to manage this student's behaviors. Then I had a sobering thought, the resource officer is only this tough on one of our students, if he knows the kid very well ... and knows how bad the kid can be. That's when I realized Robert must have a prior history with our officer and he had decided not to mentor this student but to have him removed from our school as soon as possible. I retracted the self congratulations on our team work and thought, we're in deep trouble!

Robert's attendance became spotty during his fifth week at our school and one morning he and his cousin, the students called him "Redbone," were given a ride to school in a squad car. My guess is they had been caught skipping school. I believe Robert was only pretending to adjust to our program and once his probation officer was convinced he was compliant then Robert returned to his former behavior. I had seen students do this before. Six weeks seemed like such a short time to me but some of our students could not stay out of trouble for even that long. I was certain Robert's truancy was related to gang activity and that he had progressed beyond being a baby gangster into being a full gangland soldier. I made this assumption because my other young wannabes feared him. The thought of Robert being a gangland soldier and carrying a gun sent a sudden chill down my spine. The image of this young man with dead eyes confronting another human being was bone chilling and the consequences were unthinkable for me.

Robert's attendance worsened in what should have been his sixth week in our program; and neither he nor his cousin came to school the first four days of that week. On Friday, both Robert and Redbone were escorted once again to school in a police car. I was dreading my class experience with these two because they had missed so much school over the last two weeks that I anticipated that I would have to reestablish my authority with them. However, I was wrong because it was Robert's turn to experience dread. On that Friday morning, I was confronted with two very scared young men and one of them did something that I had never expected from any of my students at the alternative school.

Robert's cousin began talking as soon as they entered the room before everyone else had a chance to sit down. His face gave away the urgency of his situation because it was twisted into a frightened look. "Mrs. OG, will you pray for me? I'm scared!" I was taken back because I had not yet shared my faith with this group of students and I didn't quite understand why this young man would ask me to pray. I looked to Robert to determine the legitimacy of the request because I knew Red Bone was not in trouble on his own account and whatever had happened, Robert was involved. Robert was not visibly shaking like his cousin but he made eye contact with me for the first time. I finally saw a glimpse of Robert's soul and it was not dark as I had expected. He was a scared child, his face had a worried expression, and Robert's eyes mirrored the prayer insistence his cousin requested. Robert sat rolling his hands one on top of the other in a washing motion like he was trying to rid himself of the blood of an innocent.

I started, "Boys you know that teachers cannot lead students in prayer or pray out loud in public schools. But we can have a moment of silence and pray in our hearts together. Anyone who wants to join us can. I will not be able to shut my eyes because I have to watch the students at all times but I will be praying in my heart. Class we are going to have a moment of silence." I watched the clock for a minute to pass and did pray for my students that God would relieve their anxiety and keep them safe. I quickly added that I was seeking his mercy to keep us all safe because I sensed we all might be in danger. That silent prayer turned out to be prophetic.

Within five minutes our resource officer and another uniformed police officer showed up at my door and asked to see the two young men. They were taken away and the other students began looking around the room to see if anyone knew what was going on. Since I knew the boys' removal would spark gossip, I decided to let the students vent for a few minutes and get the information out in the open so we could accomplish our learning objectives for the day. One young man raised his hand and said, "Mrs. G, there was a fight at the train station last night and those two beat up another boy real bad. I know the boy's family and his momma, told my momma that the boy almost died. If he lives then he will be permanently disabled. They kicked him in the head over and over."

Another student asked, "Who did it?"

"The boy's momma said it was Robert. His cousin helped with the beaten in the beginning then tried to get Robert to stop. Redbone couldn't stop him. Robert is too strong and he is a killer," emphasized the student as he shook his head and looked down at the floor.

Another student asked, "Did the boy they beat go here?"

"Yeah, he's in the ninth grade and he's Blood," reported our informant.

With this revelation, my stomach began knotting up and I had an uneasy feeling that the excitement was not over for the day because now I knew the beating was gang related.

A student who had been quietly listening up till now, asked one final question, "Miss OG, do you think they have cameras there at the train station?"

I responded, "Sure, some of our students lose their privileges to ride the train because their behaviors like fighting or causing other trouble are caught on camera. I thought all of you guys knew that." I quickly added, "Besides I heard that the city police officers look at the train station tapes and use those to identify students who might be carrying drugs into our school." I heard a soft "Damn" at the back of the classroom. Apparently, my fishing trip worked because I now had a better idea who was sneaking in and dealing drugs at our school. It was the kid who said "Damn."

Another student laughed when he realized this student who swore just gave himself away and he said, "Man, you dumb. You just told Miss O.G. your business so you better not bring stuff up in here, no more!" The other students all laughed.

The student who swore said, "I'm too smart to get caught do 'in stuff. I never get caught. I'm fly at be 'in a mobster and I got the luck working for me."

Now it was my turn to laugh. I said, "How many of you think you are lucky and you will never get caught like Robert and Redbone?" The whole class raised their hands then I said, "Look around. What are you all doing at an alternative school? Did your luck run out? You all got caught doing something wrong or you wouldn't be here. So I wouldn't be depending on the luck factor from here on out. Besides if you get caught it could be a sign from God that he wants you to change the way you are living."

The students looked surprised and were deep in thought about this last statement until one raised his hand. "Mrs. Gifford, do you always do the right thing?"

I thoughtfully replied, "All of us make mistakes but I try really hard to do the right thing because I know I will get caught and I certainly do not have the luck factor working for me. I know God wants me to have good behavior and if I don't, I will get disciplined because God loves me. God is like a good parent who disciplines His children so they will change their behaviors. So now you know, I am not always good because I want to be good but I try to be good because I am one of those who will always get caught. I think some of you are like that too or you would not be here at the alternative school."

Seeing that I had already broken protocol by offering a second moment of silence for prayer that day, I guess I figured I might as well testify. It just sort of tumbled out and I'm sure I gave plenty for the students to think about. Ten minutes of class time had been lost with the pair's removal and the resulting gossip so I redirected the group and we tackled our work for the day. The students worked quietly and everyone completed their assignment in time for lunch. I knew my decision to allow students to share what they knew about Robert and Redbone's situation was correct. If I had not aired the information, students would have been gossiping around the room and some would not have paid attention to our lesson due to the undercurrent of conversation in class.

As soon as our class was over, I lined up my students and proceeded down the hall while passing a view of our school entrance. When we rounded the corner, I became aware that there was an inordinate amount of activity at the front of our building. I hurriedly counted at least five police cars that were visible outside our glass entrance as I kept the students facing forward and moved them down the hall. I was glad the students' lunch room was at the back of our building and that it was void of windows because that location would be safer than a classroom. I puzzled to myself, "Why isn't our school on lock down?" I didn't feel safe and I was surprised that students were still moving around our building and classes were being changed. It just seemed like danger was in the very air I was breathing and I wondered why others didn't feel it. Then, I could not believe what I saw next.

After hurriedly leaving the students in the gym that served as our cafeteria, I walked to the lounge and saw teachers sitting by the windows eating their lunches. None seemed concerned about the additional squad cars outside and when I asked if anyone knew what was going on one obviously disinterested teacher replied that she had been in the front office when the police officers brought two boys in for interrogation. She said, "They told the principal they needed to use the conference room and they wanted a TV and a VCR. The principal took them toward the back of the office and that is all I know."

Next, I peered over the head of one of my co-workers and said, "Has anyone noticed the gang members across the street standing outside their cars and looking this way?" I rotated my head to the left then to the right to enhance my view of a tattooed army of individuals much older than our students. There were several cars and it appeared some cars were parked in a church parking lot on the side of our building too. I recognized the group as adult gang members and thought they probably were affiliated with the young man who had been brutally beaten. One other teacher peered out the window and said, "I wonder what they are doing here?"

I told the other teachers, "I'm not sure it is safe to sit here in full view of the windows because something is going down with those two young men and it is gang related. So, I think I will eat in my room today." I only had about fifteen minutes left of my lunch time so I hurried back to the science room which was on the back side of our building and peeked out the blinds. I was comforted to see that police cars had completely encircled our building. However, my body felt cold and I trembled a little. I knew the excitement and lack of food was causing my blood sugar to go low and I needed to eat something. I sighed deeply because there never was enough time to put up my feet or eat during the lunch hour at our school.

Bell to bell, lunch break was thirty minutes long but teachers had to accompany the students to the lunchroom then go pick them up again after lunch. Teachers needed to use the restroom during lunch time, record attendance, and sometimes run copies for afternoon classes. All of these things deducted precious minutes. However, it was the one microwave in the lunchroom and the ten teachers waiting in line to use it which prevented me from eating like I should have. Initially, I checked every day just to see if I might be able to throw in a frozen dinner but the line was always too long. Today was no exception so I made a mental note, "Buy a small microwave to keep in your classroom so you can eat properly. You can't keep up with the students if you run low on energy."

I always carried a banana to school in case I didn't have time to eat anything else. So, once I was back in my room I peeled the potassium stick, popped the first piece into my mouth knowing my muscles would not cramp tonight from all the walking I did today due to the incredible fruit. I reassured myself that the amazing banana would keep me from falling into a low-blood sugar coma in front of the students. Then, I remembered the need for protein in my diet and I frantically rattled open my desk drawer and smeared a little peanut butter on top of the last bite. However, the urgency of my need for food and the unsettling situation I just witnessed outside the lunchroom windows conflicted me so I began to pray at the same time I was eating, "Dear God, forgive me for talking to you with my mouth full but I know you will understand. Thank you for protection and for the help I asked for earlier because it is needed right now!"

After a much too short lunch period, I hurried down the hall to pick up a different group of students for my next class. I could not help but let my eye drift to the glass doorway where my two gangsters were being escorted out with their hands cuffed behind their backs. There was a short pause at the squad car directly in front of our entrance and an adult gang leader from across the street was given a hand signal by one of the escorting officers. I noticed all the rest of the police officers who were standing behind their cars, were looking in the direction of the gang members with their hands on their holsters. However, without incident the car carrying the boys sped away behind another squad car. Slowly, gang members got into their cars and drove away while the remaining police cars stayed parked around our building for another few minutes.

I breathed a sigh of relief as my co-workers, chatting and laughing, rounded the hall corner on the way to pick up their students. They seemed oblivious to what had just happened and I didn't have the heart to tell them at that moment what I had witnessed. Besides, my emotions were conflicted because the sight of Redbone looking down the hall and over his shoulder at me while being pushed forward into the squad car, had almost dissolved me into tears. I had nodded at him and faked a little smile as if to say, "It's going to be ok."

Discussion: Later on that school year, I heard that Robert and his cousin were both tried as adults for their violent crime. It was such a waste. I really thought Redbone had a lot of potential and now he would spend years in a perverted and dangerous environment. I hoped he received a lighter sentence than Robert because he had tried to stop his cousin in the middle of the beating and I was sure Redbone had not intended to go beyond a certain point of injury to the other teen. On the other hand, I was relieved I would not be seeing Robert at our school as a repeat student year after year. Robert needed more help than what an alternative public school program could provide. He was violent, mentally ill, and he was a gangland soldier who posed a constant threat to the safety of everyone in our school. My other students expressed their relief at his leaving because they were very much afraid of this young man.

Gangs and gang activity are ruining many of our nation's youth while deteriorating some of our classroom environments. A few of my students told of their induction into the gang by force not by choice. They were hailed and recruited to deliver drugs for dealers. This is a common practice because punishment for children caught delivering is less than for adults. Some of my students reported that the worst thing that happened to them when they were caught running drugs was they had to stay in lock up until their parents came. Then they were released into their parent's custody until a court hearing date was established. My students said the legal consequences generated by their arrest were not enough to deter their activities and they feared the gang members more than the law. These baby gangsters complied with gang members' orders not out of obedience or allegiance to a gang but out of fear for their own safety and the safety of their family members. Family members could be punished if the recruit did not obey. My students shared one additional disturbing fact with me about how gang membership is different today than what it once was when gangs first surfaced in our country. They stated that it was no longer possible to get jumped out of the gang; at one time a recruit could end their affiliation by taking a horrible beating. According to my students, that is not an option today and the only way out of a gang is death. Whether or not this is true is of no consequence because my students believed it was true and their actions were based on their beliefs.

It broke my heart to see good kids, only twelve to fourteen years old, who would have never been part of a gang, if they would have had a choice, be involved in this lifestyle. Gangs exact a price and their members are required to earn money for the group by committing crimes like robbery or burglary. Some of my baby gangsters tried to resist illegal activities by hiding out from gang members and they would only go home to sleep. Other students reported they had been sleeping in abandoned buildings instead of going home because they did not want to take trouble to their families. However, showing up at school put them at risk too because they were easily found leaving our building on their way home.

These kids were often hungry, unkempt and found it difficult to concentrate because they were in the survival mode and they were fearful. In spite of their difficulties some of these students performed in school and many passed were proficient on state exams. I found some of these children to be intelligent, dedicated to their families, and remorseful when forced to commit crimes. Sorry to say, these students may never reach their full potentials and some will end up dead on the streets. Many will succumb to taking drugs in order to deal with their lives' uncertainties. More disturbing is the fact, a few of these students may be enticed into becoming hard core gang members by the money, parties and free sex offered by gangs.

Teachers are no match for organized crime and the gangs. We cannot protect our students when they leave school and we can't compete with their internal drama when they are at school. Students like Robert and Redbone had potential that will never be fully realized. Gang activity is a fact of life in large cities and just like the scene I witnessed where the police gave deference to gang leaders, the delicate balance of power in large cities has to be negotiated between peace keepers and criminals. It is an advantage for police to have open communication with known gang leaders. Can you imagine what could have happened at our school if the gang members had entered to take by force the boys who committed the crime? Since many of our students were from opposite gang factions, I am sure some of our children would have involved themselves in a volatile confrontation and many of our students or staff could have been hurt or even killed.

What kind of a school or education system might work for students who are members of gangs or students who are trying to escape the gangs?

Topics for Research

What gangs operate in my city? What activities are gangs involved in? How can I identify signs that my child might be in a gang? Is my neighborhood safe from gang activity? How can I get my child out of a gang?

Things to do:

Contact your local police department and ask about gang education programs for teachers, parents and other professionals. Talk to your children or students about gang activities and explain how gang involvement may affect their life outcomes or rob them of a future. Teach your children to be individuals and help them set education goals. Create a safety plan for children and practice scenarios which help children learn how to avoid being involuntarily drafted into a gang. Parents might consider enrolling their children in private schools to limit contact with the gangs. Most important, keep children off the streets and away from gang activity.

4. Limiting Gang Influence

Do the presence of gangs increase with the size of the community? According to a Juvenile Justice Bulletin dated August 2000, the answer is yes. Forty-three percent of all students living in urban areas reported the presence of gangs in their schools compared to twenty-five percent of students attending schools in rural areas. Also, this information compares the availability of drugs in schools to the presence of gangs and showed …"Gangs were significantly more prevalent when a large number of drugs were easy to get at school" (Youth Gangs in School). In addition, this same report issued by the U.S. Department of Education and Justice found a strong correlation between the presence of gangs and both guns and drugs on campus. The above reference tells us that when gangs are present, drugs and guns are available and there is a higher prevalence of all three in larger communities.

This statistical information should help us clarify why large city school districts' students are failing to get an adequate education. Clearly, the presence of gangs and their ability to deliver drugs to students during the school day and the unsafe environments resulting from the presence of drugs and gangs are affecting student performance. One national teacher association has recognized communities need help identifying and limiting gang influence in schools. The National Education Association (NEA) developed a 'Safe School Framework' to help communities make schools safe and eliminate gang activity. They proposed a three pronged approach which included prevention education aimed to prevent students from joining gangs, intervention which contains elements of counseling and after-school programs, and suppression strategies which are constructed to: identify, isolate, punish, and rehabilitate student offenders. The association made recommendations that schools should determine first if the gang problem is an emerging one or a chronic one before forming a plan. Most large city school districts would probably state their problem is a chronic one.

The three pronged approach recommended by the NEA may have to be adjusted to fit some large city school districts' needs. Due to some family models, gang prevention education, the first prong suggested, may not be effective. Gang membership can be generational in large cities and some parents could be gang banging alongside their kids (gangwar. com/dynamics.htm). In fact, parents may act as recruiters by expressing to their own children their expectations about gang membership. This generational allegiance can be demonstrated by newer terms now heard on the streets which call infants born to gang members "Blood drops, Stains, or Rims." According to one source, children are taught to fold gang signs before they can talk and these little toddlers may never know any other lifestyle while growing up (dailynews.com/news/ny_crime/2008-06-14). For this reason, prevention education may be designated the weaker prong in the NEA strategy designed to limit gang activity in schools. Due to parent gang involvement, prevention education might not be effective with generationally affiliated students. Instead, students need to hear the message that gang activity is illegal and gang membership will result in personal consequences. Most important students who come from gang affiliated families need to find out that there are other ways to live and there are other things to do.

Therefore, the second prong which purposes intervention services like after school programs may help reduce gang membership by creating alternate activities for students. Another intervention service, counseling, could be stepped up to reduce student stress when they are being pressured to join a gang and to limit gang member confrontations.

Out of the three things recommended by the NEA, the third prong which promotes suppression strategies may have the greatest effect in limiting gang activities in schools. Suppressions usually take the form of written policies and procedures. Current policy used in some schools which have proven effective at reducing gang activity are: requiring students to wear uniforms, enforcing parental and community curfews, establishing truancy prevention efforts, and setting zero-tolerance policies for drinking, drug use and weapons at school (Youth Gangs; Findings & Solutions for Schools, Communities and Families)

School uniforms have proven to be important in establishing behavior adjustments in students. When children wear uniforms to school they are reminded to make a behavioral shift from street manners to classroom etiquette and uniforms limit gang influence by adjusting the physical appearance of students. Gang members identify each other through: clothing, tattoos, haircuts, hair apparel, jewelry, hand signs, nicknames, numbers, language use, and other things. Anything we can do, to help remind students they are at school to get an education and they are not there to carry on gang business as usual, is helpful. Since gang membership is so closely linked to an individual's self-concept or identification, changing the appearance of a student may allow that student to change their behavior at school.

There is a lot of legal controversy regarding policies and procedures governing student apparel and grooming. School districts may choose to ignore the need for stringent student dress codes and grooming requirements to avoid legal entanglements when defending their dress code choices. However, one legal argument rendered by the 5th District Circuit Court of Appeals upheld a school-uniform policy and stated if the purpose for enacting a school uniform policy is to increase test scores and reduce disciplinary problems throughout the school system then requiring uniform dress does not violate students' rights for free speech (firstamendmentcenter.org: student expression in Speech-Topic). Therefore, public schools should not fear a challenge to their codes if researched and implemented correctly.

In spite of the NEA's recommendation, only fourteen percent of public schools required their students to wear uniforms in the 2005-2006 school year (Statistics on School Uniforms, Wikipedia). I encourage every school district to revise their school dress codes to include some type of uniform dress if gangs are an emerging or chronic problem in their schools. I believe President Bill Clinton expressed the best reason for this kind of reform in his 1996 State of the Union address when he said, "…If it means that teenagers will stop killing each other over designer jackets, then our public schools should be able to require their students to wear school uniforms." Reduction of violence is probably the best reason for reforming dress code policies because gangs cannot identify each other readily while passing each other in the hall and students cannot wear expensive shoes, jewelry, or other clothing items which invite violence.

In addition, we need to control our students' environment by keeping our school buildings clean. This is a constant and ongoing battle in some public schools. As a teacher, I know that keeping your classroom neat and ordered sends a message to students that the teacher is in control. Conversely, when the classroom is messy and teachers are disorganized they tend to have more discipline problems. When our buildings look like war zones and have graffiti on the walls and trash in the halls then we might as well go home because the gangs are in control of the schools. Every day we leave the mess sends a message to the students and staff that the gangs own our schools. That is why the mess gets worse and students continue to disrespect or destroy school property.

This constant cleaning may cost school districts more money than what they would like to spend but the need should not be ignored. Some maintenance and cleaning might be lessened if there were enough people to supervise student activities in common areas at times when students are supposed to be in class. If students could not predict when they might be intercepted and disciplined for not being where they are suppose to be and students received harsh consequences for being in off-limit areas during class times then schools might need less repair. Administrators need to walk the halls to apprehend students who are wandering in the building and all staff should consider it their job to watch for and report displaced students. Keeping our schools clean and repaired is a strategy like the first, wearing uniforms, because it suppresses gang activity by controlling the appearance of our schools. It destroys gangs' attempts to territorialize school property and it sets students' expectations regarding their behavior in an adult controlled environment.

The second suppression recommended by the NEA was to limit gang activity by the enforcement of both parental and community curfews. Community curfews might be more effective in large city school districts where parent gang activity is probable and students' adherence to curfews could be related more to desire to avoid a legal consequence rather than to evade parental discipline. In addition, daytime curfews may serve a double purpose by reducing truancy and lowering youth crime statistics during the hours of school. These curfews impose criminal penalties on students, under the age of 17, who skip school and may hang out in public places without adult supervision during school hours. In addition, this type of curfew may impose fines on parents of the student or businesses which allow students to congregate during school hours on their premises.

A chairman of a council on public-safety for one large city in favor of the daylight curfew reported the ban would help police combat crimes that are associated with truancy like burglaries and car break-ins (The Wall Street Journal, March 26, 2009). Youth gang activity often takes place during the day when adults are at work and neighborhoods are sparsely populated. For this reason, daylight curfews are gaining popularity and should be promoted when school districts are thinking about reforms which are meaningful to students. School district should advocate for this kind of code to be passed. In addition to preventing student gang activity, keeping students in class during school hours could eliminate learning gaps and result in fewer dropouts due to academic failures.

The third proposed suppression strategy calls for reducing truancy. One reason why truancy may have gained popularity among urban students could relate back to enforcement. Some of the courts which hear truancy cases may be overwhelmed because they also administrate traffic violations and other civil matters. When this happens, truancy cases do not receive the attention they need and students' consequences are delayed. To solve this problem, one district I know joined forces with two other school districts to establish a different system and hire a truancy court judge to expedite student cases. This type of educational reform may be necessary in larger cities where courts are back-logged with other civil cases (self).

Also, when thinking about truancy reforms student tardiness should be considered. Some students are chronically tardy and interrupt learning when they enter a classroom. They miss important parts of instruction by walking into the middle of a lesson and they become lost. Teachers may have to spend additional time with a chronically tardy student just to bring them up to speed before continuing instruction. These youth cause classroom disruptions whether they mean to or not. In addition, these chronically late students may be tardy because they decided to use drugs before coming to school and may be coming to school under the influence of drugs which adds to the disruption. All the other students will focus on the tardy student's behavior instead of the lesson being presented when a late student walks into a classroom.

Teachers can create individual classroom rules to check unexcused tardy behavior and one I would recommend is keeping students after school minute for minute of time missed in class on the very same day a student comes late. Students will not be tardy from class often if this rule is steadfastly enforced. Of course, teachers must prioritize their after school repayment time above other school or personal activities the student or his family may have planned and the administration must support the teacher's classroom tardy rule.

In addition, tardy policies should dove-tail right into truancy policies. Most school districts already list the number of days a student can be absent during the school year before they turn the student's name in for a truancy violation. The number of truancy days add up faster when an unexcused tardy is tabulated as part of one truancy day. This one reform could effectively indentify students who: chronically come to school late, miss instruction, develop learning gaps, and drop out of school early. This suppression strategy is easy to implement and serves to discourage student drug use and gang activity before coming to school.

When some of my students came late to school they were involved in obtaining or using drugs through gang action. They came to school high or they came to school to supply! Coming late to school may allow some students to miss morning check in routines, permit them time to stash drugs on the way to class, and let them roam the school unsupervised on their way to their classroom. As long as students have an note from the office stating they may be admitted late to class, students can glean an extra few minutes in route to do whatever they want to do and teachers won't notice the small increase in time it takes students to get to class. Therefore, school policies should specifically address how tardy students will be screened and sent to class. Closely screening tardy students when they enter the school, school personnel accompanying students to their classroom, and having tardy incidents counted or rolled into truancy reports, may serve to reduce gang activity in some schools.

Some school districts count students as truant when they miss thirty minutes of a class (tardy) three times during the school year. Why allow a student to be thirty minutes late before they are counted tardy? Tardy behavior is rude behavior and its allowance disrespects the classroom teacher. Five minutes is enough of a grace period and anything more than that enables students to disrupt learning. Limiting the tardy occurrences to three may help with the problem but if you have thirty students in a class and each are tardy twice during the year then a teacher could have one-third of his school year interrupted by tardy students.

Early identification of students who may be developing a patterned tardiness is a strategy which may prevent hard core truancy. In addition, large city school districts with dropout rates approaching fifty percent may need additional steps in their truant policies to ensure the consequences are stepped up and interventions are applied at every level. One example of a truant policy which consistently steps up consequences is provided by The California Department of Education. This truant policy has added some unique deterrents: students' driving privileges with the state may be suspended, parents may have to attend school with their children, students may be assigned attendance at evening or weekend make-up classes, and students may be found "within the jurisdiction of the juvenile court which may adjudge the pupil to be a ward of the court pursuant to Section 601 of the Welfare and Institutions Code." (California Educational Code, Truancy).

The fourth suppression strategy recommended by the NEA involves setting zero tolerances for drugs, alcohol, and gangs in schools. According to USA Today, ninety-one percent of schools have implemented a zero tolerance policy for carrying weapons to school and eighty-seven percent have initiated zero tolerance for drug use and other issues (Education News, 04/13/1999). Most people would agree that slapping students on the wrist and sending them home with mama is not an acceptable punishment for gang members found using or selling drugs at school. However, the term, zero tolerance, indicates inflexibility and may become unpopular for that reason.

Problems with zero tolerance policies could relate to the course of action administrators take when enforcing such codes. Administrators do make errors enforcing zero tolerance policies. One such error was recorded in USA Today. An honor student who had never been in trouble before the reported incident, brought a drink spiked with alcohol to school. This student was assigned to go to boot camp for her offense because the school assumed a code enforcement role instead of an education role. In addition, to the inappropriateness of the student's assignment to boot camp and the ensuing legal action which cost the district money, the school district may have paid an unnecessary secondary consequence by having to fund the boot camp stay. School funds may be relinquished to other education programs when these kinds of assignments are made.

This student could have been referred to a teen drug treatment center for classes and her parents ordered to pay for those services. The student could have been placed in an in school suspension program until documentation of successful completion of substance abuse classes was provided. Clearly, a give the kid the electric chair mentality may apply when some administrators enforce zero tolerance policies. Therefore, consequences should be leveled according to offense and a resource district person should probably serve as a support to administrators making discipline decisions regarding zero tolerance policies.

However, there is another hands-off approach which might work. It is illegal for minors to use alcohol, possess drugs, or to participate in crime syndicate activities. If this approach is taken then the purpose of zero tolerance codes in schools would be to identify students using drugs, possessing drugs, and participating in gang activity. Schools might find it easier just to turn offending students over to the legal system and let the courts decide punishment. If it were only that simple!

Administrators will always have situations which are in grey areas of enforcement. Mistakes can happen when administrators assume zero tolerance policies require harsh, swift punishment and administrators do not see infractions as an opportunity to provide substance abuse prevention education and provide referrals for treatment intervention services. Failure to see the difference between a student using drugs and needing intervention services compared to a student dealing drugs and promoting gang activity in the school could cause the death of some zero tolerance policies. Therefore, one person should probably not have the sole responsibility to interpret zero tolerance offenses and administrate discipline to students.

A zero tolerance review committee could be useful to clarify and apply school policies in those grey areas where administrators tend to error. Review committees are established and used to oversee administrations of other procedures followed in public service agencies receiving government funds. A review committee could bring balance to the administration of zero tolerance policies by ensuring district guidelines were followed, students receive intervention through referrals and by serving as a learning tool for administrators. Also, schools would receive the benefit of added documentation should a student breech a zero tolerance again.

In closing, limiting gang influence in schools is not impossible and we have already had a plan set before us by The National Association of Teachers. We may only need to tweak some of the suppression strategies to make them work better. Let's review the NEA's recommendations for suppressing gangs in schools that have been discussed here.

1. Implementing strict student dress codes may help students better adjust to the school environment and lessen students' concerns with gang activity. We simply want students to recognize and respect the neutrality of our learning environments and requiring students to wear school uniforms along with other strict dress codes (haircuts, jewelry, and other things) do promote gang detachment. In addition, evidence of gang presence must be constantly cleaned, swept, and painted from our schools.

2. Enforcing daytime curfews make parents and other community members more aware of youth presence in the community during school hours and may suppress daytime gang crime. Penalties for not reporting youth present on the street during school hours should be continued because these may persuade individuals to take an active role in reporting truant students. In my opinion, evening and weekend curfews should be extended to summer vacation time in concentrated gang areas of the inner city. It is difficult to get the students back into the school mode after a summer of free-ranging, gang banging.

3. Student tardy reports should be linked to truancy reports and court action. Morning tardiness allows students to obtain drugs to use or sell at school. In cities where court cases are backed up and truancy cases are seldom heard, school districts may need to hire their own truancy judge. We need to keep kids in school in a controlled environment to eliminate gang influence and we need students to attend regularly so they can learn. When kids are absent they fail and when they experience failure they drop out of school.

4. Zero tolerance policies for gang activity, guns, and drugs or alcohol in school need to remain in place but they may need tempered to ensure students receive due process. Review committees could be established to review and enforce zero tolerance policies and these review panels could help

school districts avoid legal consequences which occur when administrators error when assigning consequences. At the very least, administrators need to enforce zero tolerance policies with caution after consulting with a school specialist or upper level administrator. Later in this book we will discuss another strategy and a different solution will be offered which might make zero tolerance policies obsolete. Zero tolerance could be replaced by a "No Refusal" code.

Resources and References

Juvenile Justice Bulletin, "Reasons for Greater Gang Prevalence in Some Schools," Youth Gangs in School; ncjs.gov/html/ojjbul200_8_2/page 2.html

The National Education Association (NEA), "Youth Gangs: Findings & Solutions for Schools, Communities & Families;" 'Safe School Framework,' 1997

gangwar.com/dynamics.htm

firstamendmentcenter.org/speech/studentexpression/topic. aspx?topic=clothing...K-12 public school student expression; "clothing, dress codes & uniforms, 04-13-2010

"Statistics on School Uniforms," Wikipedia.com

"1996 State of the Union Address," President Bill Clinton

Online.wsj.com/article/SB123802404458842181.html; the Wall Street Journal, "More Cities Target Teens With Daytime Curfews", 04-13-2013

A Review of **California**'s Compulsory **Education** Laws February 2004 ... District Attorneys' Options in Dealing With **Truancy**. **Education Code** Section48293

USA Today; "Education News," 04-13-1999

"New blood: Violent gang life is passed down from parent to child," ny.dailynews.com/ny_crime/2008/06/14/2008-06-14_new_blood_ violent_...

5. The Snake Charmer

I became suspicious of Randy because his eyes were so shiny! He was a handsome young man with dark wavy hair and he had a deep-set dimple on his right cheek which deepened when he flashed his little lopsided smile. The other students liked Randy, he was equally friendly to students of varied gang affiliations, and for this reason I knew he was not a gang member. However, he had openly reported in class that he was his own man and would never join a gang because he wanted to be friends with everyone. Then he said, "I'm a lover not a fighter and I like the ladies. I don't have time for gang stuff." Of course, all the girls giggled and the other guys were impressed with the attention Randy received from the ladies when he made this statement. Randy came to school impeccably groomed and he greeted everyone, including the police officer and the principal, with a polite good morning which enhanced his image in their sight. Some staff members might have begun to puzzle why Randy was at our alternative school because he presented himself so well. In the beginning, the only notable problem teachers reported was that Randy constantly flirted with girls in class which resulted in distractions. Randy was a charmer!

Most of the time Randy was engaged in learning and his behavior was acceptable though not stellar in class. However, I noticed on some days Randy's face had a glazed expression and he laughed continuously. I had suspected there was more to Randy's character than what the surface evidence revealed. He was too polite and he showed too much respect to adults when engaged in conversations with them. Where was his "I'm only pretending to listen to you" look that all my other middle school students displayed while they rolled their eyes in that familiar but annoying fashion? Where were his irritated responses to adult inquiries that hinted Randy knew more than his teachers knew? Something was off with this student; instead of normal teen attitude, I read humor in Randy's eyes, eyes that twinkled deception. It was his inconsistent academic performance along with his glazed expression and bright eyes in class that clued me to Randy's drug use.

I knew that Randy was not involved in any extra-curricular activities so he would never be pulled for a random drug test and his adequate classroom behavior would continue to allow him to operate under our radar. For this reason, Randy did not have to worry about coming to school under the influence. As long as he could manage to have acceptable behavior in the classroom and as long as he was not found in the possession of drugs, Randy could be high every day at school... so he was.

My suspicion deepened regarding Randy's character when it came to my attention that he was carrying large amounts of cash to school and brandishing it freely in front of other students. Since we had a school rule that students' were not supposed to have more than twenty dollars on their person, I marveled at Randy's bold show of wealth. When one of my co-workers commented to me that Randy was sweet and generous to a fault because he often purchased lunch for other students, I realized Randy's blatant disregard for our school money rule was being ignored by staff. Randy was performing indiscriminate acts of kindness toward fellow students but I suspected his generosity was just the way Randy, the business man, had devised to distribute his promotion incentives. I was almost certain that Randy was a drug dealer and my suspicions were confirmed shortly when Randy confidently over stepped a student boundary. Randy slyly talked a teacher into bringing him a coke from the teachers' lounge. In return, he bought her a coke for running his errand. I observed closely as the teacher walked away filled with girl-like giggles and when Randy saw me looking he held his soda can high like a trophy and nodded in my direction. It was if he was challenging me to do something about it and I sensed he knew I had figured out his game.

That is when I determined Randy's personality was a lot like a snake charmer's. Transfixed by his gaze, school staff members were mesmerized and allowing him to break rules all other students had to follow. I queried myself, "Hadn't I seen him come to school late for another teacher's class without stopping at the office? What about the day I saw him in the hall when he was supposed to be in PE and he told me coach let him out to get a drink? Did I check his story?" Shamefully, I had to admit that I too may have succumbed to Randy's charms and allowed him to break our school rules. Most people would probably not even think Randy's minor infractions important but in the grand scheme of things I knew every rule and every procedure was implemented for a reason. Each rule blocked students' attempts to circumvent the structure we placed to keep drug dealing and drug use out of our school.

Randy had been testing us to see how firm our boundaries were and he found out we were soft and easier to play than the snake charmers flute. I was sure Randy was a business man and he was marketing his life style to our other students right under our noses. Randy made drug use look glamorous by showing off his earnings and he was hooking other students into using drugs with his good deeds and charm. All of his benevolent acts were really like the piping of the snake charmer's flute played for the coins other students would toss in his basket. Disgracefully, I had to admit Randy had been undetected because he charmed the staff, me included, with his respectful and pleasant personality.

Other people may have been oblivious to his misdeeds because of their lack of experience with characters like Randy and I felt their inaction could be excused for that reason. However, I felt personally responsible because I had met characters like Randy before when I was employed as a social worker. In a former position, I had recruited drug dealers out of public housing to participate in a college sponsored program to gain training and change their lives. I had moved easily among the people in the projects and I knew who the main players were. Sadly, I stated to myself, "I know a drug dealer when I see one, even if he is only fourteen years old!" I hadn't seen Randy passing drugs and my only clues that led to that assumption were Randy's gregarious personality and the large sums of money he carried but I knew I probably could get Randy to confess if I played it just right. So, I decided the next time I saw Randy pull a wad of cash out of his pocket I would confront him.

"Randy, put your green away. This will be your only warning. There is a rule in our school that students cannot carry more than twenty dollars at one time and your cash could be confiscated by the police officer or principal. When that happens you may not get it back until you leave our school at the end of six weeks." I warned.

"For real, Mrs. OG? They can just take my money?" queried Randy.

I answered, "Sure, it would be returned to you but our staff will take it. You know why students are not allowed to carry large sums of cash to school?"

One of Randy's classmates hurriedly raised his hand, "Is it because other kids would steal it?"

I responded, "Maybe… but at our school there could be another reason."

A second student raised his hand, "Students could be buying and selling drugs."

"Bingo," I said as I pointed at that student. "Now, Randy, you know what I think when I see large sums of money in a student's possession. When I see money exchanging hands I am going to assume students are making drug deals. I will turn the names of everyone I see passing money into our police officer for suspicion of possible drug activity."

"Au…uh! Mrs. Gifford, that's just cold! I thought you were fly," Randy complained.

I angrily replied, "Randy, I am not cool with drug use. I worked in social services for fifteen years before coming back into teaching and I saw the destruction caused to children and families when people use drugs. Family violence, mental health issues, kids with nothing to eat because parents spend their money on drugs, addiction problems, people getting involved in crime to fund their habits, people going to jail, people having their kids put into foster care and more, all because of alcohol and drug use. I hate drugs because they destroy: health, intelligence, family life, and our society! I don't hate drug users and I do pray for all people who are addicted to any substance but I hate the results of substance abuse because it destroys lives."

A couple of students in class clapped and one timid student who never spoke in class before said, "Amen. Now, you're preach'n, Mrs. Gifford!"

"Randy, this is your only warning and I am putting you on notice. I will turn you in if I see you flashing a roll of money anywhere in the school. Twenty dollars is all you can carry to school," I warned. "Are we straight?" I asked.

"Yeah, we're straight," he answered grumpily. Then, "How come you're the only teacher knows I'm in business?"

I replied, "I guess you weren't listening to my preaching. I use to work in the social service field and visited children in their homes to make sure they were safe and that their families had resources to meet their children's needs. There were times when I walked in on drug deals, parents using, and one time I was caught in the middle of a drug bust. I'm old and I have pretty much seen it all." I explained.

"Why did you quit working there?" he inquired.

"The last time I was down on my knees, behind the bushes hiding out, so I would not be shot as police broke down a door, I said to myself, 'What is a grandma doing in a place like this?'… Also, I realized younger people are quicker. After the drug bust, I had a police officer tell me he admired my courage because he would not have gone into that neighborhood unarmed and he wanted to know how I stayed safe. That is when I realized I wanted to live to retire and I thought I had done my share of that sort of work, so I quit and came back to the teaching profession," I explained.

Randy's eyes had enlarged as I told my story and he let out his breathe with a, "Wow, Mrs. G, you must have been tough to do those things. "

"Not really, but I had to be smart and make assessments on the conditions in homes without pretending to notice the things the parents were trying to hide. As far as the parents knew, I was the old grandma that brought animal cookies and toys to their kids, helped them get groceries or diapers when they needed them, and was trying to help them find work. I always spoke to people when I went into neighborhoods and told people what I was there to do. As long as I was useful to the drug dealers' families, I was safe. Now, Randy I told you my story and there is just one more thing I want to say to you. I don't want any of your business going on at our school because we are here to learn not to buy, sell or use drugs. I know what you are about and you won't be able to fool me."

Turning to address the whole class I continued, "Students, Randy is a nice guy and I like Randy but I don't like what he is doing and I have a warning for the rest of you too. Don't be so eager to try drugs because you may find something you really like and you will: become addicted, rob or do worse to feed your habit, hurt the people you love and go to jail. You could totally miss the person you are supposed to become and never recognize your special talents or purpose on Earth. I know Randy would not want to be the cause of ruining someone else's life but he will if he continues to push his poison and tempt other kids to buy it. Now we all need to go back to work."

Randy hung his head, pouted, and became quiet for the rest of the class. After our confrontation, I never saw Randy with large sums of money again and I was watching very closely. Randy continued to have good attendance and was still respectful to teachers in class. However, he did not pass money to other students as freely as he had been doing and he seemed a little depressed at times which worried me. I wondered if his depression might be coming from gang member threats because Randy had been cutting in on their business. When Randy had told me he was too smart to join a gang and he was not going to share his profits with anyone I worried about his safety.

One day after school Randy came by my room to retake a test and I talked to him about how drug use could limit his ability to learn in school and steal his freedom. I knew Randy was destined to be arrested because gang members would likely rat him out just to get him off the street and eliminate their competition. I warned Randy about this possibility and I told him that he was a bright young man who was destined to have a brighter future if just would not sell or use drugs. Randy promised me he would think about what we had discussed and we began to build an amicable student-teacher relationship in the classroom.

If I could just have gotten Randy to give up his pursuit of the ladies during my class time then I would have been one happy teacher. All the girls in class cooed over Randy ever chance they got. Keeping the young ladies focused on learning and away from Randy had become an everyday chore that I was sick of performing. The girls could not concentrate when he starred at them, wiggled his eyebrows, and blew them kisses. Due to his amorous behavior, I kept Randy after school with two other teachers to talk about the disturbances he was indirectly causing in our classrooms. Of course, he apologized and tried to charm us! I knew he wasn't serious about his repentance because on one particularly bad day for a student to act out, he was a pain!

Our lesson was on ions and isotopes and I needed the students to pay close attention so they could compare and contrast the two atomic structures. Randy was flirting with the girls in class and they were not concentrating on our lesson so I sat Randy in the hall for a time out. After five minutes he raised his hand and wanted to come back in the room. The door was open, I could plainly supervise him, and I knew he could see the white board I was teaching from. I saw no need to bring him in so soon after relegating him to the hall because the girls were just now forgetting his presence so I decided to do a reverse chain up discipline with him. I would decrease his discipline every few minutes he behaved and let him move his desk a little closer when he participated by answering a question correctly.

My intentions were to make Randy earn his way back into my classroom and the other students became interested in the challenge. They were listening closely to see if Randy would gain another three feet forward movement by answering the next question. When it appeared he would enter the classroom before I finished the processing activity, I quickly instated a new rule to slow his progress. If another student could answer correctly when Randy failed to do so then Randy had to move back three feet. This slowed his progress enough to complete what I started and it actively involved all the students in the challenge. We had great fun that day and Randy focused on learning chemistry along with the rest of my class.

Randy continued to come to school under the influence and continued to charm his way out of drug use suspicion with other staff. He said his eyes were red because he had allergies and of course, his behavior was hyper because he had a brother diagnosed with hyperactivity so Randy thought he was hyperactive too. Whatever… But I didn't cut him any slack and I purposely made things harder for him on days that he was high. He didn't have enough time to flirt with the girls when I did this because if he wanted to leave school on time then he had to complete his work.

After being at our school for six short weeks, Randy left me with an unsolicited promise. As students were leaving that week he popped into my room to tell me goodbye. He extended a handshake and told me he was going to change his life. I told Randy I hoped he would change some of his habits because his life was precious to God and to me. When I said, "Randy, please do not throw your life away," he swallowed hard like he was trying to hold back tears. Then he turned to walk out the door and said, "Miss OG, I will never forget you." I truly saw potential in Randy and I hoped he could make good on his pledge to change.

However, one year later Randy showed up in one of my eighth sections again. He walked into the room quietly and sat at the back of the room.

I waited until I caught his eye and made a motion which was a side jerk and then up with my head. A smile broke out across his face and I got a "What up, Mrs. OG?" Quickly, Randy continued, "Mrs. Gifford, I messed up like you said and I went to jail but while I was there I got saved and I don't do cocaine and I don't deal any more. I still smoke a little weed but I want to stop. It's just hard, you know?"

I replied, "Congratulations on the salvation part because most people with addiction problems have to rely on a higher power to overcome the physical and psychological effects of drug abuse. Yes, I know it is difficult to give all of that up at one time but you will get there. I have confidence in you that if you make up your mind to do something then you will do it."

As our lesson began, I tripped back because this class was at the same point exactly one year ago and Randy should remember. Randy did not disappoint me and he began leading the class during our processing activity by answering questions about ions and isotopes. The other students were astonished and one student turned to look at Randy and said, "Man you are smart. You should be a rocket scientist or something!"

Randy broke out into a hearty laugh which reddened his face and then pointing at me he said, "You know who taught me that? You taught me that and I remembered! Remember how you made me move my desk and I could not come into the class until I got the answers correct. I remember. Man, you are a good teacher because I don't remember anything from school but I know ions and isotopes."

I thanked Randy and we continued our lesson. I thought to myself, "Sometimes it is so good to see former students when they encourage you to keep doing what you are doing." Randy's remarks meant a lot to me because I rarely saw student growth due to our student population's quick turn over. He had remembered his lesson from science and now I was inspired once again. I decided that I was not going to give up on Randy and I was thinking about his marijuana problem while glancing through the morning paper the very next day. That's when I saw it and I recognized its appearance as a God incident of monumental importance for Randy. The large advertisement enumerated the ways marijuana use affected teens differently than adults. The article was sponsored by a variety of teen health and mental health organizations. It covered a space equal to a worksheet.

It was perfect! I copied the ad and handed out highlighters to my students in our personal and social responsibilities class.

I began, "How many of you have every had an article placed in the newspaper by your family? Maybe you had a garage sale or wanted to sell a car? How big was your article? Was it as big as this one? How much money did your article cost? How much money do you think an article this size would cost?"

After processing questions were asked to ascertain the value of the information shared in the article, I started over, "Class I do not want you to read this article just yet so please listen carefully to instructions. This article was written for parents to warn them about the dangers of teens smoking marijuana. Look at the bottom of the page and you will see there are about fifteen different agencies which thought this information was important enough to pay for an advertisement this size in a newspaper. I want you to first read the names of the agencies and pick at least one name, you can pick up to three names, then highlight those. Only highlight the names of the agencies you would trust to tell the truth because of what the agencies represent. Be ready to tell me your choices."

After three minutes, the students shared their choices and explained what agencies they thought teens could believe about the effects marijuana use could have on their health. Randy chose a Latino teen treatment center as his believable agency. Next, I assigned students to only highlight words they did not recognize and students look up the definitions in dictionaries. Last, I told students, "Now let's read the article." We processed what we read with a following, hearty discussion on marijuana use and its effects on the teen body and mind. Then students were instructed to write on a piece of paper what they had learned. Randy was intensely reading and writing at the end of class so he was the last to turn in his work for evaluation. As class ended Randy said, "Mrs. Gifford, can I take this article home? I want to hang it over my bed where I can read it."

I calmly replied, "Sure Randy, and share it with your parents because it was written for them."

Then, I thought I saw a tear in Randy's eye when he asked about a friend who committed suicide, "Do you think he did that because he smoked too much?"

"Randy, I don't know. According to the article, that could be a possibility and we do know that teens are affected differently than adults by the chemicals that are created and inhaled when smoking weed. However, I would not go as far as saying all teens that smoke might end up committing suicide. Besides, suicide is a permanent answer to a temporary problem. If a person thinking about committing suicide would just wait a while their life circumstance could change making suicide a very stupid choice. Randy, you are asking about a friend, aren't you? "

Soberly he replied, "Sure, you know him because he used to go here. His name is Jay. I'm not ever going to do anything that stupid and if I get to feeling like I want to off myself then I will quit smoking for sure. Thanks, Mrs. G."

Randy went home that afternoon and asked his mother to help him get into treatment because he knew he was addicted to marijuana. He told me the next morning, "I hung that news article above my bed and I read it when I am tempted to smoke." Randy stayed two more weeks in our school then he suddenly stopped coming. I inquired with the assistant principal who told me Randy had checked into a treatment program and would not be back for the rest of the school year.

"Randy told his mother he was addicted to marijuana and he wanted to get clean," reported the vice principal.

Discussion

Some students are charming, polite and have excellent people skills. Teachers like happy students who are kind, helpful and who the other students tend to like as well. Even when a reasonable mind would tell you something is not quite right we may ignore our better judgments and overlook the behaviors of a snake charmer. Some children are benevolent in their beguiling ways and others are malevolent. The student is this story was benevolent in spirit but malevolent in actions. He was very good at recruiting other students to try drugs. **Did being a drug dealer make Randy a bad kid?**

This story is about addiction and some students will be addicted to drugs and alcohol in our inner city schools. Most of the students who shared their substance abuse history with me reported their first use was in the fourth or fifth grade. Three to four years of almost daily use may be a common occurrence for a few of these children. Students who are addicted cannot come to school without being under the influence.

It is difficult for teachers to confront students who they suspect of drug use and it may be more difficult still to confront students who are suspected of dealing drugs. Educators may think someone else should do it because educators are hired to teach not identify drug activity. However, teachers have more opportunities to observe student behaviors and interactions verses administrators and other staff members who may only view students in passing. A teacher's classroom learning environment and her students' academic performance is affected by students' drug induced behaviors. Therefore, it is in a classroom teacher's best interest to identify student drug use. Teachers may need additional training to do this and they may have to keep daily notes on certain students' suspicious behaviors. **Should identifying students under the influence or possibly dealing drugs become part of a teacher's job description?**

Topics to Research

How are addiction problems and recovery issues different for youth than adults? How does Marijuana use affect the brain and students' abilities to learn in school? Is suicide higher among teen drug users compared to the general teen population? Are certain drugs more addictive than others?

Things to Do

Learn what constitutes addiction to any substance. Search out teen addiction treatment facilities in your area and become familiar with their programs. If you are a parent and you suspect your child is addicted then try to get your children into to treatment as quickly as possible because addicted students are missing their opportunity to get an education by being under the influence of drugs while at school. If you are a teacher watch for signs of drug use and drug dealing in your classroom and just be aware some students do come to school under the influence. If a student's behavior indicates possible drug use then talk to your teaching supervisor and involve the school counselor. Schedule a meeting with the student's parents and recommend parents have the child evaluated for possible drug use. Do this especially if the child disrupts your teaching.

6. Identifying Students Drug Use

The current academic failure some students experience in urban schools may have less to do with teacher competency and more to do with school personnel not identifying and referring students who are under the influence of drugs. Sometimes it is difficult to tell where normal teen behavior ends and abnormal, drug-influenced behavior begins. In addition, we have students who are taking prescribed medications for various psycho-social reasons and they may develop "ticks," uncontrollable movements, or even become emotionally unbalanced in the classroom. Normal student behavior has taken on a whole new meaning today and illegal drug use can be disguised by students' special needs and their medication's side effects. For these reasons, teachers may be reluctant to refer students to the office for suspicion of drug use. In addition, schools may be restricted by their own policy which eliminates some groups of students from drug testing.

According to the National Institute on Drug Abuse, "The U.S. Supreme Court broadened the authority of public schools to test students for illegal drugs. Voting 5 to 4 in *Pottawatomie County vs. Earls*, the court ruled to allow random drug tests for all middle and high school students participating in competitive extracurricular activities" (Frequently Asked Questions About Drug Testing in Schools). Although this ruling expanded testing options from athletes only to include all students participating in extracurricular activities, it did not go far enough. The populations of students who have been missed by this ruling may be students who typically are not involved in extracurricular activities at school. The question we need to ask ourselves is… why does identifying student drug use at extracurricular events take priority over identifying students under the influence in the classroom?

Surly, it is equally important for students to be sober in an academic setting verses a physical competition, theater production, or a band concert. Another concern regarding the Supreme Court's decision was the age restriction of student drug testing which only mentions middle school and high school students. What happens if a fifth or sixth grader who is participating in extracurricular activities is suspected of using drugs? On the surface, drug testing very young children may appear outrageous to consider. However, the average age of first use has declined from late teens to twelve or thirteen years old students in the United States (Age of first-time drug users drops to early teens: report, ABC).

In fact, referrals to alternative education programs have been made for much younger students who were either under the influence or found in the possession of illegal drugs (self). So, there are many things to consider when developing a new policy which intends to identify students' drug use. Because new information about first use exposes the shortfall of school drug testing policies, should schools seek to enlarge their policy to include elementary aged children who participate in extra-curricular activities? Should schools further broaden their policies to include all students in academic settings? There is a lot to consider when purposing school drug testing reforms because drug testing elementary aged children, would most likely be unpopular and expanding drug testing to all groups might be ruled illegal.

Drug testing policies have been scrutinized by the Supreme Court and some have proven to be illegal according to the United States Constitution. The American Civil Liberties Union has been involved in law suits across the United States opposing random student drug testing. The specific targeting of groups of students and random testing students not under suspicion of drug use has caused the ACLU to protest (ACLU of Washington Challenges Suspicionless Urine Testing for Students; *York vs. Wahkiakum School District*). The ACLU's challenge to school policies seem to all focus around 'suspicionless' testing of random students which is another way of saying school officials did not have probable cause to test the students involved in the cases which ACLU chose to represent.

The Fourth Amendment states people have a right to be secured in their persons and other things unless probable cause is evidenced (U.S. Constitution, Fourth Amendment). According to one research conducted by a law educational faculty of a major university in 2002, the Supreme

Court challenged Tecumseh, Oklahoma's school policy of drug testing all high school students who participated in extracurricular activities and it upheld school policy. In this case, a young lady was subjected to random drug testing twice because she sang in a school choir and participated in an academic bowl, both of which are extracurricular activities. Although the school district involved in this case had a policy which withstood the scrutiny of the Supreme Court, if their random drug testing policy had been extended to the entire student body then the outcome might have been quite different.

Basically the school policy was telling students, the school does not have to provide extracurricular activities, those activities are supplemental to providing you a public education, and if you choose to participate in extracurricular activities then you choose to be subject to random drug testing. If student choice had been ignored by extending drug testing to non-participants then the policy could have violated students' constitutional rights under the Fourth Amendment (Exploring Constitutional Conflicts). From this decision, we can understand the position of the court and assume that as long as students are given a choice then random drug testing is permissible. Therefore, random testing without suspecting a student's drug use has been ruled legal but does random testing really identify student who are most likely to use drugs?

In the above case, drug use would have been out of character for the honor student who brought suit, the school district did not have probable cause to expect this student might be using drugs, and the student was subject to random drug testing twice which seems to challenge the randomness of the school's procedure. This student was taken to a restroom by school personnel and told to enter a stall, completely take off her clothes, and urinate in a container while the staff listened. The young lady involved, described her experience as horrible.

In addition, did the random testing harm the relationship between this student, her parents, and the school involved? I can imagine the girl's humiliation and resulting legal action could have left hostile feelings between the school district and the community. Therefore, when formulating random drug testing policies school districts should consider how the drug testing events experienced by students might create toxic school environments for students and erode the district's relationship with its parents. Clearly, identifying student drug use by random testing could result in legal actions against school districts and even if school random drug testing policies are upheld, school districts may be subject to law suits and spend precious education dollars defending their policies. More disturbing, is the fact that students can stagger down the halls of schools, can cause discipline problems in classrooms, and may never be subject to drug testing unless they participate in extracurricular school activities. That kind of drug testing policy is not only ineffective, it does not make sense! Why would students who are demonstrating signs of physical and mental impairments be excused from drug testing because they don't participate in sports or other extra-curricular activities? Therefore, random drug testing probably does little to deter students from using drugs because it may miss the target population completely! Let's look at one other random method.

Dog sniffs have been used in school to identify students who might have drugs on their person and in their belongings. One Appeals Court decision, held that using dogs in high school to sniff students violates the Fourth Amendment because the school lacked suspicion which is another way of saying the school lacked probable cause when allowing the dogs to sniff students and their possessions (B.C. v Plumas Unified School District, 9th Cir. 9/20/99). In this instance, random drug searches by dogs were ruled unconstitutional.

However, dog searches are still permitted and used in several states because there has not been a national challenge to the policy. If there were a challenge at a national level then the school district involved, could expect extraordinary legal expenses and for this reason, some school districts may choose not to use dogs to find drugs in school. From a teacher's perspective, I can verify that dog sniffs can cause an intrusion into academic life by disrupting classroom instruction and some students may have phobias of such animals which may cause students to fear for their safety (self). I totally agree that schools have a right to search their own premises for hidden drugs but the use of animals for searches while students are present may not be wise and it could be legally risky. Which leads us to the question, why don't schools just use probable cause to identify students who are using drugs?

It is understandable why there could be a reluctance to use 'probable cause' because its use is thought of mainly in a criminal context. Educators do not want to have to meet suspicion requirements for 'probable cause' nor do they want to act like policemen. Why then do school personnel perform student body searches, do drug testing, and search lockers? Aren't those policing actions? Besides, there could be an advantage to applying probable cause since all students attending school, not just students who are participating in extracurricular activities, could be drug tested if probable cause was applied to student behaviors which might indicate drug use.

According to a court decision rendered in New Jersey in 1985, the court should adopt a lower standard of probable cause for schools than it applies in criminal cases and the ability schools have to conduct student searches should be modified to reflect the relationship between public education and its students. The court in this student search case, may have been alluding to school personnel's' locus parentis rights and their responsibility to keep students safe and provide discipline while acting in the role of a parent. Schools do have this locus parentis rule working in their favor and 'probable cause' to search the student in this case was upheld by the court with a decision, "The court only requires officials to have something like a moderate chance of finding evidence of wrongdoing" (Exploring Constitutional Conflicts).

Although the right for schools to search students was upheld in the above instance, courts have not always agreed with a school district's choice to perform student searches. In Stafford vs. Redding (2009), the court found the school exceeded their authority to perform searches when strip searching a thirteen year old girl whom was suspected of giving a pain killer drug to another student. The Supreme Court ruled the search was too intrusive and there was a low level of threat posed. Therefore, the student's fourth amendment rights were violated. The contrast between these cases tells us that probable cause to search students can be established in some cases, not in others, and the actions of administrators who order or conduct searches must temper their decisions with rational thought. Therefore, the ability of school personnel to conduct student body searches should probably be limited because school districts face legal consequences when they are performed incorrectly. With or without 'probable cause' being upheld, school employees should probably stop acting like law enforcement officers when trying to identify student drug use.

The concept of using 'probable cause' to identify students by students' physical signs of impairments and behaviors may sound like a good idea. Its true students who have been missed by random testing could be subject to drug screening under the application of 'probable cause.' However, if using this method results in student body searches and drug testing then liability risks for school districts will remain high and educators will still be acting like police officers. I would think that most school personnel would like to get out of that sort of business. Besides, the above actions may not deter student drug use.

Drug testing especially seems to be ineffective when used alone. According to The Drug Policy Alliance, after researching student drug testing and consulting experts from the American Public Health Association and the Academy of Pediatrics, this group came to a conclusion that random drug testing does not effectively reduce drug use among young people (Making Sense of Drug Testing Why Educators are saying No, 2006). If stand-alone student drug testing is: ineffective, targets some specific groups, leaves out other groups which may be at higher risk for drug use, and sparks legal actions against school districts, then is it useful?

According to the National Institute on Drug Abuse, student testing is useful when it is a component of broader prevention program which has the goal to reduce students' drug use (Frequently Asked Questions about Drug Use in Schools). Therefore, student drug testing might be effective if used as a part of a substance abuse prevention plan which has intervention and treatment components. To limit school liability personnel should probably not do the testing and we have already decided school personnel should probably not do student body searches for the same reason. However, we can't just throw our hands up and do nothing! It is obvious that we need a new plan to reduce student drug use at schools and we need it formulated quickly because the legalization of marijuana is impending.

Decriminalizing the use of marijuana is being considered by several representatives from our government and non-drug using students clearly stated to me, if marijuana was legalized they would try it. One article from TIME in conjunction with CNN, told of legal actions going on in California, Massachusetts, and New York legislatures to legalize marijuana use (Why Legalizing Marijuana Makes Sense, 2009). Yet, The National Institute on Drug Abuse records the following effects on students, "Marijuana intoxication can cause distorted perceptions, impaired coordination, difficulty in thinking and problem solving, and problems with learning and memory. Research has shown that marijuana's adverse impact on learning and memory can last for days or weeks after the acute effects of the drug wear off. As a result, someone who smokes marijuana every day may be functioning at a suboptimal intellectual level all of the time" (NIDA InfoFacts: Marijuana). When marijuana is legalized educators could see additional decline in students' performance and they could observe an increase of students' behavior problems.

Therefore, school substance abuse prevention and intervention programs need to be in place when marijuana becomes legalized. Identifying students who may need substance abuse intervention services and educating students about health and other life consequences which result from substance abuse are appropriate roles for educators to play. If schools can reform their student drug policies to only include the following three goals, identification, referrals for intervention, and prevention education then they can make better use of their education dollars and limit their entanglements in court actions. Schools will not need to police student drug use or perform student searches if a "no refusal policy" is implemented.

Let's talk about identification first. Drug free workplace laws allow employers to ask employees to submit to drug testing when physical or behavioral signs the worker might be under the influence are documented. Employers can fire workers who refuse drug testing because their refusal is taken as admission of guilt and the workers' rights are not violated because they were given a choice to take a drug test (Drug Free Workplace Act). Therefore a school policy could parallel this model and students could be given a choice to submit to a drug test or be suspended. School personnel would only have to document the reasons why a student was asked to take a drug test and these reasons should include physical signs of impairment and behavior signs which could serve as probable cause. Unlike a police officer, educators would not have to see a student using drugs or find students in the possession of drugs. Remember, schools do not have to apply probable cause in the criminal sense and schools take their authority from locus parentis. The ability to identify students under the influence is an important function of the above school authority because it serves to keep students safe from drug injury and overdose while at school.

Since students could not consent on their own, parents would have to be notified and they would have to come to school and be involved in the process. Parents would be given referral information; they would pay for the drug testing with private insurance or by other means and a release would be signed so the test results could come back to the school. A **no**

refusal policy enforced by schools would allow a parent to refuse drug testing for their child so student choice is guaranteed and this would satisfy the students being given a choice requirement. However, if parents refused drug testing for their child then the student would automatically be judged to be under the influence. Progressive consequences for additional suspected drug use incidents at school and documentation regarding the parent's cooperation or lack thereof, could result in a referral to child protective services or parent court fines. The documentation of a parent's refusal and the assignment of progressive student consequences, along with intervention attempts in the form of referrals, would also serve as tracking mechanisms and could lead to a permanent expulsion from the school district. Of course, parents could request a hearing before final expulsion.

During the identification process, student referrals should be made not only for drug testing but also for interventions. Schools could require students who test positive to attend substance abuse education classes with their parents either at treatment facilities or with a district employee specialist. Schools would have to set their own thresholds of tolerance for students being suspect of drug use at school. Some might implement three strikes and you are out rule and others might choose to seek permanent discharge of students from their district until drug treatment is accomplished. Whatever new policies are constructed, the goal would be to: create safer learning environments by identifying and limiting student drug use at school, encourage parents to take a responsible role in preventing their child from coming to school under the influence, give students a choice to refuse testing and not violate their rights, and provide referrals for intervention services. All these actions could protect school districts from legal actions.

The advantage to using identification and a **no refusal policy** instead of random drug testing and student searches is that all students could be referred for drug testing who show physical or behavioral signs of being under the influence at school. As a society we could limit teen addiction by identifying our students who may need treatment early and by discouraging the development of student drug use patterns. Research about teens who are using marijuana is especially troubling and show children who used this drug for the first time at 14 years old or younger were classified with drug dependence at a rate of 13.5 percent compared to individuals whose first use was 18 or older at 2.2 percent dependency (U.S. Department of Health and Human Services).

If we draw an adult parallel to substance abuse and driving, as a nation we have decided people under the influence who are driving a vehicle pose safety threats and do harm to society. So, they receive consequences for their behaviors when caught. Likewise, students under the influence at school pose threats to their own safety and others. They also interfere with instruction and cause discipline problems. There is absolutely no reason why drug intoxicated students should be present in our public school classrooms and we need to formulate policies to protect non-using students from having their education opportunities limited by students who cause classroom confusion and disruptions.

The only part left to talk about is substance abuse prevention education. Many school districts are already developing health classes to meet this need not only for substance abuse issues but also for dietary concerns. As a matter of fact, childhood obesity and diabetes education should correlate with drug prevention education because children with these problems are at greater risk for harm when they abuse drugs and alcohol. Drug abuse prevention education does not have to be an entirely different course and everything children need to know about taking care of their bodies, including the negative effects of using drugs and alcohol, could be included in human health classes and most core science classes which study the human body.

In closing, research obtained by the Bureau of Justice Statistics clearly identified the relationship between low commitment to education and a higher level of truancy due to student drug use. The report stated that cognitive and behavioral problems experienced by youth using drugs may interfere with academic performance of both the users and their classmates (1992). Therefore, educational reforms should consider policies which support identification of individual student drug use, referrals for treatment, and health education which acts as prevention. I know there will always be exceptions and school personnel may have to call in law enforcement to handle students who are suspect of selling drugs at school. However, the current student drug use policies have caused school officials to act like police agents while conducting student body searches and doing drug testing. I believe this role is unacceptable for schools, I know the role is controversial, and it cost school districts money in legal fees.

Let's review our role and create policies which identify students who demonstrate a pattern of drug use and get help for those students before addiction becomes an issue. Those new policies will allow the non-drug using students to achieve their full potentials without being harassed by random drug testing policies or body searches. A **no refusal policy** would enlarge school districts' ability to promote sobriety among all its students while avoiding student right issues and legal entanglements. This policy would capture parents' attention and cause them to seek help for their children's substance abuse problems.

However, eliminating risk of legal actions against schools may become a prime motivator for change when school funding continues to experience cuts. If education reform in this one area can eliminate legal risk for school districts, improve the quality of class room instruction by removing students under the influence of drugs, and provide interventions which identify students developing drug addiction problems then why not reform our policies? There is only one downside I can think of and that is classroom teachers may have to become more aware of signs that a student may be under the influence and they will probably need additional training to do this. Teachers will also have to document student's unusual behaviors or physical signs of impairment. However, the advantages to having a drug free classroom would far outweigh the additional efforts. Conversely, teacher's efforts required to note unusual student behaviors might equal or take less time than writing office referrals for classroom disruptions.

In closing, students need to be sober to learn. When marijuana is legalized there will be more students coming to school under the influence unless school districts take action and set new policies in place now to identify student drug use. This reform is needed now.

References and Resources

NIDA, Drugabuse.gov/DrugsPages/testingfaqs.html; "Frequently Asked Questions about Drug Testing in Schools," 04-15-2010

ABC NEWS; "Age of first-time drug users drops to early teens: report," Tues Dec 18, 2007

(ACLU of Washington Challenges Suspicionless Urine Testing for Students; *York vs. Wahkiakum School District*).

Law.umkc.edu/faculty/projects/ftrials/conlaw/searches.htm, Student Searches and the Fourth Amendment; "Exploring Constitutional Conflicts," 04-15-2010

B.C. v Plumas Unified School District, 9th Cir. 9/20/99

ACLU, Drug Law Reform Project; "Making Sense of Drug Testing Why Educators Are Saying No," Kern J., Gunja F., Cox A., Rosenbaum M. Pd.D., Appel,J., Verrna A, 2006

Time.com/time/nation/article/o,8599,1889021,00. Html, "Why legalizing Marijuana makes Sense," Joe Klien, 04-02-2009

nida.nih.gov/Infofacts/marijuana.html; "NIDA InfoFacts: Marijuana," 04-07-2010

law.umck.edu/faculty/projects/ftrials/conlaw/searches.htm, Stafford unified School District vs. Redding (2009)

www.hrhero.com/topics/drug_free_workplace.html, Information on the **Drug-Free Workplace Act**, a federal law, and similar state laws: HR Topic Page from HRhero.com

Substance Abuse and Mental Health Services Administration, Division of Population Surveys; U.S. Department of Health and Human Services, "National Survey on Drug Use and Health: National Findings," HHS Publication No. SMA 09-4434

www.parenting**teens**.com/index/**Teen**+Drug+Abuse/ Graphs+and+**Stats**?lpage=2,

U.S. **Department of Justice** ... of **Justice** Programs Bureau of **Justice Statistics**

7. The Bopper

At first glance, Julie appeared to be in the third or fourth grade. She was thin, under four feet tall, probably closer to three and one-half feet in height, and her appearance in the eighth grade caused quite a spectacle when she lined up with the other students. There was something else unusual about her physical characteristics that I could not immediately put my finger on and I knew it would drive me crazy until I could remember the name of the syndrome. It was a genetic defect of some sort that I had encountered while working as a child development specialist. I tried not to gawk at the new student while assessing some of her other physical attributes. Her legs were not aligned and they appeared to turn in at her knees. She wore very thick glasses, the sort I had seen worn by individuals who were also legally blind. Her teeth appeared too large for her small face; they pushed her top lip outward and they were slightly crooked.

After I gave Julie a quick visual evaluation, I determined she was a special education student and as usual, I had not received her individualized plan before she started at our school. I knew it would not do any good to complain about the referral process for a sped (special education)student like Julie because her situation was a repeat pattern I had come to expect. Students came and left our school like they were shot out of a machine gun in rapid fire and all the staff just learned to expect the unexpected. Besides, I probably would get the information I needed on Julie within a week. The delay did mean I would have to observe Julie more closely than other new students while trying to figure out her disabilities and she initially might not receive the modifications needed to be successful in our program. Due to this, I was afraid Julie's rights to an appropriate education could be compromised for a short time period.

However, I was delighted to later find out that Julie had the ability to do my work quite well with few modifications. She probably knew her own individualized education plan better than the people who wrote it and Julie asked for help when she needed it. I thought this young lady was pretty amazing because she understood her own disabilities and sought support when she was being challenged by the demands of the curriculum. In addition, Julie was extremely polite and she was focused on her work while in class. Her ability to finish her work with time to spare and her eagerness to make friends made Julie the perfect classroom helper.

Four or five of the other students in Julie's period were struggling but unlike Julie, they were not use to taking responsibility for their own education. Many of these students had to be guided minute by minute or they would get lost in the instruction. The class section to which Julie had been assigned was designated as the special education eighth grade class. However, our staff could assign traditional and advanced placement students to this section if our other eighth grade section was filled. Due to this, Julie's class was not exclusively reserved for special education students and this created a difficult teaching situation. Six of my students needed curriculum adaptations due to their special education classifications, an additional two students were enrolled in traditional science, and another two others were taking AP (advanced placement) science coursework.

All these different ability levels and curriculum needs present in the same section of students guaranteed that most of the students would not get their educational needs met all the time. Traditional class room teachers would have no more than four sped students assigned to their class before receiving the help of a teacher's aide but at the alternative school, teachers could have up to twelve special needs students in a class without the benefit of an assistant. Worse yet, the scenario I was faced with which mixed extremes of varied ability levels could prevent me from doing my best work with these special students. I hated that possibility and I could have really gotten stressed about the situation. However, I decided I could only do what I could do for these students and I gave myself permission not to be the poster child for the perfect middle school science teacher.

Without an aide, I was very busy moving from desk to desk during seat work time and during clinical lab activities. I was thankful Julie did not need much help and I was pleased when she offered to assist me with the other students. The needy students were glad to have someone else like Julie to help them because most of them did not have the patience to wait for the teacher. Julie was capable and eager to help others. Therefore, after I instructed Julie to not do the work for the other students but guide them instead, she quickly became my classroom aide. In turn, Julie received recognition as the teacher's helper and she became accepted by the students who initially were turned off by her appearance.

When I thanked Julie for her help, on those days she finished early and was allowed to be my aide, she replied, "That's alright Mrs. G, they are my friends and you are supposed to help your friends."

Julie really did have a sweet and endearing personality. She was patient and kind while working with the other students and soon the other children in class appreciated her and respected her for being the teacher's helper. I felt good about Julie's adjustment and discovered my apprehensions about her classroom performance were baseless. Instead of requiring more teacher effort, Julie had turned out to be a teacher's blessing or so I thought!

There was only one thing that concerned me about Julie. Since she was the only girl in this section, she enjoyed the total attention of all the boys in class and I began to wonder if her eagerness to help her classmates was born out of her desire to be noticed by the opposite sex. There was one specific boy in class which Julie asked to work with every day and every day I refused her request. Since, Roger was in AP science, competent, and always did his work, I would tell Julie that other students needed her help first. She stayed busy with the other sped kids and class would end before she had an opportunity to work with Rodger. I knew my stalling would only work so long but I was concerned about Julie's crush on this young man. There was too great of a difference in their intelligence levels and I felt Julie could be taken advantage of in a relationship. In addition, their physical appearances struck a contrast that could not be ignored because Roger needed to shave daily.

Roger was a muscular, dark figure who could gave menacing looks until he submitted to my authority in the classroom environment. When I challenged his first attempt at visual intimidation, he broke out into a radiant smile revealing a full set of braces and he apologized. "Man, Mrs. Gifford, you got that look! You're alright." After our initial stare down I never had another challenge from him. In fact, Roger was almost too quiet; it seemed to me that he was guarding his behavior too closely and whatever emotions were trapped in his shell took great effort to contain. I was afraid his braces would lock up his mouth because I could see his jaw line protrude when he grinded his teeth downward sealing his lips shut. I made the assessment that this was a kid who was hiding his true self and although he was very much in control of his emotions in our school environment on the streets he might be fierce. I was sure in the right situation that any emotional response Roger gave might be accompanied by fierce blows from his large knuckled and scarred hands.

In comparison, Julie's physical development was so thwarted at fourteen years old that she showed no signs of breast development or hip enlargement. Her figure was that of a small child and was straight up and down. So, I was surprised the day she asked me to go to the nurse to get a sanitary supply because I was sure there had to be some secondary sexual characteristics evidenced before a girl could have a period. In addition, there was something else that bothered me about Julie asking for a referral to the nurse. When she made her request, Julie said it loud enough to attract the attention Roger to whom she had been showing an interest. Girls were usually discreet when asking to see the nurse and most certainly did not announce they needed a sanitary product to take care of a womanhood issue. For this reason, I thought Julie's boldness came from her desire to let others in the room know she was a woman!

That's when the name "Turner's Syndrome" came to me. Girls with Turner's syndrome do not grow very well and they do not go through the physical changes that announce womanhood. Julie could have been a poster child for that birth defect except I would have expected a lower level of intelligence from a child affected by Turner's. However, Julie's higher than expected level of intelligence was contrasted dramatically by her sweet, naïve, and child-like manners that a person would expect from a child affected by Turner's syndrome. As I pondered the possible diagnoses, I was pretty sure Julie's special education classification could be related to this syndrome. I thought to myself, "If Julie does have Turner's syndrome then that would explain her lack of physical development." At that point, I felt very protective of Julie and I did not want to cause her further ridicule so I relented and I let her go to the nurse. When I decided to humor Julie and make the referral, I thought, "Maybe Julie got the idea from watching other girls go to the office for supplies and she doesn't want to be different. I will let her go once and I will talk to the nurse afterward."

Even though I had no reason to believe that Roger or any other boy in class would be impressed by Julie's loud plea for a sanitary product, the manner in which she made the request had caused me an uneasy feeling. I did take comfort in the fact that the young man Julie was trying to impress did not appear to lack female attention. Often, I saw Roger flirting with the older girls outside while waiting for a bus home and these high school girls were not shy about returning his expressed interest. It did concern me that Julie chose to focus her attention on this one young man who was older, smarter, and more physically developed than she was. However, Roger did not appear to be the cruel type, when it came to ladies, and I hoped he would only be annoyed by Julie's attention seeking behavior. After that incident, I planned to keep Julie away from Roger in class as much as possible and I hoped he would not hurt Julie's feelings if she approached him and expressed her crush outside of our classroom.

There were some things about Roger I admired; he was an advanced placement student in science, he showed extraordinary interest in class, and he was extremely respectful to our staff. All the teachers liked his attitude because he was a serious student and he evidenced a better than average potential. However, there were other things about Roger that troubled me. He was heavily into the gang scene and he was currently on house arrest. I had seen him flash his leg ban on his first day in my room. The students often showed off their ankle monitors to each other in class like dogs show their teeth. I realized right away the emergence of the alpha male in my classroom was linked to the presence of a house arrest, leg band. I dreaded it when multiple, opposing gang bangers showed up at the same time sporting ankle jewelry because it would take a while for the students to elect the top dog. Until he was recognized and respect was given, I could expect violence to break out among the different gang fractions in class. Fortunately, there was only one other student wearing one of these charms when Roger arrived in class and he was a member of the same gang.

This student, George, had a shaved head and a wise look. The expression on his face always seemed to indicate he knew something others did not. I could imagine him as a model for the picture on a household cleaning product bottle. His white t-shirt added to this illusion and I did not doubt George would have worn a hooped ear ring in one ear if our school allowed jewelry. Like Roger, George was older than the other students, around sixteen years old, and had recently acquired his legal chain before being sent to the alternative school. According to George, "I forgot I had my gun on me and got caught with it at school… but it wasn't loaded. I went out the night before and took it with me. You don't walk around in this city at night without your pistol." George told me this when I engaged him in a conversation after motioning him to pick up his blue bandana off the floor next to his leg. I had discreetly nudged his foot with mine and made a jerking motion with my head to the side and down where I rested my gaze on his handkerchief.

George's inquisitive eyes told me his thoughts, "What's she going do about it?"

Easily, I engaged him by saying, "Since it is your first day I am just giving you a warning. Wherever, you had that, you need to put it back, secure it and never bring it again to school. Teachers will send you to the office with a referral for possessing gang paraphernalia." I didn't bother telling him I had seen our school police officer do the same thing the day before with another student so I felt justified in my action. After all he wasn't making gang signs at anyone and he wasn't flashing his affiliation. He simply dropped the cloth out of one of his pant legs.

Although I knew my principal would have come down hard on this kid if I referred him to the office for possessing gang paraphernalia, I also knew that my principal had made use of gang members when he taught. The principal had told us in a teachers' meeting about engaging these leaders to maintain order and discipline in his classroom. He did not speak clearly or tell us how he had used them but he implied winning gang leaders over and getting them to buy into what you are trying to do could help maintain order in your classroom and avoid violence. I felt I was only following the principal's lead by winning the trust of students like George.

George was a good student and he, like Roger, was in advanced placement science. According to him, how could he not be advanced? This student had been locked up for two years and had already completed work through the tenth grade level while in jail. I was really sorry for George's situation and I did not understand what our school district was thinking when they put him back years in his education. George was sitting in an eighth grade classroom and studying stuff he already knew. I feared that eventually George would become a discipline problem or drop out because he would turn seventeen this school year. Without his ankle attachment, I doubted George would have even come to school. Some days he did cut school in favor of other pursuits. When George was truant and caught on the streets, he would show up in the back of a squad car and receive a police escort to our school office. He would be warned not to skip school again and he would be threatened with a return to jail. However, the officials who were picking George up must not have been reporting his school truancy to his probation officer because he continued to receive police escorts to school at least once a week his whole time of attendance at the alternative school.

I would say that George's attitude about the work we had to do in my classroom was not enthusiastic but he complied with my wishes and was respectful. Bored out of his mind, George occupied his time by finding humor in the adult logic that developed our alternative school program and he made one comment which caused the whole class to erupt in laughter. "Mrs. Gifford, don't you think who ever decided to put all the bad kids together in one school might be special? They must have ridden the short bus to school themselves when they were young!" I had to laugh along with my class because the teaching situation I faced was preposterous some days.

In addition to being a humorist, George was a watcher. He was always observing the other students and seemed to have a heightened awareness of classroom situations. George had time to watch because he finished his work quickly and since he had no interest in helping his class mates, I allowed him to read library books. Once finished with his work for the day, George would open his current read and occasionally peer over the top of his book to observe the classroom. Intermittently, with a twinkle of his eye or a discreet side jerk with his head he would direct me to situations which needed a teacher's attention. When this happened, he always rewarded the class with a hardy laugh as I busted students' attempts to break rules or play me to get out of work. "You know you can't play Miss OG! Why you even try? When are you little kids gonna learn, Mrs. Gifford knows what's up?" In this way, George actually helped me maintain discipline and order when he was present. He was a benevolent critic who made assessments but gave positive suggestions for the betterment of our class. George's ever watching presence in the classroom proved useful to me because I learned to watch this student, "the watcher," to be aware of disguised student activities which could have taken place directly under my nose in the class room.

Although I enjoyed the presence of a student with a comradely spirit in my classroom, I would have liked to see George skipped up to high school where he belonged. I had arranged a meeting with the school counselor and I had tried to get George promoted. George seemed appreciative of my efforts and I reasoned he became loyal to my cause in the classroom due to my attempted intervention. However, I believe he became discouraged and his increasing number of truancies could have been related to our failed meeting with the school counselor. Our school counselor was in agreement with me about George's ability and the inappropriateness of his placement in eighth grade but she was unable to convince the people responsible for his assignment. The school district refused him promotion based on his jail curriculum completion. Apparently, George's studies while in jail, did not meet our district's curriculum standards. George was disappointed and he took an extended leave from school for one full week after this meeting.

On one particular day, I was glad George decided to come back to school because I had a face-off with an extremely low functioning sped student who announced that he was going to fight me. Donny was an older student, sixteen years old like Roger and George, but unlike those two students Donny was developmentally delayed. Donny's eyes were wide-set and drooped at the outside corners giving him a sleepy appearance. His ears were deformed and rolled forward at the tops. His teeth were all pointed, even his incisors, which gave the appearance of a sharks' mouth. He had an upper lip that was so thin it could have been drawn with an eye liner pencil with one quick whoosh. Donny was a child who was born with genetic defects and he probably had fetal alcohol syndrome. Julie often worked with Donny and he sometimes would do things for her that he would not accomplish for me or any other teacher.

Occasionally Donny could not be persuaded to do anything and would refuse Julie's help or become angry at me for not letting him just sit or sleep. When Donny announced, "Mrs. Gifford, I'm going to fight you," I knew he could pose a real threat to my safety and I was hoping that one or two students in the class would respond to my unexpressed need should Donny follow through with his threat. I thought George and Roger, because of their maturity and intelligence levels, were the two most likely students who might intervene.

It had happened before and I was always amazed at the students who stepped forward to protect the teacher. The last time this happened a Katrina refugee, a young man by the appropriate name of Michael, came to my defense. He had reacted quickly and prevented a young lady from knocking me out. This girl was assigned to one of my class sections that was overflowing with Katrina refugee students. All these children had attended alternative education programs in New Orleans. These youth had been in trouble with the law or had caused disruptions in traditional educational settings in Louisiana before coming to our school district. Some may have even been in juvenile lock up when the hurricane hit and had to be removed quickly.

Shana was tall, muscular and thick. She wanted to run her mouth all period long and I was tired of trying to talk over her. I had moved her seat, I had talked to her in private, and I had written her up on a discipline form. She had been assigned to the ISS (in school suspension) room for one day because her behavior was bad in all our middle school classrooms. Still, she continued to disrupt my teaching. Since we were not allowed to keep students after school for detention at this point in my employment, I was severely limited in the discipline I could prescribe for this young lady. Making an effort to understand how I was supposed to maintain order, without keeping students after school, I conference with my supervisor. He asked me, "Are you afraid to kick the desk and tell the students to shut the hell up? Because that is what you need to do. Humiliate them and call them out. You're the adult. You are in charge not them."

That was the extent of advice and help I got from him. This was not my first year teaching but this was my first year at the alternative school and after talking to my supervising principal, I realized I needed to adjust my demeanor to relate to the students in a manner which resulted in them respecting me in the classroom so I could teach. Now, when I look back at his urging me to be physical he probably was only telling me to act tough but at the time I thought he meant for me to literally kick the student's desk and swear. However, the use of profanity with children was not a pleasant idea for me and I did not do as he instructed for several days more.

At last, my meeting with the school authority only helped me realize I could not send this young lady to him for discipline again because the he wanted me to handle the students' behaviors on my own. So when her disruptions interfered with my lesson that last time, I walked back to the girl's seat and did what my principal said but my action did not ring true to my character. It was not my style and Shana knew my attempts to intimidate her were puny. She stood up and postured to make a blow upside my head and I just closed my eyes because I knew it was coming. The only thing I had time to do was pray and I did.

Then I heard a desk turn over at the front of the classroom and here came Michael who placed himself between me and the girl. Michael got up in her face and said, "Oh NO! Not my mamma you don't. This is her classroom and she runs it. Now you sit down and let her teach. I'm learn'n in here and I like science. Now shut yo mouth or I will shut it for you." The girl sat down and she was respectful in my class from that day forward.

My relationship with this one student had kept me from being hurt. I had been kind to Michael because he had confided to me he could not read well when I had encouraged him to do his work in class. I told him I could make a referral to a special reading program at our school and in the mean time, he could copy down notes off the overhead and we could go over those together. No one in class needed to know that Michael could not read. I promised Michael that he would not fail due to his reading deficit and I would help him understand the work. He told me I was the only teacher who did not make him feel dumb. I believed, that Michael felt loyalty toward me, defended me and even called me mamma, an honorary title that still warms my heart today, because I did not make him feel dumb.

After that first episode, I realized I could not intimidate students with swearing and I really wasn't any good at hurling expletives. Now, I looked around the classroom and I wondered if any of these students were like Michael because I was in the middle of a situation again that could prove dangerous. I did not believe this young man, Donny, had a grudge against me because I tried never to offend my students. However, I did know I irritated this student by not relenting when he feigned he could not do the work in class. I refused to let this young man just sit or sleep and I had been working diligently with Donny to show him he could do the work. My guess is that Donny made up his mind that I would not coerce him into doing anything that day.

Donny approached the front of the classroom and began starring me down with his fists clinched in front of his face evidencing he was ready to deliver blows and his position blocked my path to the infamous black button that teachers were supposed to push if a threat of violence occurred. I quickly assessed the situation and decided I would have to brush past

Donny to reach the button and that would surely initiate an unfavorable response. Not knowing what else to do, I posted up; I raised my fists in the air and I took a boxing stance that would have impressed the heavy weight champion of the world.

I felt like I was in a movie scene where the characters were moving in slow motion. The sounds in the room intensified in my ears as I heard the clock ticking loudly. Then there was the quiet whooshing sound of air rushing over vocal cords, as all the other students in my room sucked in their breaths. After a very long minute posing toe to toe and nose to nose with Donny, he gave up, put his hands down, and walked away saying, "Mrs. G, You scare me!"

The other students in class were buzzing, "She' tough! Did you see her face? She was going to take you out, Donny. Miss OG don't play! She's gangsta."

When I look back now I can't imagine having the courage to do what I did that day but I had to handle the situation on my own. I'm sure if Donny would have seen fear in my face instead of glimpsing my determination then the ending would have been quite different. Donny sensed he could expect a real fight from me. Although I would never want to purposely hit a student and I knew from my earlier experience that God would provide deliverance, I wondered if He really expected me to fight. The thoughts that went through my mind while I stood posed against Donny were: "Use what you know, look into his eyes, and don't blink. You have walked in on drug dealers while doing client home visits and your personal safety has been threatened before but you are still standing. So just keep standing!"

Later I thought my self- increasing faith talk, was a little like King David's when he called out Goliath and said to himself, "I've killed a lion and a bear..." it's true I didn't understand the purpose of my confrontation with Donny but I understood the results. I gained the respect of the other students in class that day including the gang members because I showed them I was not afraid. Although, I have to admit my courage partially came from seeing George move from the back of the classroom to position himself on Donny's left side. George was still across the room but I knew if Donny had landed a blow he would not have gotten a second chance. There was no doubt in my mind that George would have reached him quickly. Also, Roger who was sitting in the front row had taken a position on top of his desk and could have easily propelled himself into the fray. Building a respectful relationship with these two students had given me some security. So, I had to admit that part of my supervising principal's advice really did work and I learned that building a respectful relationships with my student gang members was not only necessary to gain their compliance to my classroom rules but mutual respectful relationships with these students could prove useful for my own safety.

I was glad the confrontation with Donny ended the way it did because getting involved in a classroom brawl could have cost both Roger and George their freedom. Students, who are wearing an ankle monitor and have a probation officer, should not get into fights at school. These two young men had used good judgment when they chose not to immediately get into my dispute with Donny but I had the distinct feeling that if I would have needed their help then they would have intervened.

Then Roger completely lost his ability to make good judgment calls and he threw caution to the wind by committing an unthinkable act. It was a day when my lesson plans were so varied for the different ability groups in the same class that I could not keep the whole group together. So, I decided to create a computer research lesson for my traditional and advanced placement science students. They could do their work at the computer stations on one side of my room while I helped other students like Donny who needed more attention. I only had two computers but they were placed on a long table which allowed enough room to accommodate four chairs. The only thing I would have to do was make sure students were on the correct web site then they could follow their worksheets to find the information they needed.

Occasionally, I looked up and observed that area in the classroom. I was not too concerned about close supervision of these AP and traditional science students because my students were notoriously well behaved when they were allowed to work on the computer. Besides, they did not dare slip off site because they had been informed I would retract their computer privileges for at least two weeks if they attempted to do this. By this time, students realized I would do as I said and my students were convinced I would follow my own classroom edicts. My divided classroom plans would have gone just fine except one of the traditional students was called out of class for a dentist appointment vacating a chair next to Roger at one computer.

That is when Julie begged to use the computer saying, "Please Mrs. G, I love using the computer. You know I will do the work."

I had apprehensions and there was a gnawing sensation deep in my gut that screamed, "No!" However, while disregarding my feelings, I said, yes to Julie's appeal. There was only about twenty minutes of class time left and I really wanted to reward Julie for being such a good worker and for being a help to me. Even if the assignment was too difficult for her, I reasoned Julie would be able to find some answers and I could give her extra credit for those. As Julie took her seat next to Roger, I turned to assist my less capable learners.

When George and his learning partner finished at their computer station, I offered Julie the chance to sit at the vacated computer alone to finish her assignment. That's when Julie explained she didn't want to find the web site again because the other boys had shut down their computer. Again, I relented even though the knot increased in size in my stomach. Now only Julie and Roger sat at the computer station. I really didn't have reason to suspect anything unusual was going on between these two students until I looked in the direction of George's desk.

I became aware that some kind of student deception might be taking place on the computer station side of the room because twice when I looked up while helping a student, George was looking in that direction. Also, he had a weird expression on his face which I studied for a few seconds before determining its meaning. George was unaware of my watching him and his face revealed a trance like gaze combined with a crooked smile. After watching my classroom watcher, I carefully repositioned myself so that my back was against the wall and I could easily make a half turn to view the working area across the room. When I heard a pencil drop, I jerked my head up and I was just in time to see Julie pulling her head up and away from Roger's lap. At first, it looked like she was just bending that direction to pick up her pencil and I chastised myself for a wayward thought, "You have worked so long with perverted characters in social work that you are imaging things. Little kids don't do stuff like that!" However, my darker side took over and convinced me to lay a trap.

I walked to the front of the room and pretended to go through papers on my desk like I was trying to find something. I could feel the tension in the room was mounting and I could sense that George was somehow a part of a conspiracy as he raised his hand and requested help with the processing questions from his computer research. Casually, I walked from my desk which turned me away from the computer stations. I took two steps toward George, then unexpectedly, I whirled around to see Julie drop her head into Roger's lap again and this time she didn't even bother to pretend she was picking up her pencil!

I calmly said, "Julie stop and come over here and sit down," as I pointed to her desk.

"You too, Roger," I ordered and made a motion toward his desk.

I knew that other students besides George were aware of the interaction between Julie and Roger because I had caught them looking too. So, I felt I needed to address the whole class regarding the action they had witnessed in my classroom. After asking the students to rearrange their desk from group positions into straight lines and everyone was seated I began, "How many of you know that it is against the law to have sex in public?"

Not one student raised a hand. I continued, "What just happened in our classroom is illegal and it is considered offensive public behavior." For the next three to five minutes I talked frankly to the students about my need to report the incident and the possible resulting consequences. Some of the students wanted to argue with me what Julie had been doing was not really sex and others had questions about locations where they would get in trouble for having sex. One child wanted to know if it was alright to have sex at the car wash and another asked about having sex in the park.

My answer was always the same, "If you are in a shared area where other people are present or could be present then that is considered a public area. It is illegal to have sex in public."

What I was saying finally sank into Roger's mind as he gazed down at his leg monitor and a look of horror crossed his face. He got up out of his chair, hit the floor on both knees, and began begging by clasping and raising his hands into the air. It was really a quite dramatic display! I told Roger I did not have a choice but to report the incident and I could lose my job if I did not tell. I assured him someone in the classroom or someone who heard the story from someone present in the classroom would tell regardless of my report. Roger kept saying he did not know having sex in public was illegal and I told him I believed him but I still had to report it. I did assure

Roger that I would tell our principal that he did not force Julie into doing anything and that she was participating of her own free will. Julie said she would say the same.

Next, I asked the students involved why they thought they could get away with such behavior in my classroom because it concerned me that they thought I would not notice. Their answer was simple, "We were doing it in the lunch room before coming to your class and the other teachers there didn't notice." The students went on to proudly tell me how the boys had stretched out their legs to block the view while tiny Julie slipped out of her chair to perform oral sex under their table. I was right; there was a conspiracy of students who were covering for the activity.

I was curious to see if anyone had reported the lunchroom incident to any other teacher because it would have grossed me out if students were doing that while I was having lunch. However, I knew if a student had made a report they would not want anyone to find out, so I did not ask. As I looked toward the window in my classroom door I saw another middle school teacher walking down the hall and I motioned to her. I asked this teacher to escort the remainder of my students to their next class while I retained Roger and Julie for the office. I wrote up the discipline report while my two students sat silently on opposite sides of the room. The whole time I was writing I was dreading the talk I would no doubt have with my principal about kids having sex in my classroom while under my supervision. However, I thought, at least I was aware and I caught them. Then I fumed to myself, "This would not have happened in my room if the staff supervising the lunchroom had been paying attention."

As I finished writing the discipline report, the helpful teacher who had escorted my other students to their next class came back by my door and caught my attention. She informed me, "The students told me what happened in your classroom and I wanted you to know that one student had told me earlier what happened in the lunchroom." I asked this teacher if she had made a report of the incident and she said, "No, I didn't see it so... I didn't think I had to report it." I was confused by her answer but I thought I really could not blame her because none of us had ever encountered this problem before and there wasn't a protocol written somewhere that told us what we should do if someone reported children were having sex in the school.

When I thought about it, I chose not to villainize my coworkers and I did not think they were at fault. None of the middle school teachers, including myself, had received an explicitly designed training for teachers at the alternative school. Certainly, we had not received written instructions in a handbook dedicated to explaining all possible student misbehaviors. For these reasons, I came to the conclusion if it seemed like I was always dealing with discipline problems someone else chose to ignore, I probably was. I had to admit it was in my nature to handle things in a direct manner and I did not shy away from dealing with difficult situations like this one. Maybe that was why I seemed to be the person who most often discovered and confronted the bizarre behaviors of our baby gangsters.

However, I also knew I was too pragmatic at times and that I just jumped in to do what I thought needed done without concerning myself with personal consequences. At that very moment, I realized any mention of sex to students or discussions like the one I just had with my students could be open for interpretations and I could receive a consequence for my straight forward conversation with these kids about the consequences of having sex in public. There just weren't any good options in my opinion.

I abhorred inaction when it came to student discipline and someone had to address this behavior because other students might try engaging in the same behavior or students might report the incident to their parents. I could just imagine the consequence I would receive if a parent called and said "My child said students were having sex in Mrs. Gifford's classroom and she did not even notice." Either way, I could be fried and served up on a platter at a school board meeting so I might as well do what my conscious told me was right and talk directly to the students. The students needed to know this type of behavior could not continue in our school and after confronting my students about their conspiracy, I was sure no one would try that behavior again in my presence. Of course, I would have to meet with the middle school team and tell them what happened or these young people would just carry on their activity in another teacher's classroom. Sharing students' misbehaviors and discipline information was very important to me.

At the first of the year, I would notice children sitting out in the hall or I would hear complaints of a particular student's behavior in another teacher's class but the child was never written up or sent to the office. Through the school grapevine new employees were warned by other teachers not to write up too many kids for misbehavior because it might go against our evaluations. There was just one problem which surfaced due to this philosophy; the students were not getting disciplined! Teachers were just passing the kids on to the next teacher and the next teacher did the same. Until, a group of students came to me who thought they owned the school and I would have to deal with their misbehaviors which would have been much easier to squelch earlier in the day. Once empowered by the lack of discipline, these students mocked our classroom structure and used class time to talk about drug and gang activity. Naturally, when I refused to let the students circumvent the rules in my class and made office referrals, it appeared as if I could not manage students' behaviors on my own.

In an effort to get the middle school teachers to at least share the students' misbehavior information, I talked to the principal and was given permission to create a clipboard system. Each group of students had its own clipboard which was handed off with the class to the next teacher. We began tracking student behaviors and identifying problematic students. The system I was given permission to use, allowed me to reference the student's history of disturbances in other classes when I made the office referrals. At least, the front office could see I referred students who were chronically misbehaving for everyone. I looked at the clipboard setting on my desk now and decided this was one behavior I would not circulate in a written format and I would talk to my coworkers directly about what had happened in the lunchroom and in my class.

Now, in reviewing our communication system I wondered if maybe we should not transfer the clipboards to the lunch room supervisors when the students were handed off to them. In light of the happenings today, I realized lunchroom supervisors probably did not have a tracking system for student behaviors and maybe they had been told the same rumor we had been told about personal consequences received by staff when disciplining students. Whatever the problem might be, our student supervision failed today and supervision might need to take a higher priority than learning and teaching for quite some time in my classroom. As, I raised my eyes off the referral form to gaze at little Julie and distressed Roger who were both sitting quietly and looking down, I muttered to myself silently, "Who would have thought it possible for this to happen in an alternative middle school?"

After I finished the discipline forms, I took my two offending students up front, and I sat them with the receptionist while I conference with the principal. After talking to him, I had another reason to be puzzled. Julie had been doing the same thing at her home school with other boys and the principal had blocked sharing that information with us. The principal said he felt it was a "Need to know" situation and there was no way of determining she would continue the same behavior at our school. Later, I would be further dismayed by the principal's decision to suspend Julie from school on a lesser charge and not to inform Julie's parents of her behavior. He cited his reason, "Julie cried and said her mother would beat her. You know she is from a different culture and they are different that way."

However, Roger was sent back to jail for breaking the law when his probation officer was notified of his transgressions. I did tell the principal that Julie was not forced to do anything and in light of the information he shared about Julie's past history, Roger may have been the victim. It did not matter; Roger still paid the price. I supposed Julie's special education status played into Roger's return to jail. Secretly, I felt that the principal was looking for a way to send Roger back to jail because of his heavy gang involvement. What principal would not want to rid their school of a gang leader when given the opportunity?

When Julie came back to school after a three day suspension the boys in middle school began treating her with extreme disrespect. When we had the students lined up transitioning them to other classes or waiting for bathroom breaks, the boys standing next to her would turn around to put their crotches in her face, she was the perfect height for this, and they would press her into the wall. The boys started calling Julie a "Bopper" which is a slang term for girls who perform oral sex on boys, making fun of her appearance, and laughing about what she had done with Roger. When I gave the boys discipline for their behavior, Julie would beg me not to get them in trouble saying, "It's alright Mrs. G. They are my friends." Of course the boys were disciplined but Julie's attitude really bothered me because she did not seem embarrassed nor did she seem to mind her new label.

Discussion

Educators are cautioned to be careful when conversations with students bring about the subject of sex. Teachers cannot be careful enough when it comes to this one taboo subject. Most school districts try to avoid controversy by providing a special class for human sexuality that requires a parent's signature if a student participates. However, these classes are usually weak and mostly inform students about physiological changes the human body goes through as children pass into adulthood and they may contain limited HIV/AIDS information. After my experiences with middle school students, I believe more pertinent information may be needed and sex education classes for students should probably include information about: sexualized conduct in public, sexual harassment laws, sexually transmitted diseases, the effectiveness of different types of birth control, and sexual deviations which may prevent pregnancy but still can produce disease and cause health risk for students. Most alarming is the trend among teens to participate in oral and anal sex to prevent pregnancy. Just like my students, other teens may believe that oral sex is really not sex at all and oral or anal sex allows a girl to remain a virgin until she is married (reported by female students to me).

It appears that students may still be learning about sex the same way most of us learned, by talking to other children and by experimenting. Of course, kids are getting misinformation and today they may be placing their very lives at risk. Due to the incubation period of the HIV virus, new cases of AIDS could be the result of teen exposure to the virus. Young people really do not know what they are risking when they have unprotected sex. Due to the teen belief system recorded in this book and youth's acceptance of street lies as the truth, many young people believe there is a cure for AIDS and may not be concerned about contracting the disease. Even if parents are inept at talking to their kids about sex and teachers are afraid of getting fired for mentioning sex in the classroom, the very least any of us can do is inform our teens that AIDS is still a killer and new cases are being diagnosed all the time. **Should middle schools be allowed to publicize information about the risk of STDs and AIDS on bulletin boards or in their hallways?**

While it is true that some parents do not want public educators talking to their children about sex, it is also true that most school districts do not want their classroom teachers talking to students about this same subject. For this reason, parents should probably take the responsibility to become informed about current teen sexual trends and they should initiate conversations with their own children about sexual behaviors. Some parents might appreciate help doing this. **Would parents attend**

school district sponsored trainings about current teen sexual trends and how to talk to their kids about sex?

In our story, Julie's behavior poses additional concerns. When children like Julie are particularly naïve due to their emotional immaturity or due to their developmental delays then they may be at a greater risk for harm and may not understand fully the risk they are taking by engaging in sexual activities. Julie wanted to be accepted and wanted male attention like the other girls her age received and she found out sex was a way to get attention from boys. In addition, this story about Julie has a twist that most people would not recognize as a possibility. Julie was seeking acceptance and membership into a gang. According to other male students, Julie met male gang members after school in a certain location and provided the same service for them that she gave Roger, a known gang leader. Girls who get involved in gangs often get "sexed in" instead of "Jumped in." Teens like Julie, who are rejected due to their appearance or intelligence, may find acceptance through sexual favors and get a sense of belonging through gang membership. **If girls live in neighborhoods where gangs are prevalent, what should parents do to prevent their daughters from being recruited and initiated into gang membership this way?**

Topics for Research

How big of an age difference does there have to between young people before a teen can be found guilty of sexually abusing another youth? What are the other special circumstances that determine if sexual abuse has occurred when both parties are minors? Are there any classes offered in your school district to teach children about human sexuality? Does your church offer this kind of education in youth groups? Are there any parent books you could use to teach your children about human sexuality? What do you think could happen to a teacher who knows students are having sex in the school and doesn't report it?

Things you can do

Begin teaching your child about human sexuality before they enter middle school. I had many students who were already parents by the time they were in seventh grade. Don't be afraid to say no to your child when they want to go to a party or hang out with older kids. A twelve year old should not be hanging out with high school age students. Talk to your kids about substance abuse and its connection to date rape and pregnancy. If gang membership might become an issue then talk to your daughters about the personal consequences they might face while seeking membership in a gang.

Research and find parent materials to help you teach and review the materials used by your school district. You may still want the educators to provide the classes but you might want to add moral teaching to their material at home. TALK TO YOUR CHILDREN!

If you are a teacher who teaches the human body always insist that students use scientific terms to ask questions about human sexuality. Create a question box so students can submit questions without asking out them out loud if they don't know how to ask the questions using scientific words. Defer any delicate questions to the school nurse, the child's family doctor, or public health department. Most important when faced with a situation like I experienced, document everything you said to the students. You can inform students without major discussions and repeat the information in a broken message style like I did when I stated, "It is against the law to have sex in public."

8. Sexual Harassment

Students do experience sexual harassment at all levels of education according to Equal Rights Advocates, an organization in existence since 1974 which has been a leading force in fighting for women's equal rights (Equal Rights and Economic Opportunities for Women and Girls). This organization has stated that sexual harassment creates a hostile environment at school for students, makes students feel unsafe, and interferes with student's ability to do their school work. Another source, has reported that verbal and physical harassment begins in elementary school and 6 out of 10 students will experience some form of physical sexual harassment (Wikipedia.org/wiki/Sexual Harassment). This source explains that most sexually harassing behavior happens between students in school.

Although adults can rationalize sexual harassment between youth is born of inexperience because student's may lack the social skills needed to gain the attention of their love match, the American Association of University Women reported the true reasons are power assertion and fear generation (2006). Therefore sexual harassment is more in line with bullying. Some schools may choose to replace sexual harassment charges against students with bullying language because of this assessment. It might be easier to talk to parents about their child bullying another student verses their child sexually harassing another student.

According to one source, sexual harassment is discrimination under Title IX of the education Amendments of 1972 and it involves everything from "Mild annoyances to sexual assault and rape" (ed.gov). The Equal Rights Advocates elaborate the definition to include: "Comments about your body, spreading sexual rumors, sexual remarks or accusations, dirty jokes or stories, physical touching or exposure, displaying pictures or obscene gestures." In addition, I would add singing or humming words to some contemporary songs which are offensive. Students at my school often tried to disguise sexual harassment by singing sexually explicit songs, some of which were extremely insulting to women.

Verbal sexual harassment and gesturing could be precursors to unwanted physical touch. Therefore, teachers should watch for this form of harassment and it should be addressed. Failure to correctly identify these types of behaviors as sexual harassment and warning students of consequences could lead to students feeling empowered to physically touch other students. In an alternative school setting the knowledge that unwanted physical touch could lead to assault charges is a good deterrent for most students. However, students need educated what constitutes sexual harassment and not just punished when they do it; they may never make the connection between their inappropriate behaviors which led up to their bold physical act. Educating our youth about sexual harassment laws makes sense because this type of education will prepare them for their work life after school. Students are being educated about bullying but they may never make the connection of verbal and non-verbal sexual harassment to bullying without education.

However, informing youth about the definition of sexual harassment and how to conduct their behaviors toward each other at school may be unpopular due to parent objections regarding sex education. The two things are really different because one is about social conduct and illegal activity and the other is about sexual body functions. One prepares students for the work world environment, sexual harassment education, and the other prepares students for procreation, sex education. One benefit of providing sexual harassment education could be to create a safer environment for students because a hostile environment develops when students are allowed to sexually harass each other.

According to the Safe Schools Coalition, "Fear is not conducive to education. Nobody can teach in an unsafe place and nobody can learn in an unsafe place (http:www.safeschoolscoalition.org/). Like the whole of our society, schools have become concerned about hate crimes committed against individuals whose presence may be less tolerated in a population of people. Today the interaction between gay and straight students in schools may generate into hate crimes and may contribute to students feeling unsafe in schools. Gay students may be more often the target of disparaging sexual harassment remarks. Therefore, educating and enforcing school policies regarding student sexual harassment may prevent the commission of some hate crimes in public schools.

Our school atmospheres have changed and heterosexual males along with homosexual males may now experience sexual harassment. One source asserts that girls have a tendency to think boys like their forward manners and boys enjoy the harassing (I Proceeding of the National Union of Teachers, United Kingdom 2007). From this source we can determine that sexual harassment in schools is not an exclusive problem of the United States of America. We also might infer that the problem has evolved to include females harassing males. Recent studies have indicated that sexual harassment occurs against gay and straight students, may lead to the commission of hate crimes, and leave children feeling scared and anxious as long as the behavior is allowed to continue (Safe Schools Coalition).

Large city school districts may experience more sexual harassment activity. One such city school district in Memphis Tennessee reported 76% of their female students experienced sexual harassment. According to a risk assessment conducted in the Memphis schools in 2005, students experienced sexual harassment above national rates and were more likely to have multiple partners, become pregnant or impregnate a partner than their peers elsewhere in the country (Tackling Sexual Harassment in Memphis Schools). Memphis is probably not the only large city school district which has experienced an increase of sexual harassment incidents committed by students.

When you consider the increased gang activity evidenced in some of our large city districts and that girls' initiation into gangs could result in them being "Sexed in" then we can understand why sexual harassment may occur at higher rates in school districts like Memphis where gang activity is also a documented problem. The possibility of gang members attending the same school with girls who are being initiated into the gangs could create a general atmosphere which promotes sexual harassment (self). Therefore, if there is a large population of gang members present in schools there might be more of a need for students to receive sexual harassment education along with school staff being made aware of the heightened risk.

The fact that students may be sexually active at increasingly younger ages, evidenced by students being parents in middle school, may add to a sexually charged atmosphere. Students need educated about proper conduct in public and they need advised regarding sexual harassment laws. In the absence of a district approved curriculum on this topic, I found it necessary to create my own lesson plan because I was having episodes in my student population which disrupted learning and compromised the safety of my classroom. I sought intervention from my administrator, school counselor, and police officer to no avail. Everyone side stepped the issue or knew of no resources I could use. After, I developed my lesson plan, I was careful to share it with the appropriate authority and ask for their input. However, I knew if a parent complained about my speaking to students on this subject then I would probably be hung out to dry because I was not teaching a district approved curriculum.

I purpose it is not fair to make teachers choose between maintaining a safe environment in their classroom and receiving personal consequences because they choose to educate students about sexual harassment laws. I was fortunate that no complaints were issued. However, other teachers may continue to have their jobs jeopardized while trying to educate students about this legal and social issue. As long as school districts continue to treat sexual harassment like bullying and do not incorporate sexual harassment law information into their student packets as a separate issue or require students to be educated about the law then students are not being prepared for citizenship or their adult work life.

My students seemed truly astounded when they discovered there were laws addressing this kind of behavior and after our training my students' behaviors not only improved but students begin to police each others' conduct. Students came forward expressing concern over uncomfortable situations where they felt sexual harassment was the issue. Once the students were aware I was listening and watching for inappropriate behaviors along this line and after I had some students suspended for inappropriate sexual conduct then students began acting more respectful toward each other (at least in my presence).

The education I provided my students raised the expectations for acceptable behavior in the classroom and school. Schools need to make students feel safe so they can concentrate on learning and students who are subject to sexual harassment by other students do not feel safe. It is true that sexual harassment is a type of bullying which may lead to psychological distress and even suicide in some students. However, we need to name that type of bullying "Sexual harassment" so students will understand the difference between the two.

According to a New York Times article written by Tara Parker-Pope written in March 2010, More than one third of middle-and high-school students may be victims of sexual harassment by their classmates. She quoted one source, Fineran and Gruber from the University of Michigan who surveyed 522 children between the ages of 11 and 18 about bullying and sexual harassment in public schools. This source argues that sexual harassment is a problem which needs addressed separately because an education law Title IX has already been passed which would allow schools to address this topic.

References and Resources

"Sexual Harassment at School: Know Your Rights," Equal Rights and Economic Opportunities for Women and Girls, equalrights.org/publications/kyr/shschool.asp, 05/06/2010

"Risks and Consequences of Sexual Harassment," American Association of University Women. Hostile Hallways: The AAUW Survey on Sexual Harassment in America's Schools. www.maec.org/sexharas.html ·

Title IX, Education Amendments of 1972 (Title 20 U.S.C. Sections 1681-1688). www.dol.gov/oasam/regs/statutes/titleix.htm

"A Teacher's guide To Surviving Anti-Gay harassment," http:www.safeschoolscoalition.org

In a national survey conducted for the American Association of ... United Kingdom, 2007 ^ kspope.com ^ retrieved January 15, 2009 ^ Sexual Harassment in Education, (Wishnietsky, 1991) en.wikipedia.org/wiki/Sexual_harassment_in_education

"Tackling Sexual Harassment in Memphis Schools," Patricia Hawk for www.school-12.com

"Sexual Harassment at School," New York Times; Well, Tara Parker-Pope on Health, 05/2008

9. Too Big for My Heart

The Jolly giant arrived in my eighth grade class with a booming voice and a domineering presence. He was taller than all the other students in class and dwarfed my five foot seven frame. I guessed he was at least six foot-four and his weight was dangerously out of proportion to his height. Definitely, Jolly would be classified as morbidly obese. He was a pleasant looking young fellow, about fourteen years old, whose evenly dimpled face and extroverted personality could have won him many friends if he had not been so annoying! He insisted on demanding the attention of all the other students in our room. However, his needs were not limited just to acquiring his classmates' attention; he issued regal proclamations which required his classmates to do his work for him. Princely in his demands, he waved his royal hand as he dismissed and passed his work over to his subjects' desks for their completion. The other students appeared intimidated by Jolly's size and demeanor so they complied without hesitation.

Jolly made no pretense of hiding his lack of activity in my classroom, "Mrs. G. I don't do my own work. I was born with a heart condition and I had surgery," he emphasized while pulling his shirt down to reveal the top of a thick, raised scar which I assumed ran down the middle of his chest. He continued, "I have almost died three times in my life. Once when I was born, once when I had a heart attack, and once when I had surgery. I had a heart attack because I had high cholesterol and because I was too big for my heart. I went to fat kids' camp and lost one hundred and twenty pounds but I have gained some back and I need to go again! Ha…Ha…Ha…Ha."

This student was really big, too big to sit in the normal sized student desks arranged in my room, and I had to accommodate him some other way. I did not want him to sit in the back of the room but I could not sit him in front of other students. I would not be able to see behind his huge body and I had to observe all the students at all times. His desk had to be a separate piece of furniture, the chair had to be a large adult size, and the chair had to be strong enough to hold him.

I reasoned to myself, Jolly could sit slightly to the side of a desk and still write on it. He would not be able to fit under any desk or table while sitting on a chair large enough to hold his weight. I did not like it but had to admit to myself, Jolly would have to sit at the back of the classroom! Every teacher knows that when you have a trouble maker you should sit them in the front row; it's easier to watch them and manage their behavior. I definitely thought Jolly would be a trouble maker because he was loud and demanding on his very first day of attendance.

Jolly felt empowered as I cleaned off one of my demonstration tables for him to use as a desk and as I opened my classroom closet to retrieve an adult size chair. When he positioned his kingly girth at the rear, he complained, "Haven't you got anything bigger? I can't sleep like this." The rest of the class laughed at Jolly's joke.

I quickly responded, "I don't think you will have time to nap, Jolly. Besides, I keep students after school when they try to sleep in my class."

Jolly taunted, "I won't stay because my momma won't let me stay. Teachers can't discipline me and my momma won't discipline me either. She is afraid that my heart will give out and I will die. I tell my momma: what to do, what I want to eat, when I am going to bed and when I go to school. I probably won't be here much…if I don't feel like coming."

I was curious, "Do you participate in PE?"

He answered, "Only if I want to. I don't run but I play a little basketball. If a Coach ask me to do anything I don't want to, I refuse because of my heart condition."

There was no doubt that Jolly had a serious health condition that was being made worse by his obesity, inactivity, and maybe his parent! If what Jolly said was true about his mother then he would cause constant disruptions. Without a parent's support teachers find it difficult to manage children like Jolly. However, I was not ready to give up just yet. All I had to do was design a plan or trick him into doing his own work. Since Jolly appeared to be a master at manipulating people and situations to his own benefit, I ran the risk of him figuring out what I was doing. If he did, no doubt, he would be angry at my playing him and the situation could turn ugly. I surmised it was worth the risk because normal classroom strategies were not going to work with this intelligent but super lazy student.

As I puzzled in my mind what to do I remembered another teaching experience at a developmental preschool and a student by the name of … Timmy. Yes, his name was Timmy and he was going to be kicked out of the nursery school in our birth to three year old program. The developmental nursery teacher came to me because I was the case manager for his family and asked me to develop a behavioral plan for Timmy that would help extinguish his unacceptable behaviors.

First thing every morning when Timmy came into the nursery room he would directly run up to whatever children were present and take away their toys, hit them in the head with the toys, or bite them. Since some of Timmy's classmates were more severely affected by birth defects than he was, they were easy victims. Most of our Down syndrome clients were physically delayed due to their floppy muscle tones and if they walked, they were unsteady on their feet. It was easy for my pugnacious little client to topple them over and pummel them.

Some of our other children had epilepsy and Timmy hitting them in the head was unthinkable! If I did not come up with a plan then Timmy would be staying at home every day with his low-functioning, developmentally delayed mother and he would never gain the language skills he needed to start school. I asked the nursery teacher to give me two days to watch Timmy's behavior through the one way glass in our observation room before I set a plan in motion.

I observed Timmy as he came in the side door of the nursery. His mother who was very needy herself engaged the nursery staff in conversation and Timmy took off running toward a group of four or five other toddlers. No one had helped Timmy acclimate to the nursery surroundings and nursery workers had not greeted him or even acknowledged his presence. His coat was not removed and he was not given an opportunity to use the bathroom. Since Timmy was toilet training and the nursery staff complained he wet and soiled himself before school started each morning, I thought it was unusual the staff did not immediately see to Timmy's creature needs.

However, Timmy did just as the staff reported. He ran to a weaker Downs child whom could barely sit up, knocked him over, and started to bite him, as a nursery helper hurried, while screaming Timmy's name, to save the fragile child. Now Timmy's presence was acknowledged and he rewarded that recognition by promptly pooping his pants! Once he got the nursery staff's attention he was going to keep it.

After our small charges were gone for the day, I conference with the nursery staff and tactfully suggested that someone greet Timmy in the morning instead of spending so much time with the mother. I explained it would be alright to say a quick good morning but their focus should be on the child. They explained that they were conferencing with Timmy's mother about his behavior. I suggested that they let me conference with the mother while they attended Timmy. I wrote Timmy's behavioral plan and it included all of us. The staff would change their behavior and greet Timmy in the morning warmly then they would take him to the restroom and meet his creature needs. Finally, one of the nursery helpers would take Timmy to the toy area and model correct play with the other children.

For my part, I would model the behavior plan the very next morning for the staff and we would assess its effectiveness before they tried it. Also, I would conference with the mother, at a separate home visit, regarding Timmy's possible removal from our nursery program if his behavior continued to jeopardize the safety and health of other children. In addition, I would evaluate the type of discipline the mother was using with Timmy. (It did not surprise me when I discovered the mother disciplined her children by biting them.)

I modeled the plan and it worked and the nursery staff changed their interactions with Timmy. As long as the staff followed Timmy's behavioral plan it worked perfectly. However, all it took was one morning of relaxed behavior on the nursery workers part and Timmy would go right back to bullying and hurting other kids. Consistency was the key.

What made me think of Timmy? How were Timmy and Jolly alike? I compared their behaviors in my mind and decided that both needed acknowledgement and attention! My guess was Jolly was an only child, did not interact with other kids outside of school, and had a parent who was so focused on his physical needs that his emotional needs for child companionship were ignored. I was sure Jolly wanted the attention of the other students and he wanted to be accepted. I would talk to Jolly a little bit more about his home life to find out if this was true. In the meantime, I would need to find a way to allow Jolly to obtain the attention he needed without disrupting my class.

On the second day in my class Jolly took his position at the back of my room and immediately started to tell a story about a street person he saw on the way to school. His voice boomed and he accentuated the tale with his own loud gales of laughter. At first students were amused and found Jolly's account entertaining. However, when Jolly noticed his classmates had their notebooks out and were ready to start their work, he began to deviate from his original tale in almost a frantic manner. He took on the appearance of a frenzied comedian who had lost his audience. Since his classmates had been programmed to immediately begin their work for the day, they eyed me to see if I could rein in his performance. I could tell Jolly's fellow students were annoyed that his one man show was being allowed to continue.

When Jolly paused I said, "That was a very interesting story, Jolly. I like to start the day with a good laugh and hope tomorrow morning you will have another entertaining tale for us. I will allot three minutes of my class time just to hear your morning story because I enjoy your humor so much. That will be your job in my class. I want a three minute story everyday! Now class we will begin our lesson." Jolly looked puzzled then his expression changed as a grin gradually broadened across his face and I noticed he was silently studying me like an opponent sizing up his competition. Jolly was intelligent enough to realize that I had just stolen his thunder and regained control of my classroom and I was smart enough to know my diversion would be short lived. I passed out papers and turned on my overhead projector while anticipating Jolly's next attempt to derail my lesson plan for the day.

I heard the giant king in the back of room proclaim, "Hey, I've already done this stuff. Well not me, I didn't do it but my home school teacher already taught this. I don't want to hear it again."

"Jolly, I realize that you may have already heard this information and you should remember it because it is not new information. We are reviewing for a chapter test we will all take tomorrow," I replied.

Quickly addressing the rest of the class, "How many of you remember the organization of periodic table?" Not one student raised their hand. "Alright, Jolly, your friends and fellow classmates do not remember studying the composition of the periodic table. Some of them may have been absent from their home schools when this was taught so they really need this information. However, because you have told me you know this, I will make you a special deal."

Immediately, I gained Jolly's interest with this proposal and as he straightened up in his chair to listen he displayed cautious anticipation by raising one eyebrow and quirking his mouth to form a lop-sided smile, "Yeah…I'm listening. Tell me more."

Since Jolly wanted special attention, I knew an offer of a special deal would cancel any suspicion he might have and I knew he would take the bait. "If you can help your friends out by not being bored during the review and by listening to the information again then I will only require you write your name and today's date on the top of the worksheet. I will give you a passing grade for your class work today if you do this."

Immediately, another student raised his hand and spoke before Jolly could answer, "I know this stuff too, Mrs. G. Do I have to do the worksheet?"

I responded, "Yes, David, you do have to do the worksheet because I gave you a chance to tell me if you remembered covering these concepts and you did not raise your hand. No one raised their hand or said anything other than Jolly. He is the only one who said he knew this information so he is the only one who gets this deal. What do you say, Jolly? Before you answer I want you to know if you do not pass the chapter test tomorrow then you will have to look up all the answers to the questions you missed. That's my rule in this class room because we use our mistakes to learn."

"Do it, bro! I wish I didn't have to do the worksheet," piped in the David.

"Alright, Mrs. G, I'll take your deal but I want to sleep not pay attention," he replied.

"Sorry, I cannot let you sleep in class but I can let you close your eyes as long as your head is up and you can answer a question when I call on you," I replied.

Jolly said, "You're tough but I'll do it." I was able to complete the review and Jolly did respond when I called on him twice and I could tell he was marginally listening.

During the review, I had been assessing the other students' knowledge of our subject matter and I felt most of my students would pass the test on the next day. However, there were two boys who had been placed with me a week before Jolly came, and they would probably fail. They had been truant from their home school and were really far behind in the curriculum. I would need to give them individual attention during the test correction session I would hold and use that time to re-teach the information. However, I could use the knowledge of their eminent failures to assist me with the Jolly problem. Right before I dismissed the class I reassigned seats and placed the probable fails on either side of Jolly.

Test day came and I instructed the class in test procedures, cautioned them about talking during the test, and gave a strong warning about cheating. I hoped I could at least get Jolly not to talk during the test but he began just as soon as I passed out the papers.

"I don't wanna do this test. It is dumb!"

I immediately said, "Jolly would you please come out into the hall with me to talk about this? Get up now and stop disturbing the other students."

Jolly thundered his dinosaur sized thighs and shuffled his pigmy sized feet to the door of my classroom. I supposed he thought I was calling him out to make another deal. Once outside and I positioned myself to see the other students through the glass at the top of the classroom door and I began, "Jolly I am not going to make another deal with you. We made a deal yesterday and I expect you to be a man of your word. I don't like being played. Now you need to do what you promised to do and go in and take your test. If you don't pass your test the worst thing that will happen will be that you will have to attend a test correction session and look up the answers in your textbook."

Jolly pouted, "I ain't com'n to no test correction that's why I'm not taking the test!"

Alright Jolly, "I can't make you take the test but I want you to take it because you are going to get awfully tired standing out here in the hall for forty minutes while the rest of the class sits comfortably in the room."

Jolly asked, "Can't I have a chair?"

"No, our school rules say we cannot give chairs to students who are placed in the hall for discipline. You will have to stand and when the principal or the police officer come walking by, they will ask you why you are in the hall. I promise you they will not be pleased you are out here," I answered back. Jolly stuck his lip out and made a pouty, baby face so I knew he was not ready to cooperate. "I am going back into the room now. When you are ready to come in and take your test just come to the class window," I instructed and thought to myself that should do it. Size seven feet can't hold an elephant sized boy for long! I didn't have to worry about Jolly sitting down on the floor because there was nothing in the hall for him to hold onto nor would he be able to get up once he sat down. He would have to stand.

However, Jolly extended his stay in the hall longer than I anticipated and I decided to check after three minutes. I peered into the hall to see how Jolly was coming along just like I was looking into an oven to see if a cake was done. He was almost ready! He teetered in his balance and rocked up against the wall. Did I see him wince in pain? Good, he is done, I said to myself. I heard the oven buzzer go off in my brain as Jolly came to the door pleading, looking like his feet might be causing him pain, and displaying a defeated expression on his face.

Now, the next part of my plan would work perfectly. As Jolly took his seat he looked left then right while deciding which one of the students, I had transplanted the day before, he would require to complete his test and I pretended not to notice. I had anticipated Jolly's royal hand would not write today and his subject would circle his answers for him. As class ended and I collected the chapter tests, Jolly had a triumphant look on his face. However, Jolly would not get the last laugh. The next day I passed back the test and Prince Jolly had failed as did his royal subject. Now, they both would stay for a test correction session.

I knew this session would frustrate me more than benefit Jolly but I wanted Jolly to come to the conclusion it would have been better for him to do his own work and not rely on other students to do it for him. Now, he would have to make corrections by looking up the answers in a textbook which required a lot more effort than taking a test. In addition, Jolly would have to document where he found the information and explain the concepts fully. However, this test correction session was only one part of my plan and if it succeeded then Jolly would start thinking about doing his own work. I groaned, "I should have a dentist license instead of a teaching certificate, getting Jolly to do his own work will be like pulling teeth, a long and painful experience and I am afraid I will be the one in pain!"

That day, I pulled all three boys from PE at one time during my planning period and gave them an opportunity to correct their mistakes. Our correction session was difficult but I convinced Jolly that I would keep him after school if he didn't complete his corrections. I said, "Don't complain at me because I am giving you an opportunity to correct your work during school time instead of staying after. If you would rather stay this afternoon, just tell me and I will walk you on down to PE. I could be sitting in the teachers' lounge with my feet up and I could be drinking a coke. I don't need this. I'm just trying to do you fellows a favor. If you don't want it tell me now. I have to stay after school anyway. Teachers don't leave when students do, so it does not matter to me."

The other two students thanked me for allowing them to do their corrections during the school day and they began working. Jolly sulked a while and then asked if all three could work together to find answers they had missed. I considered this and came up with a rule they each had to answer one question before sharing their answers and I reminded them that they could only share the answers to the same questions all three had missed and I cautioned them to take their work seriously because they would be retaking the exam individually. I monitored the students' progress and thought, baby steps; I've got to go slow because Jolly has not done any work for a very long time.

The next week proved to be better with Jolly doing some of his own work and increasingly more, he was paying attention in class. Occasionally, he forgot himself and actually participated by asking or answering questions. I began to see a spark and I was hoping for a full fledged flame when another test day came. I knew Jolly had the ability but he had been allowed to become lazy and that is why he no longer knew how to participate in his own education. Like a dance instructor with an inept learner, I was dancing with this student while piping music to him. I hoped he would take the lead and discover for himself that learning is a beautiful thing. However, I was determined to win this dance contest even if the big boy tromped my feet.

As difficult as it was, I had blocked Jolly's attempts all week at being lazy and I had obstructed his attempts at disrupting my classroom. Now, Jolly was not even telling his morning stories in my room. Instead, he would open his folder and begin writing down his objective for the day. I was making slow progress but it was progress never the less. Every day was getting just a little bit easier but now the true test was coming. Would Jolly take his own exam and perform as I expected?

I went through my usual speech about following instructions then passed out the test while making one final announcement, "Remember class, it is much easier for you if you take your time to read and answer the questions carefully the first time than correct answers and retake a test. You won't have to do test corrections if you pass the first time." I looked at Jolly when I said this and I thought I saw a flicker of acknowledgement in his eyes. I carefully observed him. Would he regress and hand off his test to a student on either side of him? I watched intently and restrained myself from jumping for joy as Jolly completed his own work. I was very excited to see the outcome. As soon as the students went to PE, I graded the tests and Jolly's was first. When finished, I hopped out of my seat and did a very unusual dance across the floor that sort of looked like I was trying to get my Dougie on and do the Stanky Leg at the same time.

I sobered myself and said, "M y students would rock out if they knew I could do their dances!" As I laughed out loud, I wrote in large red numbers across the top of Jolly's page, ninety-seven percent. I could not wait for the next day because I felt like a real scientist instead of a science teacher. I was going to do a launch like a rocket but it was going to be a human being! If my plan worked, Jolly was going to finally realize how smart he was and he would fly high. Once launched this student could reach the stars. Jolly would find out what little effort it took on his part to receive good grades. Jolly was intelligent and I wanted him to succeed and quit being lazy!

The next day came and as I passed out test, I placed Jolly's on top. He sat shocked as he looked to his fellow class mates on each side of him and discovered their test grades were much lower than his. He ventured, "Mrs. G, who got the highest grade in class?"

I responded, "Would anyone in class who received the highest grade care if I told?" All the students said they would not care so I said, "Why Jolly that would be you!"

"No way, Mrs. G, I couldn't have. I haven't ever had a good grade like this and...," he paused momentarily, "I didn't copy. It is my own work!"

"Fool, you been failing cause you been copying off of people dumber than you," exclaimed one girl in class.

Jolly erupted into laughter as other students joined in and for about five minutes the class room was total chaos as other explosions of mirth bounded around the room with the additional comments students made about Jolly's surprise. One boy fell out of his chair on the floor and was holding his sides. One girl was laughing so hard she said, "Stop you all, I'm about to pee myself."

Of course this made us laugh harder. Tears were in my eyes that were part real and part laughter. Then a sobering moment happened when the principal opened the door, chastised me with a look, told the class to settle down and told me I better get my class under control. I thought if he only knew how much control I really have over the children's' education he would not have said that! I ignored his rudeness and continued to laugh with my students (as soon as he walked down the hall).

However, my triumph was short lived because Jolly missed the next two days of classes. I was concerned that when Jolly had time to think over what happened in science class, he would realize I had played him. After all, he was a smart guy. I really had hoped that when Jolly became conscious of his own abilities, he would be inspired to discover his potential in school and to get a good education. Now, I had an ominous feeling that darkened my days while waiting for jolly's return to school.

Jolly came back in the same mood as he had demonstrated on the first day of class and this time there was no taming him. His behaviors and my attempts at blocking his loud outburst and self-defeating behaviors were at a stand-off. I was running low on energy and he was gaining ground by being disrespectful to all the teachers in the middle school. I had to stop it and the only way I knew how was to try to reason with Jolly's parent and petition her for help.

First, I talked to Jolly in private and asked him what had changed and what had caused his behavior to deteriorate. Jolly reported that on the very day he made his good grade in science, he had gotten into trouble in a different class room and was given an after school detention. Jolly walked out of the building, did not serve the detention, and decided not to come back to school for a couple of days. Jolly reported, "That teacher said I was an idiot and that I would never amount to anything and that is why I called her the name of a female dog. I didn't want to come to school because of her; I was afraid I might hit her and go to jail."

I chose my words very carefully, "Jolly I am sorry about what happened to you and I am glad you did not hit the teacher. Sometimes when you attend school you learn academics like reading, writing, math or science. Other times you may learn something about life and this lesson is about life. Jolly, all of us are going to run into people who show hate instead of love. You kids call them 'Haters' and you will have to learn how to overcome their evil by doing good. I want you to look at this magnet on the side of my file cabinet. What does it say?"

Jolly read the magnet, "Success is the best revenge. I don't understand, Mrs. G. What does it mean?"

"It means that when you make something out of yourself and you are successful, all those haters will be put to shame. You don't need revenge because your success will shame those people and their opinions of you. Do you understand now?"

Jolly started slowly, "I know what you're saying but... I think I would feel better if I hit that teacher!"

I tried to help Jolly process what had happened without defending the teacher because the way Jolly had been treated was wrong! I certainly understood my co-worker's frustration with this student but I was aghast because this teacher jeopardized the hard earned progress I had made with Jolly. The only thing my coworker had generated was anger in our student. In Jolly's mind, this one teacher had ruined his academic success and tore down his self-esteem in one blow. Jolly did not recover from the experience.

During our meeting, I had explained to Jolly the behaviors I wanted to see in my class room and he promised to change. However, the very next day he was so loud and disruptive that I had to send him out into the hall so I could give instructions to the other students. I decided not to keep Jolly after school because the other teacher, after humiliating him, had tried to exact that punishment. I thought a detention would just serve to remind him of that experience and he probably would walk out on my detention anyway. I really didn't see how assigning Jolly extra time after school would help him learn to control his behavior. In addition, he would retaliate by being truant from school for a couple of days more, and he would probably come back more angry.

Instead, I called his mother and I should have waited because I was fired up after a tough day with her son. "You got five hundred dollars lying around your house?" I quizzed before introducing myself. Then, I continued, "I am getting ready to have our police officer issue your son a ticket for class room disruption." I immediately regretted my hastiness because I realized I was judging this parent's reactions based upon her son's description of her parenting skills. I thought I should have at least waited to hear her voice before assuming that I needed to take such a direct tone in our conversation.

"Who is this?" The voice on the other end asked.

I apologized, introduced myself, and went on to explain all the separate issues our middle school staff had with Jolly. I explained Jolly was totally disrupting learning for other students and we could not allow that to happen. When the mother acted like she was powerless to do anything I resorted back to my former direct method, "Well, if you can't support us by helping us manage his behavior at school, you can at least tell Jolly when he comes to school not tell your family business." Then I gained her interest and I explained that Jolly had told all his teachers he did not have any rules at home and he bossed his mother around.

I repeated what Jolly said, "I tell her what to cook, when I go to bed, and if I go to school. She don't do nothin' about nothin' cause I'm in charge." Also, I reported that Jolly said his mother was afraid to spank him because of his heart condition. The phone went silent a few seconds after I made this statement and then Jolly's mother responded with a shaky voice which brought a vision to my mind of a woman doing her best to hold back tears, "I've almost lost him three times and he is my baby. I was afraid he would have another heart attack if I spanked him and now he is too big to punish that way. I don't know what to do."

I felt discouraged by this parent's attitude, felt she was responsible for Jolly's problems at school, and I made one more appeal for her help and said, "I'm sure if you can't manage your son's behavior at home then teachers cannot manage his behavior at school. Jolly is at risk for failing because of your inaction. You are his parent and we are only substitutes for you when he is at school. If you allow him to disrespect you then he will certainly disrespect us. Therefore, if we issue the five hundred dollar fine I told you about, it will really be a judgment on you as a parent. I hope we don't have to write a ticket tomorrow and I believe you can reason with your son if you try. Please don't give up because Jolly is worth your efforts. He really is a smart young man who is capable of doing much better. However, he will never get an education unless you support his teacher's actions and discipline him yourself at home. Can I count on your help?"

Jolly's mother angrily slammed down the receiver after saying, "I'll take care of it!"

The very next day, Jolly came to school with one black eye. He asked me, "Are you the one who called my mamma? She doubled up her fist and hit me like a man! My mamma's big! She is six feet tall and she done this!"

"Yes, Jolly, I called your mother because she is the one who would have to pay the five hundred dollar ticket which you were about to get. She needed to know. Remember, I first gave you a chance to change your behavior and you gave me a promise to do better in class. When you failed to follow through with our agreement then you left me no choice… but to call your mother," I calmly replied.

Jolly continued, "I told my momma to shut up when she tried to talk to me and told her to go make dinner and that's when she popped me. I didn't know she would hit me but I've never told her to shut up before. I am going to be good because I don't want to be hit again. Mamma scared me because I've never seen her that angry and she yelled at me all night long. She even yelled at me outside the bath room door while I was trying to take my shower. This morning she made me promise I would go to school and apologize to my teachers. I told her I would apologize to you but not to the other teacher. Then I told her what that teacher said to me. My mamma is going to talk to the principal about her and that teacher better not say anything like that to me again because my momma said she will come down here and give her some of what she gave me! I am sorry I was so bad, Miss O G and I 'm going to try and do better."

"Jolly, I did tell your mother you are an intelligent young man who is capable of doing good work in school. I would really like to see you succeed and I know it would make your mother proud if you had good behavior," I encouraged.

"Yeah, but you know, Mrs. G, I am lazy, I like be' in lazy, and work ain't my thing. When I work for you then I'm too tied to do stuff for the other teachers here. But… I don't want you call'n my mom again. If you could just tell me when …" replied Jolly.

I anticipated Jolly's request, "We can develop a signal and the other students do not need to know. Whenever your behavior is getting to be unacceptable, I can walk over and pick up my desk phone and you will remember I called your mother." True to my word, I did just that and Jolly would apologize really fast and correct his behavior when I went for the phone. Jolly did a minimal amount of work in my class for the rest of his stay but he no longer caused loud disruptions or intimidated other students into doing his work. He continued to pass tests on his own.

Discussion

Although laziness is not a problem limited to obese children and most all students will whine and try to get out of work, obese students, like all other children, can be lazy. One of the biggest problems teachers have at school is motivating lazy students to do their work. This causes concern because students who do not put forth effort and participate in their own education do not learn as much as those who are motivated and involved. Some teachers may believe the student's laziness is a reflection of their parents poor parenting skills. **Do lazy children have lazy parents or do they have busy parents?**

Children want to know that an adult is in charge because it makes them feel safe. Jolly could not control his weight, his heart condition, or the way other people acted toward him because of his weight. Instead, Jolly sought to control the classroom, whether or not he would do his work, and the other children by making them laugh. Students like Jolly test teachers to see if they are in control and if they are not, then students will take control in order to feel safe. Teachers need to control the classroom environment but that environment should be responsive to student needs. A delicate balance has to be maintained to promote learning. Jolly was allowed to feed his need for attention when he first arrived at our school so he would feel safe and accepted. **When was Jolly allowed to exercise control of the classroom and get his needs met? How did I set the perimeters of his behavior to assure he did not ruin the learning environment for everyone else?**

Parent and teacher relationships can be difficult. Most of the teachers at our alternative school phoned parents as a last resort because a parent's reaction could result in violent acts toward our students. Although some may question the action Jolly's mother took, it was effective and my classroom environment improved as a result of her deed. **When Jolly came to school with a black eye should his mother have been turned into a child protective service agency for abuse of a child?**

Teachers are human and I admit my original demeanor when talking to Jolly's mother was inappropriate. However, after my first rude display, I developed a positive relationship with Jolly's mother by updating her about his subsequent good behavior in class. During one of my calls I advocated for Jolly to be allowed to have friends come to his house to play video games or even stay all night. The mother had kept Jolly isolated from other kids because she was afraid they would carry illness to him and make him sick. Through my intervention, Jolly was finally allowed the peer interaction he craved and he caused fewer discipline problems after he was permitted contact with other kids outside school. **From this example, can you tell why building a relationship with students and parents is important for teachers?**

Topics for research

How might childhood obesity affect student motivation and school attendance? Why do some parents feel helpless when confronted with their difficult child's behaviors? How do requiring test corrections and test retakes act as classroom incentives?

Things to Do

Parents should teach their children to be self-sufficient, self-disciplined, and respectful at home. Parents could help by establishing a work routine in the home, by requiring their children to accept responsibility for their own behavior, and by insisting children complete what they start. By the time children are in middle school they could be doing their own laundry, cleaning their own rooms, and helping with other family chores. Children who are allowed to be lazy at home will be lazy at school, too lazy to get an education.

If you are a teacher, document all your parent contacts. When confronted with a difficult parent have a co-worker sit in on your conversation and use the speaker phone. Not only can the co-worker testify to what was said but that person could help you retain your professionalism. Write and communicate to parents what actions the child specifically took in your classroom to disrupt learning and don't generalize. Tickets for chronic classroom disruption cannot be issued without this specific documentation or without the parent being contacted.

10. Lazy or Discouraged Students

Teachers should be aware that some children rule their families, tell their parents what to do, and fully intend to implement that same dysfunctional model in their schools. Classroom organization and rules can block these types of students from continuing behaviors which are self-defeating and disrupt learning for other students. The following classroom strategies and rules worked for me in an alternative school setting where students have documented behavior problems and extraordinary social concerns. For that reason, the methods described here should work for every middle school teacher. Anyone who wishes to implement these ideas or use the forms I describe has my permission to do so. However, this article is meant to be only a description of how I managed my classroom and how I engaged my learners. I am not claiming to be the supreme authority on classroom management techniques but I know these things worked with some of our most difficult students placed at the alternative school. Middle school students often need help organizing their work and managing their own behavior; they need help with one task and they need motivated to do the other.

I used simple paper folders with pockets and brads down the middle to organize students' work. Students were not allowed to remove these folders from the classroom because they served to document the level and quality of work the students completed while assigned at the alternative school. Student folders were either given to the students to take back to their home schools on their last day of attendance or were sent through our inner-office mail to their home school teachers. I relied heavily on student folders to track students' level of engagement in learning. The folders were useful to middle school students because they could track their own attendance, behavior grades, and academic progress by referencing their classroom folder.

The first thing I required my middle school students to do when they walked into the classroom was copy down their daily learning objective onto a form they kept in their student folder. This form had two columns which said "My learning objective is" and "What I learned today." This form covered one whole week and it was designed to be used as both a class opening activity and a class closing activity. After students recorded their daily objective they could anticipate what we might be studying for the day and they could predict how it related to the previous days' lessons. At the end of class, students wrote down what they learned in class about their daily objective. Students were not free to leave class until I saw this one sheet that I named the daily evaluation sheet. I allowed three minutes for class closing, called on students to share what they had learned about our topic, and I quickly walked up and down the aisles to make sure this form was completed. If a student had not completed this form then I put them on a detention list for that day. In addition to helping students focus on the task at hand, using this one form assured me that I would always have an opening and a closing activity in every class I taught. It was a simple daily procedure but it worked well. I'm sure other teachers have used similar forms but the way I used this form may be a little different because of the importance I assigned to its completion and because I used it as both an opening and closing activity.

After the students copied down their daily objective, we reviewed briefly what we did in class the day before and we predicted how our objective for the current day might tie into our studies. Then, the class read the list of processing activities written on the board (the activities we would complete in class) which were designated for our lesson. All these quick routines served as our class opening and did not take any longer than five minutes. This organization worked so well that students would automatically open their folders as soon as they walked into class and would not talk while they busied themselves writing down their study objective for the day. By the time they finished, I had taken attendance and was ready to review the activities listed on the board with them.

Compliance was easily obtained because I reminded students daily about this requirement until they initiated writing their objective without a reminder. I explained "If you don't complete this very simple form you are telling me you did not learn anything all week therefore you don't deserve a good grade. I will deduct points from your score and I will keep you after school to give you time to complete it. It's only my responsibility to design your learning experience and it is your job to learn. You are not doing your part if you can't write down your learning objective and tell me what you learned each day." This learning objective requirement helped students not only focus on the task at hand for that day but it also kept students from getting too involved in social exchanges at the beginning of class. They had something to do as soon as they walked into the science room.

Another classroom structure I implemented which helped maintain the students' focus was an assignment checklist (participation sheet) which I passed out at the beginning of every week. Students would check off their listed activities as they were completed. This not only served to keep students focused on the tasks at hand but this one form enabled me to tract students' progress and assess their level of engagement. If I saw a student start to slack from working I would ask to see their completed assignments along with their participation sheet. Students could not hide from me their inactivity and they had to produce the completed items they had checked off from their list for my review.

Students were unable to sit and stare without working in class because of this form and I would set time limits on the completion of specific task if it appeared a student was delaying or being lazy. I would tell students who tried to play me this way, "You have ten minutes to complete this one page," and I would write the time I told them this on their paper. I would circle back and check to see if they completed the task and I might have to say, "It appears you may need more time or individualized help to complete this classroom assignment so if you cannot finish this assignment in class then I will keep you after school this afternoon and we will discover what you don't understand together." It was amazing how many students went to work quickly to avoid an afterschool stay!

However, most students enjoyed checking off their assignments on the participation sheet and felt accomplishment at the end of the class period when they realized they had completed all their work for that day. Often students would tell me they did not do school work of any kind at their home school and they would marvel at how easy it was to keep up in my class with this one form. Although students valued this form, the student participation sheet, I valued it more because it allowed me to keep on top of the individual students' progress in real time. In addition, since the completion of their work for the day was linked to students' ability to assign themselves a participation grade, students wanted to complete their assignments each day.

Along with tracking their completed assignments, students were allowed to grade their daily performance on their participation sheet. The last column of this form contained a space for recording students' self-assigned participation grade. Students were allowed to give themselves a 100% each day if they completed all of their work (check-off list) and they demonstrated good behavior in class. Students who had never earned a passing grade in science before could record a one hundred percent for their participation grade in class, every day, if they met my criteria. All my students took pride in grading their own classroom performance and tried to improve their participation grade which accounted for 15% of the classroom grading matrix. The system was easy to understand and students could assign their own grade for the day's performance by answering three questions which I posted in my room. Are you in attendance and not tardy? Did you complete all your work for today? Did you have good behavior in class today? If students could answer yes to these three questions then they could give themselves a 100% classroom participation grade. If not then they had to ask me what I thought their grade should be and I told students I reserved the right to raise or lower their grade if their self-assessment was not accurate. I would tell students, "Trust me, I will remember if I had to give you discipline during class."

There were two organizational strategies I used to establish student engagement and the working atmosphere in my classroom. The first was the student classroom folder which held the current objective sheet (daily evaluation form) and the participation sheet (assignments list) in the left pocket along with students' graded work which was held in the right pocket. Down the middle of this folder and fastened with brads was the students' science journal. The use of brads made it easy for the students to insert additional material. All class notes and science diagrams were placed in the journal in chronological order. Students used this self-constructed journal for test reviews and for open book or open note tests. Our school district science chairperson initiated the use of journals and although many teachers groaned at the prospect, the journals turned out to be useful to motivate students as well as keep students organized. Most students valued the work placed in these folders and they enjoyed showing the work to their traditional classroom teachers when they returned to their home schools. A simple paper folder which kept student's work organized instilled pride in many students who had never taken school seriously before coming to an alternative education program.

The second organization strategy I used to engage students in learning was a requirement that students' had to construct a learning packet every week that was due on Friday. The packet consisted of all the daily work completed in our classroom for the entire week and included: clinical lab reports, computer research worksheets, homework, tests or quizzes, and the daily evaluation sheet and assignment sheet. The last two documents were placed on top and had to be filled out completely. The work was stapled together and I reviewed each packet to make sure everything was included before allowing the students to turn it in. Even though students received immediate feedback in class on the correctness of their work, I did not officially issue grades until Friday and students would have to attempt to complete any missing assignments during our Friday class period. I would not accept an incomplete packet as long as class time remained. When students tried to get out of work by saying, "I already turned that paper in. You must have lost it!" I would laugh and say, "You know I don't collect any work from you until Friday and that all of your work is stapled together and turned in at one time. So if it is lost then you lost it and you will need to do it over by the end of this period. For other students who had completed their work Friday was a reward day.

I developed science research worksheets that were aligned with our curriculum for students who earned privileges on Fridays. Those students who had their work certified complete by me were allowed to listen to music with head phones as they researched science topics on teacher chosen web sites. Since we had at least one learning activity on Friday, privilege time was limited to no more than half the class period. Soon students who wanted that privilege pushed themselves to do the required work so they could earn Friday computer research and music time.

Although, all students worked on the computer at least one day a week during learning power class, students prized the extra time given on Fridays as a reward. Students received a grade on their computer researches and had to verbally tell me what they learned at the end of the period. So, students were rewarded when they successfully turned in their completed weekly learning packets. Students had to stay focused all week on their lessons and assignments to do this successfully and their grades improved when they did these things. The check-off list on the student participation sheet kept students organized and they never had an excuse to say they didn't have anything to do or they didn't know what to do. If they were absent then they knew what work they missed and they were required to make it up. I established a folder system with days listed Monday through Friday that contained copies of work that students could access easily. Due to our classroom organization, students found it was possible to get all of their work finished and earn privileges in science class.

Formerly discouraged, learning disabled, and lazy students performed equally well with this system. Of course, the work requirements were adjusted to meet the modifications listed in individual education plans of some learners and lazy students were prodded to work or they could receive after school detentions every day. Once students understood the rules and structure in my classroom, I often had students say I was the only teacher for which they had done any work. Many stated they were allowed to sit and scribble on paper or talked to other students at their home schools. Clearly these students had not been engaged in learning and may have thought they had no culpability in the learning process before attending the alternative school.

One thing I did not do was grade students' daily work for content mastery. I only assigned daily work grades based on the percentage of work students completed and I purposely set the volume of daily work assignments higher than what average students could complete in one period. I did this to determine the true ability of all students. I would tell students if I saw they were working the entire class period and were not wasting time then I had the option of reducing their work requirements. However, my advanced placement students were challenged by the additional assignments and they were competent enough to complete the quantity of work I assigned.

I scanned through students' daily work while they were doing it in their seats to make sure they had not written down ridiculous answers so they could say they were done. When someone tried this deception, I would share the bogus answers with the entire class as examples of how not to try to trick the teacher and the offending student got a clean work page to do over. Students were allowed to work in groups and often the whole class worked as a group to complete learning or review activities. However, I had to maintain a high level of supervision when students were doing this to keep students on task. If students could not handle the extra freedom then I would dismiss the group work and students would have to work independent of each other. Homework was assigned two to three times a week and consisted of simple and concise worksheets which covered concepts that we had studied that same day. Supplemental material was used because students were not allowed to take their textbooks home. We graded our home work and corrected the work together in class which served as a review. We were always reviewing concepts then building on them.

It was not unusual for students to make comments to me about my class structure. One student said, "Mrs. G., how come you always on your game? Your class goes fast. I wish the other classes went like this one." Students soon realized that science class had learning objectives to cover every day and there wasn't any down time in class. Some students initially may have felt overwhelmed because the routine could be rigorous at times. However, when the students learned to use their participation sheet as a guide and began to see an improvement in their grades, they would ask for the sheet if they were absent and missed the handout. They knew the only way they could keep up was to use this guide.

Since the daily work grade was a reflection of the percentage of work completed and students were given a fifteen percent advantage for being engaged in learning (participation grade), the only activities which could lower students' grade averages in my class were poor test grades, inaccurate lab performances, and failed computer research or other class projects. Computer research skills were gained through weekly computer lab research experiences and clinical lab skills were improved through teacher demonstrations of proper techniques. These demonstrations were followed by student activities where students not only performed their own labs but completed processing questions about their work which connected our classroom objectives to their lab performances. Improving test scores took more effort.

I did two things to help students improve their test scores and unmotivated students saw the merit of both these interventions. The first thing I did was to tell students if they did not pass tests in my room they would be required to attend a test correction session, look up every question they missed in their textbook or other resources we used, and fill out a test correction form for re-evaluation. If they did this then they could earn a passing grade of seventy, even if they were still five points or less away from the 70%. As long as students were improving their score by doing the test correction and they were within a five point range I would give them the 70% passing score. This test correction was not an option; it was a requirement when students failed tests. However, it was an option for students who wanted to raise their test scores. The correction form was a bear to fill out and students hated doing it. Some students had to attend more than one after school session to correct their tests.

Students perceived this test correction rule was fair and I thought it was necessary to help students start taking test seriously. Since all students have become so use to taking objective test it seemed to me that they lacked motivation to really learn the concepts I was teaching in the classroom. Some students stated they knew the answer would be on the paper somewhere and all they just had to guess the right one. Since all state level performance tests were objective, students had to be taught how to choose, not guess, the correct answer. Motivating students to choose instead of guess is easy when one method involves more work than the other. My test correction rule definitely required more effort so students began to analyze questions instead of guessing answers to avoid making test corrections.

The second thing I did for students was to teach them strategies for taking objective tests and I gave them sample questions periodically at the beginning of class for an opening activity. It was just a three to five minute oral class activity in which I put one or two sample objective questions on an overhead projector while discussing with students strategies they could use to analyze and choose the correct answers. This activity served to improve students' test taking skills and motivated them to actually learn concepts instead of guessing answers. Some students valued test practice enough that they chose to attend sessions before the annual state test so they could review what they had learned about taking objective test.

However, just the avoidance of additional effort and time were powerful motivators for most students taking chapter tests. Staying after school was not something students wanted nor was it something parents wanted their children to do. My students gained test taking skills through: developing, reviewing, and using objective test strategies, and through attending test correction sessions. The single best thing I implemented to effect change in students' tests scores was my classroom rule which required students who failed test to attend correction sessions after school. Students' attitudes changed due to this requirement and they quit guessing answers!

Most teachers I know put in extra hours after school with students (often without extra pay) so why not make students' completion of daily work and student test correction sessions top priorities for the time invested? My outlay of time deterred students from being lazy in the classroom and caused them to put forth more effort during the school day. Also, my strategy adjusted students' attitudes about taking test and caused them to develop some analytical thinking skills. However, my classroom policies were sometimes met with passive aggressive behaviors and some behavior deviations.

A few students became chronically tardy from my first hour class. Our office did not count them tardy unless they missed more than thirty minutes of class which allowed them to miss thirty minutes of instruction and seat work time. I suspected these students' unexcused absences related directly to their need to be lazy and circumvent my classroom rules. Two things resolved this problem, the school district began to count three tardy days as one truant day for reporting truancies to the court and I developed a new classroom rule.

My rule "If students comes into class late and their tardiness has not been excused by the office then those students will stay after school and give me minute for minute of class time missed on the same day they were tardy" confounded the students' attempts to derail my other classroom rules. However, my tardy rule came into conflict with the school's policy of allowing students not to be counted tardy until they were thirty minutes late and not to be counted absent until they missed all of their first period class and part of their second.

Since students will manipulate any policy to their advantage, students reported, "They say we are supposed to come to school at this time but we really don't have to be here until thirty minutes after that and we can miss one and one-half periods of instruction before being reported absent from school. (I believe most school districts have a similar rule which probably relates to school funding issues.) To combat students' referral to this policy, I explained to students that I was in charge of my classroom and I did not want them to enter my classroom if they were more than five minutes late because they disrupted learning for the other students. If they were thirty minutes late then they would be too far behind in the lesson for me to catch them up before the class ended. For this reason, I made students apologize when they came to class late even if it was just five minutes. Whether or not they meant to, tardy students disrupted learning, they needed to take responsibility for their own tardiness, and I would keep them after school to make up the time they had missed if their tardiness was not excused by the office.

However, as a result of this new classroom tardy rule, students who were going to have an unexcused tardy would skip my class altogether and just be absent. This was only a problem for my first hour class because once our students were at school they were escorted from class to class and could not leave their groups unless accompanied by a staff member. When students skipped my class, I just refused to let students make up the work they missed because they had unexcused absences even though they were not counted absent from school for the day. I conference with parents to try to resolve the issue because sometimes students were absent because parents would not get up or bring them to school on time. If students were just ditching my class to avoid class work and parents enabled them to do that then students just failed my class. I would tell students, "The only way you can fail my class is to be absent from it and not make up the assignments. You are not allowed to make up your work if your absence is unexcused. If you are present then you will do the work."

Tardy and truant students can be a huge problem for all middle school and high school teachers. I believe more needs to be done at the district level to hone school policies which may enable students to miss half a class period before counted as tardy or miss an entire first period without being counted absent. Students interpret all school and classroom policies to their own advantage and it didn't take long for my students to develop their own interpretation of our school tardy rule. Unfortunately, these types of policies put more of a burden on classroom teachers to track students attendance but my participation sheet helped with this task also.

Remember the student evaluation sheet that required students to write down their objectives along with what they learned that day? Students who missed class did not have the information they needed to fill out this form completely because old objectives were erased and a new one written each day on the board. In addition, when they were absent, students were missing daily worksheets and homework from their learning packets. If they didn't come on Fridays, their learning packets were conspicuously missing from my grading and recording routine. Missing work was easily checked against the students own participation sheet stapled to their weeks' work and missing information on the student evaluation form triggered my checking the attendance register. Again, these two forms enabled me to stay on top of student absences and evaluate their classroom performance based on completed work and classroom participation.

Unexpectedly, there was one additional advantage to my classroom structure and paper management style that was revealed after two years when our school district started requiring all educators to post their classroom assignments on teachers' personal web pages. Most technologically advanced school districts probably have this requirement by now and if not already mandated, this soon could be a national model. The students' participation sheet (Assignment check-off list) I created every week was useful to me for this purpose and I pasted it into my school district website so parents and others could see what my students were doing in class every day. The teacher version of this sheet was my lesson plan and it listed the district objectives, text page numbers, and other resources used for the lessons. Once my lesson plans were created, it was easy to construct the participation sheet which listed student activities. I just referenced the teacher's plan to construct the students' version. The high level of accountability required of teachers today can be a burden but this one participation sheet I created for students ended up benefitting my need for internet classroom transparency.

Teachers today need to be aware that computer use, specifically internet, has changed classroom accountability into a district wide or community wide event and building supervisors may not be the only ones evaluating teachers' performances for this reason. However, web page requirements should not generate anxiety for teachers because they give them an opportunity to create a virtual "Dog and Pony Show" (Teachers know what this means). Classroom educators can demonstrate their adherence to district learning objectives and show their creativity for developing student processing activities by posting their lesson plans and innovations via the net. In addition, teachers who can make learning fun with varied and creative activities can toot their own horn on their personal web site.

However, the general public and school district administrators will continue to use the ultimate teacher evaluation, student performance. Did student performance increase with the classroom structure I implemented? Most students grades improved while in my class and students did gain self-efficacy because they had academic success. In addition, their classroom behaviors improved and they understood the need for keeping track of their assignments and organizing their work. Often, students expressed amazement regarding their improved grades and I would say: "If you: attended school every day at your home school, did all of your class work and home work, had good behavior in class, corrected all the answers on tests that you missed, wouldn't you have better grades at your home school?" Of course the students answered yes to that question.

All students need structure but may resist it initially. Teachers have to be smarter than their students by organizing the learning environment in a way that helps students stay focused and blocks their attempts at being lazy. Students often lack self-discipline when it comes to doing school work. Middle school students would rather be socializing instead of working so maintaining their interest is challenging. Students attending alternative middle school programs may have more distractions and be more challenging due to their drug use and past histories of academic failure. Therefore, alternative teachers have to create classroom structures which block them from continuing their self-defeating attitudes and behaviors. I hope some of my suggestions here might prove useful for that purpose.

Personally, I considered my classroom structure to be successful because discipline problems decreased while I gained more time to teach, students became engaged in learning and accepted responsibility for improving their grades, and students gained self-efficacy. One principal said she didn't think I had any discipline problems with any students and she was almost right. Like all teachers I had discipline problems but I learned to respond quickly and consistently to limit their impact on the learning environment.

When students did misbehave even if it was unintentional (students do forget where they are at sometimes and what they are supposed to be doing) was a reminder about the rule. The student consequence was an apology to both their class members and to me for disrupting learning. I posted instructions how to properly apologize to help students do this. Students had to stand and address the class and take as little time as possible performing their acts of contrition. I informed students that I would accept their apology as long as their behavior changed because their behavior correction was the only evidence I had they were being sincere. This also served as a warning that a detention would be issued should they continue to disrupt and they would be in danger of losing their good day. Losing a good day would mean the student would not get credit for participating that day in our program due to their poor behavior and this meant they would have to stay one extra day at our school. Since many of our students wanted to return to their home schools and be with their friends as quickly as possible, losing a day because of misbehavior could motivate some students to have good behavior.

If a student persisted and I had to place them in the hall so I could give instructions to the rest of the group, a student conference was needed and a detention was issued. I did not call the first time I kept a student after school for a detention. Instead I named it a teacher-student conference and I would talk to the students to find out what motivated them. This first meeting also served to build a relationship with my students. Usually, a reminder issued to the student about their assignment to an alternative school program worked well when the students realized they could receive additional legal consequences or be referred to a more restrictive environment. It was my policy to meet first with students before calling parents because I wanted the students to take responsibility for their own behaviors. I would tell the student that calling their parent would be my next step if their behavior did not improve. If students had probation officers I would tell them I would contact probation officers before I contacted their parents because clearly their parents had little influence over their behaviors. I informed students I expected them to be a man or woman of their word when I accepted their apology for disrupting my class. I informed them I would do everything possible to help them get an education because that was my job and I wanted them to be successful in our program. However, I cautioned if their repentance was faked and they caused more trouble in my room then I would notify the principal that they were not adjusting well to our program and I would contact the school police officer with my concerns. I ended by saying "And...we will not be friends anymore!" When the students stayed that first time we focused on their academic goals and reviewed their transfer grades. Often we could determine the exact percentage they needed to either earn a passing grade for the grading period or what percentage they needed to pass the semester. We developed a plan and this served to motivate students to achieve. After our initial student-teacher conference students usually did not have to be detained after school again, they changed their behavior, and they adapted to my classroom routine.

This initial conference was a one on one experience and was much more effective than a detention assigned for punishment with a room full of other students. I did not like traditional detentions because they wasted precious time that could be used to motivate students and provide tutoring services. When a detention was necessary I only kept students long enough to make them miss their ride home, usually fifteen minutes, because that would inconvenience both the parent and the student enhancing the likelihood there would not be a repeat performance. I documented my attempts to notify parents the day of the detention and the student stayed the very day they committed the offense. If the student had other commitments it was of no concern to me. My detention came first and I would not negotiate the time or day the detention was owed. I felt the consequence should not be delayed or it lost some of its impact. All staff watched the hall when students were exiting and reminded students on their way out of impending detentions and their need to stay after school to avoid further consequences. If students walked out of a detention they were not allowed into class the next day, could be placed in ISS for one to three days, or they could be suspended if their behavior they received the detention for merited that decision.

Occasionally, a student would try to destroy the learning environment in every classroom and teachers would hold a conference together with an individual student. Although this may be frowned upon and some school policies could prohibit teachers from doing this it can be very effective. When presented with a united front, these types of students cannot claim that one teacher is treating them unfair or doesn't like them. These types of meetings should be well documented and parents should be notified of the meeting. However, the meeting should not be delayed if the parent does not show up. Again, the student should apologize, they should be extolled for their merits, and specific behaviors for change should be targeted. This can be verbal initially but should be written down and shared with the parent and a behavior modification plan developed that all teachers follow.

Mainly, the thing I learned about classroom discipline and classroom structure while employed at the alternative school is that it needs to be consistent, swift, but forgiving. Don't hold grudges against your students because they have the ability to change their behavior with your help. For those rare, out of control students who pose safety concerns in your classroom or who chronically disrupt learning there is a limit to what you can manage by yourself. Take a team approach to discipline and when the team cannot manage the child then turn all your documentation over to the principal or director of special education. Getting these students identified quickly so they can get the help they need should not reflect poorly on your ability to manage a classroom because they should be few and far in between. However, alternative school teachers often receive a classroom of students who have a history of disrupting learning and some groups are worst than others. Speak up and tell the administration that you need an aid to help if you have too many special needs students with histories of violence in the classroom. Document your meetings where you asked for this help and go to your department chairs with your concerns. Your team members may not really be aware of your difficult teaching assignment unless you share the information.

I am reminded of a time when a school counselor opened my class door to pick up a student for a session and gasped in horror at the overcrowded situation in my classroom. She was in charge of accepting kids into our program for placement and she had assigned eighteen children to that section when the room only had a physical capacity for twelve. Middle school teachers shifted seats between classes to have enough desk for students and my desk and desk chair were both used by students. I had reported the overcrowding to our principal who said we were being forced to accept all the students referred because it was time for our district's yearly exam. These trouble makers were not wanted at their home schools and they were being referring to our program at lightning speed. Even with the counselor's acknowledgement of the overcrowded situation, I would have been forced to accept the arrangement if other team members would have not joined me in making a proposal based on safety issues in our classrooms. I believe we mentioned calling the fire marshal because the number of students placed exceeded the capacity of our small rooms. After this, some students were removed to a vacant ISS room and I pulled those students during their PE class for instruction (my planning period) and left work with the ISS teacher for the period she had them.

The point of telling this story is that there are always going to be classroom management challenges and teachers have to be flexible to meet the needs of their school districts. The most important thing a teacher can learn to do is create a classroom environment that enhances learning opportunities for students. Certainly, my organization, rules, and management style were somewhat rigid and were totally teacher initiated but this was due to the student population assigned to me. I learned through experience. However, there is one curriculum I would highly recommend for all teachers. CHAMPS (www.pacificnwpublish.com). This curriculum trains teachers in some of the strategies I incorporated in my classroom due to my experience.

11. Humpty Dumpty

Bernard was a short, portly-shaped, seventh grade special education student. His broad face, slanted eyes, and unusual haircut gave him an odd appearance. His hair was shaved short on both sides but he had ringlets of curls piled high on the top of his head. It sort of looked like Bernard tied to create a Mohawk effect, failed because his hair was too curly, and instead, fashioned himself a pointed head. However, it was Bernard's missing neck that made him conspicuous because his head sat directly on his chest. This student shuffled and rocked side to side when he walked. His unsteady gate plus his bizarre appearance caused students to stop working and gawk when he entered our room. Bernard seemed to realize all eyes were on him as he wobbled like an egg across the floor and bobbed into an empty front row desk.

That morning when I introduced Bernard to the class, I looked around the room for an interpreter because I had been told he was not proficient in English. Hernando did not like group attention because he was shy but he would help if other students were called on for assistance and complied. I posed a request to another student first and said, "Ashley, will you please close the window blind for me? The sun is shining on our white board and I am afraid the class will not be able to read our objectives for the day. Thank you, Ashley. Joe, would you please pass out student folders? Thank you for your help, Joe." Then it was Hernando's turn, "Hernando, I need your help too. Would you please come forward and talk to Bernard for me? Could you ask Bernard in Spanish the name of his home school and the name of his last science teacher?" As Hernando made his way to the front of the classroom Bernard surprised me by answering my question in English.

"Appalwo and dun't know teacher." The other students in class were startled by the sound of Bernard's deep nasally voice and they began laughing uncontrollably. I nodded at Hernando giving him permission to sit back down and I analyzed Bernard's response. I thought his dictation sounded like it was affected more by his thick tongue rather than by his unfamiliarity with English and I realized it was not Bernard's pronunciation that triggered the class room hilarity. Instead, Bernard's lack of ability to modulate his voice had caused the students' to howl. He had an extremely loud and deep voice but the monotone quality was unexpected and it had caused the mirth. This student clearly knew more English than what I had been led to believe but I became worried that he might become reluctant to communicate if other students kept making fun of him. I was ready to address the class about laughing at Bernard when he acted like he had something else to say.

He began by smacking his thick, generous lips like he was practicing for speech. Then he knitted his brow together causing wrinkles to appear between his eyes like he was putting a lot of thought into what he was going to say. His words took several more seconds to materialize. Everyone in the class was intensely waiting for his vocalizations and I had the distinct feeling students wanted to hear Bernard's strange voice again. Now, at the same time Bernard cleared his throat with a "Hu-u-um" he narrowed his eyes to form slits barely distinguishable from the other wrinkles which were now deepening across his forehead. All of which gave him the appearance of a large cracked egg. Poor Bernard was straining and the anticipation our class experienced while waiting for him was maddening. I was ready to end all our sufferings when Bernard opened his mouth to speak and simultaneously began bobbing around in his seat to get comfortable. It appeared Bernard's midriff bulge was caught fast between the chair seat and his desk top. He began rocking side to the side in an effort to free himself and came dangerously close to dumping the whole thing over. One of the students called out, "Slow down Humpty Dumpty you will turn your desk over and break your big egg-shaped head!" All the students laughed again and I prepared to issue a hot reprimand to the rude student when Bernard stopped rocking in his seat and spoke, "Dun't know teacher. Fat and bald. Dat's all." Of course, all the students in class laughed harder than ever before because Bernard's loud monotone voice assaulted all our ears. Bernard's face reddened but he laughed with us!

Sammy, the student who named Bernard Humpty Dumpty quickly stood up beside his desk and placed both hands over his ears and said, "Stop it Bro, you're going to make my ears bleed." Other students were holding their ears too and Bernard's facial expression saddened. Sammy owed Bernard an apology for his name calling and I called him into accountability. Since he was already standing, I informed Sammy he needed to apologize to his new classmate for saying hurtful things and for calling him a name. Sammy looked toward the "How to make an apology" poster I had placed on the side of a bookcase closest to his desk. He was familiar with the routine because he often had to be prompted to take responsibility for his inappropriate behavior in class toward other students and Sammy knew he would have to perform his act of contrition flawlessly or he would be kept after school for additional disciple.

Before Sammy began he slammed Bernard with another insult, "You better call all the King's men or this boy is going to stay in your room all day, Mrs. G. The only way he is going to get loose from his desk is to fall out of it and break his big head!" HA...HA...HA...HA.... I hurriedly interjected some cautionary words before Sammy went any further, "Don't you talk about my son that way!" I was hoping my unexpected statement would make Sammy think about what he had just said and he would correct the direction of his behavior. However, Sammy did not have a chance to open his mouth before Bernard jumped in the conversation and testified to the veracity of my comment.

Passionately, Bernard asserted, "Dat's right. I'm er son. I'm da baby!" He sputtered in his deep voice while thrusting both thumbs back toward his chest. Bernard's words were understood by everyone in class but his dictation and supporting loud emotional vehemence caused all the students in class to pause. There was an interval of silence before the laughing began again fresh and some students almost believed Bernard's testimony. I could clearly read the students' expressions as their mouths gapped open and their eyes widened. A few students were showing confusion and others were displaying utter disbelief. Bernard's statement was timely, funny, and disarming to everyone including Sammy, the wannabe bully. Even I had to grin a little because this unusual student, Bernard, was turning out to be quite a trip.

Sammy promptly apologized when I pointed at the 'How to Make an Apology' poster and Bernard began grinning from ear to ear. As soon as Sammy finished with his penitence, Bernard rocked out of his desk, bowed from the waist and said, "I cept your apowogy," in a formal and gentlemanly way. Astonished once again, the class snickered and I used

Bernard as an example of how to properly accept an apology. Then, I quickly changed the tone of our classroom by giving instructions before I became mesmerized by this very interesting student. That first day, it became plain to me that I really would not know what to expect from Bernard in my classroom.

When we started our work, Bernard seemed attentive during the lab demonstration but began to lose interest during seat work time. I worked individually with Bernard at his desk and I determined he could read and understand English quite well. I was thrilled because more than half of my students in this class could not read above a third grade level. Only one other student in this section could read better than Bernard, his name was Bobby, and I was thinking about pairing the two together in a learning group when I reached my limit for hearing the familiar but now intolerable crane whooping sound next to me. I was not surprised when Bernard complained, "I dan't dink! Whad's wong wid dat boy?"

I turned to the young man on my left and stepped aside a little so Bernard could see him and said, "Bernard, this is Bobby." The student extended his hand and when Bernard went to shake it, it was promptly withdrawn for a few seconds while Bobby resumed his multiple bird calls accompanied by a couple of wing flaps. Bernard looked puzzled and annoyed as Bobby redirected his wing, turned it into a hand, and caught Bernard's hand shaking it enthusiastically. Bernard gave me a pensive look which conveyed his feelings of uncertainty about this classmate. Then, Bobby explained to Bernard he had Tourettes syndrome and it caused him to do silly things. Bobby looked at me and I nodded while walking to my desk to write out a referral to the nurse. Bobby then started clicking his tongue while he folded his arms across his chest and tucked one hand inside each pit. Also he rocked and jerked in his seat. As Bernard stared cautiously at the student seated next to him other kids in class hardly seemed to notice Bobby's new movements because the clicking and rocking were much quieter than the bird calls they previously experienced.

As I wrote out a referral to the nurse for Bobby, Bernard spoke out loud, "Booby oou div me eadache!" The students all laughed again at Bernard's mispronunciation but this time Bernard clinched his fists tightly and he appeared not to enjoy the laughter at his expense nor the added head pain it caused. After I filled out the paper, I made a phone call to the office to let them know Bobby was on his way down. Bobby flew a wild zig-zagged pattern up the corridor while warning other middle school teachers of his uncontrollable state with a loud whooping crane noise as he passed by their doors. I watched from my classroom entrance until Bobby turned the corner and met another staff member head-on who then walked him to the office. I turned in time to see Bernard slump his head in his hands and I decided not to disturb him because I felt like doing the same thing. I spoke to myself, "Bernard would have to start our program on a day when Bobby forgot to take his medicine."

The other students and I had become use to hearing a certain amount of background noise made by Bobby and we really didn't notice it until a specific decibel level was breeched. Then, I would signal Bobby he was getting too loud and he would make an attempt to gain some control. Some days he could do this better than others. Bobby did not mean to disturb and at times, he was hardly conscious of his own movements or how they distracted others from learning. Regardless of his intent, Bobby disrupted his fellow students enough to cause them not to like him and I thought part of the reason he was rejected or ignored was that his behavior was so unpredictable. Bobby's classmates would mostly ignore him until he began flapping or flailing his arms in their personal space. Then, I became worried for Bobby's safety. Students could not ignore Bobby's arm motions when they came close to hitting them. Since, some baby gangsters in our program were always ready to fight, Bobby's uncontrolled arm movements could cause a classmate to pin him on the floor and he could be pounded. For this reason, I referred Bobby to the office whenever he started moving his arms erratically.

I turned to look at Bernard after I had given him a short three minute time out and it appeared that Bernard had fallen into a deep sleep as soon as his head met the top of his desk. When he choked on a loud snore two minutes later and jerked awake, the entire class once again hooped and hollered with laughter. This time Bernard giggled a little with his classmates and looked sheepishly at me. I asked, "Feel better?" Bernard nodded and smiled. I said, "Good. Bernard, I don't let students sleep in my class and I only let you put your head down today because you complained of a headache. Make sure you get enough sleep tonight because I will give you a detention if you try to sleep in class tomorrow. Now students let's put our things away and get lined up to go to our next class."

All in all, Bernard had earned a good day in my classroom. "Cute kid," I thought to myself, as the students lined up and filed out the door. Bernard's eyes were twinkling as he politely nodded goodbye. I instantly liked this young man and thought, "I can work with Bernard." He had, recognized the lesson of tolerance I was trying to teach other students when I called him my son and he had shown intelligence by reinforcing that message with a statement of his own. In addition, Bernard had made the other students laugh and they were now smiling at him. I hoped the rest of his day would go as well as science class but I worried about the interaction between Bernard and Sammy, the student who had named him Humpty Dumpty. Bernard's physical appearance could attract bullies like Sammy who might not only name call him but might make Bernard a physical target of their hate.

Then Sammy passed before me in the line going out the door. Although programmed to apologize, Sammy could not leave well enough alone and he added a departing hit, "I'm sorry I said what I did. But I can't help it. Your son is ugly." From his statement, it was evident to me this student was still not going to take responsibility for his poor behavior, he did not like apologizing to Bernard, and Sammy thought Bernard was my real biological son!

Sammy was a different type of student; he was turning sixteen in the seventh grade and he was discouraged. I didn't really understand how his multiple grade retentions were justified. I knew Sammy's attendance had been poor so I guessed that his truancy eliminated the possibility of him receiving social promotions. However, now he was so far behind his peers that his placement no longer seemed appropriate for him or for his classmates. He was placed with students who were three to four years younger than him and I worried about his contact with less mature, twelve-year old girls in class. The most troubling aspect of Sammy's seventh grade placement was the blame he assigned to classroom teachers. Sammy wanted teachers to suspend him from school for his bad behavior so he would not receive consequences for being truant. His desire to get kicked out of school motivated him to become a master at creating discipline problems in the classroom and he often started fights by hurling insults at other students. While everyone one else followed instructions and began their daily work, Sammy would try to start a fight with another student just so he could get kicked out of school. When teachers gave discipline instead of referrals for a suspension, Sammy would say, "Why don't you go ahead and just kick me out? I don't want to be here anyway. It's your fault I'm here because you won't let me go home." Dealing with Sammy's self-defeating behaviors every day exhausted all our staff.

I was doing the best I could with Sammy but he was not motivated and he was just biding his time until he could quit school at age seventeen. Sammy had told me if his parent did not let him quit school when he turned seventeen then he was going to run away and live on the streets. It appeared to me that Sammy's anger was growing stronger every day he was forced to attend a seventh grade classroom and I felt it was only a matter of time until someone at school received the full measure of his anger. Bernard's unusual physical appearance and his funny voice made him stand out as being different and I was afraid he would become the main target of Sammy's frustration. Bernard could be hurt and Sammy could end up in jail. While thinking about Sammy I confessed," There is something wrong with our special education system when students are placed four years behind their peers and cause major classroom disruption and safety concerns."

Sammy did not have good attendance and although I was relieved to see him gone, I wondered how a student sent to an alternative program for misbehavior could get away with not coming to school. I posed this question in a teachers' meeting to our principal who explained our current lame truancy court system. It seems our truant students were placed on a list for court appearances that never or seldom came to fruition. The courts were overrun with other civil cases which took priority. Without enforcement, students like Sammy were choosing not to come to school. The system needed fixed, our school district was aware of the deficit, and eventually, the district initiated a contract for a separate truancy court by combining funds with two other school districts. The process took a while and many of our students took advantage of the truancy loop hole until the system was fixed.

In the meantime, there was a troubling question on my teacher evaluation form which asked, what have you done to encourage attendance? Truthfully, I did not know how to encourage students like Sammy to attend school. When I asked Sammy one morning why he had missed school the day before he responded, "I don't have to come because my president, George Bush, said so." Sammy insisted that he didn't have to come to school because the president of the United States had passed a new law which said Sammy could not be left behind. This was the second time I heard this excuse from a student and I was perplexed. Middle school students certainly had their own spin on the no child left behind act.

I knew once a middle school student started a rumor like this that other kids would accept the idea as God's holy truth. It appeared Sammy had fully embraced this perverted interpretation of an education law which was meant to help special students. Therefore, Sammy now had two good reasons for not coming to school; he didn't want to go to jail for hitting someone and his President had passed a law saying Sammy could not be left behind. I felt outranked by the president after talking to Sammy and I wasn't sure what I could write on my evaluation form regarding the encouragement of student attendance. Sammy's logic was flawless because it was better for him to stay home from school verses go to jail for felony assault and Sammy would be promoted, at some point, regardless of his school attendance.

After talking to Sammy, my attendance encouragement policy took a different direction and became more direct. I told parents, "Trust me, I have five children, who are all precious to me, but I do not want to support any of them forever. If you want to retire before you die and you do not want to take care of children all your life then you need to make sure your child gets an education so he can take care of himself." I felt I gave parents both the motivation to promote student attendance and a reason to hope through this encouragement talk. However, I still didn't know how to explain my strategy on the teacher evaluation form.

In addition, I developed a parallel strategy for students, "Trust me, that woman who you call momma, who says she loves you, won't support you lying around her house when she is old and tired of working. You will be young and healthy and she will kick you to the curb. She will be over taking care of you, a grown person. She will be like that woman on the TV commercial who doesn't even come down to see her son off to college. You know the one, the dad lies for when he tells his son, 'Your Mom is just too broken up to come down.' The whole time the mom is measuring the son's bedroom trying to figure out where to put a hot tub. Listen, you have to do your best in school because you are only going to be able to count on yourself to earn a living when you get out of school. Parents are not supposed to take care of their kids forever! If you don't believe me go home and ask your parents if they are going to support you when you are grown and they are old." This also became part of my attendance encouragement plan for students because they needed a dose of reality.

However, when I talked to Sammy and used this strategy it did not work because he was determined that he would be a bum, sleep under a bridge, and eat his meals at a local shelter for the homeless. At least that is what he told me were his plans for the future. I contacted his parent and she attended a meeting with all the staff and assistant principal. She yelled at her son in front of us for taking her time away from her work. It was plain to see this poor woman was functioning at a survival level and she was bemoaning her own life's situation. Sammy's mother volunteered personal information that she was a teenager when Sammy was born, Sammy's dad had never helped with his support, and she had given up her own education to work and take care of Sammy. Now, she said she sacrificed for nothing because Sammy was failing to get his education. This mother was seeking to improve her own life by attending community college. Sammy's mother ended by saying she was moving on with her life just like Sammy's dad had done, "I tried to do the right thing by this boy but he isn't smart and he won't even try. I'm changing my life and I'm leaving the old life behind." She might as well have added, "Sammy can go to hell!" After this meeting I put Sammy at the top of my prayer list and I had empathy for both their situations.

In contrast Bernard's story was much different than Sammy's. He had excellent school attendance for the whole time he was assigned to our program. Bernard's father was in jail for dealing drugs but he knew who he was and he was able to visit his father regularly. Bernard's mother did not speak English so we used an interpreter to communicate his progress and she expressed genuine appreciation of the help teachers were giving Bernard. She assured us Bernard liked coming to our school. Bernard did seem happy but he consistently demonstrated one behavior that was difficult to overcome. Barnard feigned a lack of understanding due to a language barrier when he did not want to do work.

I knew he did in fact understand much more than what he let on because his reading comprehension in English was excellent. So, one morning when he tried to do this I said to him in my best ghetto voice, "You play'n me? I don't like be' in played. You are going to do your work in here or I will be keeping you after school every day, starting today. Do you understand?" Bernard said he understood but he just wanted to draw.

Many of my students were good artist and I found ways to incorporate their interest in art into science class but drawing was all Bernard wanted to do. I told Bernard he could draw, as a reward, after he finished his work. He complied and things went smoothly for a while. Once his interest was identified I gave Bernard plenty of opportunities to draw, color, and label visuals in his science journal for processing activities.

I continued to have students cycle in and out of the classroom while Bernard was in attendance. Sammy and Bobby were still in Bernard's class but there were other new students present and all of these new students started calling Bernard "Humpty Dumpty." Bernard told me he now liked his nick name the kids gave him because all of the other students had special names. I thought to myself, "Bernard doesn't understand that the special names are nick names used in the gangs." However, in view of Bernard's limited understanding and his sheer joy of feeling like he belonged, I decided not to correct other students when they called him Humpty or Dumpty. The assignment of this nick name became a positive for Bernard and the new students in class treated him with a fondness due to his humor and good nature. Bernard blossomed in friendships and academic performance in just a few short weeks. I thought he had adjusted well to my classroom and I could now move on to help other new students who needed more attention.

However, I was wrong because Bernard crossed a behavior line that even alternative education students could not ignore and his classmates became appalled by his conduct. Bernard began to put his hands under his desk and touch himself. I think he was doing this because we had a new girl in class that he liked. It was the girl who noticed Bernard first doing this, "Mrs. G, make him stop! He is grossin' me out. Bernard is touching himself!" Janey cried out.

The boy sitting directly across from Bernard jumped out of this seat and said, "Tell him to go wash his hands! Man, that ain't cool. You don't do that in public."

I did send Bernard to the bathroom across the hall to wash his hands and I told him, "You have lunch next period and I do think you will want to wash your hands."

While Bernard was out of the room I talked to the other students. I told the students that we should not make a big deal out of what happened.

Bernard probably didn't know better than to do what he was doing in public and that I would talk to him about his behavior. True to my word I kept Bernard for five minutes when the other students went to lunch and told him, "From now on Bernard, you have a new rule in my class. You must keep both your hands on the top of your desk. I will help you learn this new rule by reminding you, Bernard put your hands on your desk. When I say this, both of your hands have to be moved to the top of the desk." Bernard said he understood and repeated what I had said to him in English. I walked him down to the lunchroom and went to find my fellow middle schoolteachers to inform them of Bernard's new entertainment and how I purposed to control his behavior in the classroom. Bernard would respond better to the plan I had for extinguishing his inappropriate behavior if all the teachers responded the same way.

However, Bernard's behavior had caused some intolerance to surface in the classroom again and Sammy was now more hateful than ever toward Bernard. As soon as the students walked into the classroom the very next day and as they were sitting down Sammy said, "I told my momma what you did in the classroom yesterday and she said I could hit you and she wouldn't care. Even if I get sent to jail my momma won't be mad at me. You deserve it, Humpty!"

Before I could intervene, Bernard said, "O Yeah! Dat's not what yo momma said last night when she kiss me wight ere on my neck. She div me ickey right ere!" Bernard pointed at the side of his neck while he said this.

As the other students bellowed laughter all around the room, Sammy was taken back and appeared paralyzed not knowing what to do. One of my more tolerant male students gave Bernard a high five hand slap and said, "You're ok Bernard! Ms. Gifford, Bernard just made a Yo Momma joke!" I just shook my head and smiled at this amazing sped student who had gained the respect and support of hardened baby gangsters with a Yo Mamma joke! After the class recognized Bernard's humor, Sammy had no place to go with his aggressive behavior and he became a coward without the support of the other students. Bernard's unique sense of comedy timing had diffused a dangerous situation and I had been spared violence in my classroom.

As the next week progressed, Sammy became a run-away and he was not found for the remainder of the school year. My little noise maker, Bobby moved to another state and I could now hear myself think in the classroom. I still had students above the capacity of what the room allowed but now only one-half of my students were special education students. Things became a little easier for me when Sammy and Bobby left and I had more time to work with my other students. With the passing of each new week, Bernard's English and academic performance improved. He now could copy notes off the overhead and read them back to me in English and he could use his textbook to find answers for worksheets which were fill in the blank type of questions. He loved doing clinical labs in science and he took his work there very seriously. He was using his drawing skills to create diagrams in his science journal and I was feeling good about the progress Bernard had made in just five short weeks.

Of course, there were days when Bernard complained of headaches and he was especially loud and monotoned. On those days his voice took on a thick tongued pronunciation of words and he giggled a lot. When I noticed theses effects and a pattern emerging which correlated to his non-compliant behavior, I began to suspect Bernard might be under the influence of drugs or alcohol. I asked the special education teacher if she thought Bernard might have been drinking before coming to school. Then, I told her I had noticed Bernard's voice was not always loud and his word pronunciation was not always slurred or imperfect. Although, I had never smelled alcohol on his breath, I told her that Bernard's inconsistencies in classroom performance evidenced to me something else could be wrong with Bernard that did not relate to his special education diagnosis and I suspected alcohol use.

The special education teacher said Bernard had problems with alcohol in the past but she thought the characteristics I mentioned were just part of who Bernard was. I was not convinced and I decided just to watch him on those days he seemed a little bit off and document his behaviors. We covered substance abuse topics in our personal and social responsibilities class and I hoped Bernard would ask questions or make comments but he did not. His academic performance had improved so I thought maybe I had misread this student's behavior cues like the special education teacher said. His stay was drawing to a close and I realized I would be sorry to see this student go because working with Bernard had been very rewarding. He had improved both academically and socially during his stay at the alternative school.

However, during Bernard's last week he had one more surprise for me. Like the rest of the students in his class, Bernard had complained to me about creating a science journal and said it was too much work. I realized the students didn't understand the journal's purpose. So I decided to let the students' use their science journal notes and diagrams as a test modification. When Bernard took his first test this way, he scored the highest score in the class and only missed one question. Bernard proudly held up his returned test paper while saying, "I'm the smartest! I got the best grade! Who's the dummy now? Humpty Dumpty is the best!" Other students in class laughed with Bernard then some stood and applauded his success. The students really had learned to like Bernard and they celebrated with him.

When Bernard left my class to return to his home school I felt accomplishment for me and joy for him. I really thought he would meet with some success on his return to his home school because: his self-esteem had increased, his social skills had improved, he was speaking better English, he could use a textbook and his own journal to find information, and he had improved his lab skills. However, his success was short lived because he returned to the alternative school later that year and finished the seventh grade in our program.

When Bernard came back, he continued to fit into my classroom structure and did not cause any behavior problems. When I told him I was glad to see him but was worried because he was sent back to our school, he looked down and said one word, "Alcohol." It seems as if Bernard had gone back to his same pattern of drinking once surrounded by his former friends at his home school and he had been identified as being drunk at school. Our school staff had missed Bernard's use of alcohol due to his physical appearance and his special education classification that led us to believe Bernard's behaviors were related to his disabilities. I discovered Bernard was probably developing the disease of alcoholism when he shared his history with me.

Bernard was like many of our students who lived in families where drinking alcohol was a way of life. He told me he drank alcohol as a baby because his relatives put it in his baby bottle to help him sleep and that now he had to drink alcohol ever day to just feel well. I don't know if his statement was true or not but I had known cases, while working in child welfare, of parents pouring beer into their baby's bottles to put them to sleep. So, I had no reason to disbelieve what he said. It was difficult for this thirteen year old boy to get up and come to school each day because he drank the night before, every night, and he had a headache upon waking until he drank some more. I explained to Bernard it was possible that he was becoming an alcoholic and that he might need to go into a treatment facility to kick his habit. He told me that kids can't get addicted to alcohol and only adults had that problem. I asked Bernard to promise me he would seek help if he began to think he was an alcoholic and I told him his future and his education could depend upon him getting help for alcohol abuse.

Bernard did not come back the next year for the eighth grade but I saw him two years later walking down our high school hall. He was then in the tenth grade. When I said hello to Bernard, he shamefully cast his eyes down and did not speak to me. I went to find the special education teacher and ask what had happened to one of my favorite students. She told me, "Bernard is an alcoholic and was released to us from a juvenile substance abuse treatment program. He is feeling really low right now and said he never wanted to come back to our school. He did not want his old teachers to know what happened to him. Also, Bernard is wearing an ankle monitor because he was arrested for stealing. He is not taking good of care of himself and he often comes dirty and smelly to school. He said he just doesn't care about anything anymore and he really seems depressed."

After hearing this, I made it a point to say hello to Bernard every time I saw him in passing and tried to make eye contact with him because I did not want him to think I no longer valued him as having worth. Once he came to my room and we talked but it did not go well. He was not the same bright and happy child I knew two years earlier. All the staff tried to encourage Bernard to keep fighting his addiction because he was capable of getting an education but Bernard appeared permanently depressed about his situation and he no longer engaged in comedy in anyone's classroom.

Our other troubled student, Sammy, also reappeared as a freshman in high school and he had turned eighteen years old. Since special education students can attend school until they are twenty-one, Sammy was still receiving services. However, the high school teachers in our program said Sammy's behavior was truly unmanageable. He was contentious and disruptive in all his classes. One hardened alternative high school teacher said she considered turning in her retirement papers because Sammy and other special education students placed in her room that year were impossible to teach. I winked at her and said, "Now you know what I was going through a couple of years ago when I first started teaching at this school. You have many of the same students I had exactly two years ago. Come by my room because I've got a poster you can use with Sammy and I will tell you what I know works with him."

Discussion:

In the beginning, I recognized Bernard's unusual voice could be a characteristic which accompanied a specific human genetic defect. So the moment he spoke, I thought I had an idea of what his learning disabilities were. Later I would find out I was totally wrong with this educated diagnosis and Bernard's loudness and thick tongued communication was related to him being under the influence of alcohol. Bernard was a child alcoholic and his use of alcohol was disguised by his developmental delays and mongoloid appearance. His unusual look did place him at risk for being bullied.

Sammy was another story and his behavior placed others at risk. Sammy was not intelligent enough to do the work required in middle school. His academic ability topped out at the third or fourth grade level. His assignment to a traditional seventh grade science class should never have happened. Grade retention was a punishment for Sammy who was not able to understand basic middle school science concepts. Children like Sammy continue to be assigned curriculum mandates which are inappropriate considering their intelligence levels. These unsuitable curriculum placements discourage severe learning disabled students and when they are retained in grades they often become angry and cause discipline problems.

Both of these young men were special education students but they had very different abilities and needs. At the same time Bernard and Sammy were attending my class I had other students in my room like Bobby who needed my individualized attention. One day I looked out on this class to see all my students engaged in typical special education pursuits which included displaying various repetitive motions called ticks. Some students were rocking or humming while others were cracking their necks from side to side or drumming on their desk tops. Bobby was shrieking loud bird noises while flapping his arms like wings, Sammy was posting up to knock Bobby out and ... Bernard was self-pleasuring.

Too many times teachers may be blamed for students not learning when in fact teachers may be set up for failure. A system that placed fifteen special needs children in a classroom designed to physically hold no more than twelve and not provide a teacher's aide to assist with the class needs was a broken system. The scene I witnessed in my classroom that day would have been overwhelming for any traditional classroom teacher who did not possess mental health related training or experience. Fortunately, I had both along with personal determination. However, I was often called on the carpet that first year for not maintaining discipline in my classroom and other teachers may have been left with the impression I was not a capable teacher because of the noise level generated in my room.

The next year things changed and special education students could not be sent to our alternative education program without a review to determine if their home school teachers were following the students' IEPs correctly. If their behaviors were related to their disabilities then students were not supposed to be assigned to us. Things improved for a couple of years then special education students once again were referred to our program in record numbers. This proved to me that special education students are still not getting their needs met. There are many things wrong with our special education system because these students drop out of school at higher rates than other groups. **What kind of a system changes do we need for our special students to be successful?**

It is difficult for a child Bernard's age to recover from an alcohol addiction problem. The latest research on addiction reports if the first use of alcohol or other drugs can be delayed until a child is eighteen then the chances of that child becoming an alcoholic is dramatically reduced to about 10%. However, if a twelve or thirteen year youth uses alcohol then the risk for becoming addicted increases to 50%. Alcohol remains the drug of choice for a lot of children because they have easy access to it. Even if a parent does not drink or keep alcohol around, their child has friends whose parents have alcohol in their homes. Some of these parents believe that they are allowed by law to give alcohol to their child and your child if present, as long as they are supervising. The law which exempts punishment for parents who allow their child to drink alcohol was designed for religious ceremonies some faiths hold in the home. The law does not give a dad the right to pop a beer tab with his young son while watching a ball game or for a mom and daughter to relax and have girl talk with a brew. Some parents are deceived and they are deceiving their children into thinking that underage drinking of alcohol is safe and legal. **Explain how you would talk with other parents about not wanting your child to drink alcohol when they are in that parent's care.**

More than likely, Bernard was a fetal alcohol affected kid. His mongoloid appearance, learning disabilities, and social behavioral problems may have evidenced his mother's use of alcohol while pregnant. Students with Fetal Alcohol Syndrome are easily identified by social workers and teachers because they all have a similar look. Students who are born prenatally exposed to alcohol and have disabilities like Bernard's are at a higher risk for addiction themselves. Most disconcerting is the fact students who are coming to school both with limited academic potentials and under the influence further disable their own learning. Often, these students are uncooperative and some may be prone to violent outburst. **Explain why you think teachers should or should not talk to parents regarding student alcohol/drug use and its ability to further limit their special education child's academic outcomes.**

Sammy no longer wanted to come to school and he was convinced he could not learn. Sammy may have felt humiliated every day he spent in a traditional classroom with students who were four years younger. Sammy did not progress beyond the third to fourth grade level because he simply could not understand or process information above that level. **What purpose did Sammy's grade retention serve?**

Topics for Research

What is the difference between fetal alcohol syndrome and fetal alcohol effects? Is there a responsible way to model and teach alcohol use to children? Can a parent be arrested for delivering alcohol to a minor if that minor is using alcohol in their home without their knowledge? Is it legal to suspend educational supports to learning disabled students when they are sent to an alternative school program for their misbehavior? Under what circumstance should special needs children not be placed in traditional classrooms?

Things to do

Support special education reforms which make curriculum relevant to students' needs and eliminate grade retention.

12. Individualized Education Model

A federal law (IDEA) requires that school districts meet the individualized needs of special students. All special needs students are entitled to receive a free and appropriate education and should be placed in a least restrictive environment. Basically, what the law really means is that special needs students should receive public school learning opportunities close to what is experienced by their peers, be placed with their peers when possible, and accommodations should be made to assure these students have equal opportunities to learn. Gifted or talented students qualify as special needs students. However, programs for these types of special children may not be readily available because more funding is required on the other end of the continuum for disabled students (K12 academics).

Special education takes up between one-fifth and one-fourth of our current education budget. Students who have a permanent or lifelong disability classification are less numerous than students who are classified learning disabled. This one particular student group, learning disabled (LD), has increased by 233 % and contrasted with all other special education groups, which combined increased only by 13%, may be a crisis in the making (Ensuring High Quality Education for Students with Special Needs). Testimony given before the Senate Appropriations Committee verified more special education dollars are being spent on students who are learning disabled than on any other group of special needs students, "It appears that this "Lowest incident disabilities group carries the highest costs" (Andrew J Rotherman).

The evidence is clear regarding special education services and funding in public schools. Our learning disabled student population uses a higher proportion of special education funding. In addition, LD spending could be limiting services to students who are at both ends of the special needs continuum, those students who do have life-long disabilities and the gifted or talented special needs students. If this learning disabled student population continues to grow exponentially then all special needs students may be at risk for receiving less services.

According to one source, we may want to create a new educational model to meet the expanding need for special education services. Our current model of education, the factory-model, was designed to produce factory rejects (The Providence Journal). The factory-model moves children through sets of knowledge divided into grade levels. These sets of information are called curriculum. Our factory-model system is unforgiving and students, who cannot keep up with our lock-stepped curriculum, because they need to work a little slower or need a different type of instruction, will run the risk of falling behind and may have to be retained in a grade level. Retention in the same grade is called failing, students who fail become discouraged, and students who repeatedly fail have an increased risk of dropping out of school. "Students who drop out are five times more likely to have been retained that those who graduate" (National Center for Educational Statistics, 2006).

Special education students and/or children later identified as needing special education assistance are being retained in the same grade because retention is the accepted way we give these students additional time to acquire information and skills. However, the only alternative to retention in our current factory model is social promotion and this practice has been criticized for producing high school graduates who are illiterate (Retention and Social Promotion...). It is clear that our current education model uses retention and social promotion as a band aid fix for LD students. If we want to provide a quality education for this group and not produce dropouts or graduate students who are illiterate then we need to change our model of education.

According to one forward thinker in education, "Getting the model right will prove not nearly as important as getting the right model" (Competing Models for Public Education). One solution I purpose would replace our current factory-model with an individualized education system of instruction for all students. Regardless of academic ability every child would have their own IEP, Individualized Educational Plan. In this model students' abilities would be assessed by a standardized test and they would be placed in curriculum according to their level of performance in each subject. The test would be administered at the beginning of each academic school year and at the end of each academic year it would be repeated to evaluate student growth. Students would no longer pass or fail grades in school, they would remain with their peer groups which would be determined by the students' chronological ages, and they would master curriculum before being assigned the next level of instruction. Gifted or talented students could work ahead of their chronological age and LD students could work at levels below their chronological age while being placed with their true peers.

Under this individualized concept, there would be more than one way of completing high school and there would be more than one type of diploma or certificate attainable. Examples of long-term educational goals could be: earning a high school diploma for college readiness, varied technology diplomas for specific work opportunities or additional training, job readiness for students who would be entering the job market, basic academic skills certification and literacy trough a specific grade level, or life skills training. These are just suggestions of categories which students and their parents might choose as educational goals based on the student's abilities and family preference.

In addition, grade retention would no longer serve a purpose because students who work slower and need more assistance would continue to work on their selected educational goal every year. Progress would be measured by their mastery of curriculum content assigned to their goal area. In addition, if a student appeared to be falling behind their goal then Saturday school support would be available along with tutoring and those services could be mandated for some students. Also, a student's educational goal would be re-evaluated every year and could be changed based on the student's academic growth and their parents' preferences. Social promotion would never happen because mastering the curriculum would be the focus of our new individualized educational system. Students would stay with their peer groups but work on their own unique educational plan.

However, the development of technology would be the key to this new system and we might want c to individualize instruction through computer based curriculum so students all assigned to the same teacher could work on individual goals at the same time and in the same room. Computer-Based Training (CBT), sometimes called Computer-assisted Instruction (CAI) would make this individualized education system possible.

The first public institution to create a computer learning based system was the University of Illinois at Urbana-Champaign. This first CBT was called Plato and it has continued to evolve with the help of other entities like the Science Research Council and Virtual Systems to create additional programs like Wicat which have become the forerunners of e-learning. Computer based instruction is possible today because personal computers have more power and come equipped with some form of CBT, tutorial training (K12 academics). Public schools are beginning to offer computer based instruction and some high school students may be taking college courses through virtual learning experiences. We need to use this education tool more than what we have and step it down to include traditional curriculum offered at elementary and middle school levels. We need our mandated curriculum to be designed at different ability levels and made accessible through school web sites.

The advantages of implementing an individualized educational system using CBT are: students could receive immediate feedback, students could redo instruction and retake test to improve their grades to assure mastery, students' assessments could be completed on line and the results could be transferred to the teacher's grade book automatically, and students, parents, and teachers could track academic progress through assigned levels of instruction through the computer. This kind of instruction could truly help students achieve their highest academic potential. Students in middle or high school could still be working at elementary levels if they were learning disabled and needed more time to master the information. While younger students could be working at higher levels and could advance to take college level courses in middle school. In addition, teacher aides or parents could be trained to serve as computer lab monitors and would only need to be familiar with the computer based curriculum program to assist students. One benefit to school districts might be that some districts who are currently struggling to meet special education students' needs could use this CBT system to provide individualized instruction to LD students while staying within a budget.

Few highly qualified teachers would be needed in the actual computer lab and classroom teachers would be freed from the mundane task of grading and recording computer-based student progress. Instead, educators would be hired to teach advanced or specific academic courses (college prep, auto mechanics, etc.) and there would be enough funding to hire special education teachers to provide services for the life-long disability group. In addition, our gifted students would no longer be limited and their special need for advanced instruction would be met. There might actually be money in school budgets to enrich advanced students learning opportunities and money enough to hire the highly qualified instructors these students deserve.

If our old factory educational model was dumped in favor of individualized education for all students then all of our special needs students would be getting their needs met and school districts would be in compliance with the law. In addition, students would be better educated because they would be required to master the content at one level before being assigned work at the next level. Allowing students and parents to determine which educational path of instruction they would follow, which high school degree they would pursue, would empower both the parents and the students. Finally, parents, students and educators could become real partners if we converted to this new model.

Continuing, if students could see they were making progress and their educational goals were more relevant for them then they might not drop out of school because of failing classes or imminent grade retention. We could eliminate the words failed, retention, and social promotion from our academic vocabulary. This new system would only seek to measure student growth; students could not fail an academic year. Instead, new terms word be coined to signify students' performance and those could be "Mastered the information" or "Do over." If students were not making acceptable progress then a reassessment of their long-term educational goal (college prep, etc.) and a possible assignment of Saturday school attendance or tutoring enrollment might be instituted to help students correct their deficits. If a student's long-term educational goal proved to be inappropriate it could always be changed to something which is attainable without reflecting negatively on the student. Measuring student growth is more positive than failing students and adjusting a student's long-term educational goal to something which is attainable for them makes sense. For this reason, I believe drop-out rates would decrease if we adopted an individualized educational system for all our students.

Currently, learning disabled students like Sammy in the preceding story: are not always placed with their peers because of retention practices (Sammy was sixteen in the seventh grade), are being taught traditional curriculum which is neither pragmatic nor compatible with their mental abilities (Chemistry and physics), become overwhelmed and drop out of school (Sammy said he would run away and live on the streets if his parents did not let him drop out), and are using up special education funds needed for students who have life-long disabilities. Students like Sammy could be placed with their chronologically aged peers if CBT was part of his individualized program.

I know there is a lot to think about when considering the use of technology and the development of tutorial computer based curriculum would have to be completed before the system could go into place. However, we need to start now and develop an individualized educational system that is pragmatic for our nation's future. If we want to compete in the world market and produce a minimum level of education in our citizenry then we must consider that our current model: does not focus on mastery of information, it is designed to produce student failures, is not adequate to meet the needs of our gifted and talented students because their programs do not receive adequate funding, and our learning disabled classification of students is growing and taking away funding from our students who will have life-long impairments and need more services than what they are getting now. It is time for action and the problem can be solved if we use our funding wisely. CBT can reform our entire educational system and make individualized education a reality for all our students.

We have many good reasons for abandoning our factory-model education system. These reasons all have names and Sammy, Bernard and Bobby are just a few of them. However, there are others like, John, the fourteen year old eighth grader in my class who had a 165 IQ but was failing school because he was bored with the work and would not do it. Department of Education statistics record that gifted students have a higher than expected drop out rate. John chose to stay up all night studying his interest on the internet and wanted to reserve his school time for sleep. When John was awake (he had developed the uncanny ability to sleep with his eyes open) I sparked his interest in astronomy and he asked higher level concepts than what I had time to teach. I had to delay classroom interactions with this student and ask him to come after school to discuss his interest. I did this because I could not deviate from the learning objectives, the other students would not have understood our discussion, and it would have used up precious classroom time devoted to covering our massive, composite science curriculum.

When John demonstrated to me his interest and his depth of understanding in astronomy I was bound not to deviate from the prescribed curriculum requirements, which were not relevant for him. My hands were tied and truthfully, I knew any discussion I had with John would confuse my other learners because they had not yet mastered the basic objectives we were studying. In our district, John would have to wait three years to study a subject in depth for which he had exceptional aptitude. John should have received an appropriate education because he was a "Gifted" student and his needs should have been met under special education law. Students like John are rarely allowed to skip up to a higher grade nor are they allowed to earn high school credits through taking community college courses. He serves as an example of why the United States may be trailing behind other developed nations in science or math.

After talking to John I understood why he was sent to an alternative school. John was functioning at a much higher academic level than his peers. At his home school, John harassed his classroom teachers when they refused to answer his questions or diverted his inquiries in favor of the mandated curriculum. John assumed he was smarter than his teachers and they could not answer. Therefore, he saw no need to attend school regularly and he lost respect for his educators. When he was present in class he showed disrespect by playing mind games with his teachers and he tried to disrupt learning for others.

From John's story, it is plain to see that we are cheating students at both ends of our education continuum. Therefore, we should not complain about our national report card or whine as we compare our performance to other developed countries. Our education model was designed to fail exceptional students along with our learning disabled. If we want to keep pace in education with the rest of the world we need to individualize education for all students, we need to begin now to create a new model, and technology can help us do this.

References and Resources

K12 academics.com/alternative-education/computer-based-training

"Special Education Dropouts," Eric digest # 451; ERIC Identifier: 295395

"Ensuring High Quality Education for Students with Special Needs; Testimony before the Senate Appropriations Subcommittee for the District of Columbia," Andrew J Rotherham, 2002, dic.org/ndol_ci.cfm?kaid=110 &subid=900030&contentid=250389

"A Bright Idea," New Dem Daily, dic.org/ndol_ci.cfm?kaid=110&subid= 900030&contentd=253037

"Class Struggle," voices.washingtonpost.com/classstruggle/2009/10/why_ squelching_gifted_students

"Are 20% of high school dropouts gifted?" Gifted Exchange, giftedexchange. blotspot.com/2008/09/are-20-of-high-school-drop-outs-gifted.html

"How to Skip a Grade in School," *e*HOW, ehow.com/how_2077747_skip-grade-school.html

"Competing Models for public Education; Which Model is Best?" Common Dreams.org, commondreams.org/views05/0226-25.htm

"Special needs, a costly debate; Schools seek state funds to meet rising expenses,"boston.com   News,boston.com/news/education/k_12/ articles/2007/02/18/special_needs_a_costly_...

Education; "Our factory-model schools are soul-killers for students," The Providence Journal, projo.com/education/juliasteiny/content/se_ educationwatch9_12-09-07_3E857...

National Center for Educational Statistics, 2006

"Retention and Social Promotion: Research and Implications for Policy," ERIC Digest # 161; ERIC Identifier: ED449241

13. Dumb, Dumber and Dumbest

Rainstorms were forecasted daily for that week and I feared I might reflect the weather's dark and gloomy mood as I looked out the window. This school week would not be easy because we were receiving new students today and current students would not leave until Friday. I expected our classes would be extremely overcrowded and as I looked outside a mob of students exited the city bus proving my apprehensions true. Congested classrooms could lead to discipline problems so I reminded myself not to smile or show any weakness as I walked down the hall.

I cut a path through the high school area of our building and gained a little bit more time to think. I had something gnawing at me and I was having hard time letting go of my thoughts as I walked toward the cafeteria. The new group of students I received today would be taking the state test with me and I would have exactly two weeks to prepare them. I was stewing because the test was comprehensive; it covered the entire year's curriculum. Our discipline school received students from all the middle schools in our district, we taught them for six weeks, and returned them to their home schools. I never had a group of students take the state test with me that I taught more than six weeks straight out of the year.

A monetary incentive was being offered to teachers this year if they had at least one-half of their students in each section passed the state exam. Originally, our staff was told that we would receive an average of the awards other teachers earned because alternative teachers' performances could not be tracked accurately. Due to students being placed individually and at varied times throughout the year; the district was unable to determine what objectives were taught to which students while placed with us. I verbally agreed to the district average when I met with the grant administrator but when the final contract came the incentive criterion had been changed.

Now, only students attending our school at the time of the test would count and my incentive would be based only on their performances. I would teach some of these students for only the two weeks prior to the assessment, the students I would pick up today, and other students I had taught earlier during the year would not be counted.

I didn't have to sign the incentive agreement but by doing so, I had contracted to work a rigorous tutoring schedule without extra pay. Although it was true our students were not usually the best or the brightest in the district, most were capable of learning, and I was use to going the extra mile for them. I was already doing above what the incentive contract required but I was upset about the way the terms were changed from the original verbal agreement. I thought the incentive offer made to our alternative school teachers was merely a pretense dangled in front of us to make it look like we were being given the same opportunity as other district educators. It really made me sad to think our contemporaries did not value our contributions to the district enough to consider our special teaching circumstance and that they conspired against us to make it harder for us to earn a share of the grant money. I halted my progress in the hall and took a deep breath; I knew what I had to do next.

I forgave all the people involved in creating the scam and put the outcome squarely in the hands of someone who could do something about it, God. I didn't need the money because God is my source but I needed to forgive and once I did that, my mood changed for the better.

When I arrived at our student pick-up point I noticed my co-workers were showing signs of dread by shaking their heads at one another. I smiled brightly then spoke to a teacher standing next to me, "This is just a temporary situation and we can handle this group for one week." She winced and gave me a half-hearted reply, "I don't want to but... we can do it." Then, she jerked her head to the side and rolled her eyes in the direction of the new students that were joining our lines.

As I looked over the crowd and issued marching orders to my students, I noticed a familiar face. He sheepishly looked in my direction then broke ranks to give me a hug. Along the way, he stopped to hug other teachers and by the time he reached me his face was glowing. Gypsy was smiling so brightly that the bling off his braces almost blinded me. His partner lumbering beside him instantly brought back memories of a circus scene, now relived, a handsome gypsy showman leading a bear walking upright. As I tried to contain the joy of the moment, the bear shifted a little farther to the side and revealed a monkey like student who completed the trio. I recognized the bear and thought the monkey looked familiar too.

I tried not to laugh or be obvious about the joy I felt because alternative school teachers were not supposed to be happy to see students returning to our program. I did remember telling Gypsy if I saw him coming back then I would throw rocks at him to keep him from coming into the building. He had laughed when I told him that but he understood my meaning. Now, I pretended to check my pockets for rocks and said, "Darn, I'm fresh outta rocks or I would have nailed you," just as Gypsy walked up. When my new students dutifully joined the line, I quickly reasoned and spoke to my friend, "These three amigos must have gotten into trouble together." She nodded in agreement while calling her group to line up properly.

I looked across the cafeteria to see our administrators looking in the direction of the middle school procession and I was sure they had noticed the warm greeting we had received at the hands of our returning students. One supervisor threw a disgruntled look in our direction. No doubt, it would be obvious to our administrators we were not doing enough to discourage student re-enrollment and teachers would hear about it during our next in-service. However, more than one teacher must have needed a student hug that morning and I for one, was glad they were provided. Student appreciation is sometimes all you get when you become discouraged as a teacher. Besides, we did not initiate the hugging and I would claim victim status if I was questioned about the physical show of affection. My excuse would be... I had my arms full of a clipboard and the student grade book so I could not defend myself!

As soon as we were in the room, the monkey boy raised his hand. "I did good Mrs. OG? You haven't seen me for a long time." he quizzed.

"Yes, you stayed out of trouble for how long?" I replied. Orlando informed me it had been two years since he had been sent to the alternative school. He said he was surprised I remembered him because he had been much smaller his first year in the seventh grade. "So you ended up repeating the seventh grade?" I probed.

"Yeah, but I passed science. They held me back because of reading and math. I went to a special reading class and I can read better now but math is still hard for me. Eighth grade is easier than seventh and I am sure I will pass this year," he answered.

"Well, I'm certainly glad you passed science because you were a good student for me. Do you want to tell me why you are back at our school now?" I posed. Then, I quickly added, "Maybe you should ask your friends before answering because you were all three sent together. Right?"

Bear looked down silently as Gypsy spoke, "Miss OG, I was do'in business. You know I gotta make the green."

Proceeding cautiously I posed, "Were you doing business for the gang?" With a worried expression and a direct, burning glance, I quizzed, "You weren't using were you?" Gypsy shook his head no and made eye contact with me. At that point, I believed him and relaxed a little because I knew this student well enough to determine he was not lying. I perceived Gypsy had expected my direct questioning because he had attended our school sporadically both in his seventh and eighth grade years and he knew all his teachers' personalities as well as we knew his.

Gypsy was a teachers' favorite student because he was always respectful to our staff and he was an excellent student. In fact, Gypsy was a joy to have in class because he attended to instruction and he participated by answering questions, correctly. Gypsy was clean now but I wondered how long he could resist the temptation to try drugs when he was involved in dealing them. I had never seen Gypsy under the influence but I feared he would use drugs if he continued to live in his same gang infected neighborhood. His part of town was Crip territory and Gypsy was recruited by this gang to carry drugs when he was just in the sixth grade. Gypsy told me how he was grabbed by a leader off the street and forced into service by threats of violence. Now, in the eighth grade he was a baby gangster and he was dealing. The next step in gang affiliation would result in Gypsy committing crimes like home invasion or burglary to get money for the gang and he would carry a weapon. Once he proved himself he would become a gangland soldier. I did not understand how a young person like Gypsy could function very long in the gang culture and I was sure he could not commit violence toward another human being. He was too empathetic and too intelligent to remain in a gang.

While taking attendance, I saw Gypsy stretch to reveal an ankle monitor under his pant leg and just above his shoe. He noticed I saw the attachment and his complexion deepened in color as he glanced away. When Monkey realized I had caught a glimpse of Gypsy's leg jewelry he broke the awkward silence, "Since Gypsy has been caught with drugs at school before... I was carrying the stuff. I was helping out my friend."

Then another student spoke up, "Gypsy was dealing, Monkey was holding, and Bear, were you...using?"

Bear choked on his own salvia while starting to laugh as the student speaking turned around and pointed at each boy separately, saying, "Dumb (Monkey), Dumber (Gypsy), and Dumbest (Bear)."

The laughing had just ended when I asked Dumb, Dumber, and Dumbest to lead us in our morning pledges to the flags. The mirth of the situation threatened to resurface as our three amigos stood. However, their good examples quieted their classmates and I could not have been prouder while they led the class in respectful flag salutations. That morning during our opening routine I discovered the reason why I liked to see students return. These guys were already programmed to follow classroom rituals and rules; I would not have to engage in any power struggles with them. These young men knew what was up and they would be respectful to me.

During our lecture and question time when anyone of the three boys raised their hands to comment, I would say yes, Dumb, Dumber, or Dumbest that is a very good answer considering your Dumb, Dumber or Dumbest. The three boys laughed every time I did this along with the rest of the class and we had great fun. At the end of the period, I made sure the whole class understood our new class members were very good science students and I assured the boys that we all would call them by their real names from that day forward.

Then, Gypsy topped my morning on the way out of my room by saying, "It's good to be back, Mrs. G. I wish I could stay at this school because it is fun and I know I can do good."

After class ended I began to have hope about my situation. I knew all three new students in this section would have an excellent chance of passing the state test. Two of them had attended tutoring with me when they were assigned a stay earlier in the year. I reasoned, "If I can get the circus trio to put in a little extra time with me over the next two weeks I am sure they will get promoted to high school." I really wanted that to happen for these young men because they were all smart and had lots of potential. I had seen their abilities in the past and I was convinced they could be college graduates some day if they didn't fall prey to the culture of drugs that surrounded them.

I started counting... right now I have a class of sixteen students but four are leaving on Friday. Then I will have a class of twelve, I would need six students to pass the exam in order to get the teacher incentive, and I have: Gypsy, Bear, Monkey, Jerry, Juanita? Kirsten? During my calculations my conscious took control and chastised me, "This is why teacher incentive programs should not exist! You are thinking about your own rewards and not about the needs of the students." I could not argue with that logic and I sincerely apologized to my conscious and made a promise that I would not let those thoughts possess my days again. All my students would get the same attention without regard for their ability to pass a state exam!

The next couple of weeks were hectic, some of my students did not have good attendance, and some students did not like using the review curriculum developed by the district. Many complained there was no way that we could complete everything prescribed for each lesson. Sadly, I agreed we hardly could complete the review as it was designed because unlike the other students in the district, our students were not allowed to take textbooks or other classroom materials home with them. I tried to compensate by using my two elective classes, both my Personal and Social Responsibilities class and Learning Power, to finish the work left undone in the morning science class.

However, since some of my students were pulled out of those two periods to attend Spanish or computer classes, they never completed the review sessions. I encouraged these students to come after school for tutoring and some did. Then I developed an added concern because the lost of my elective classes began to show in the attitudes of my students. Our PSR class was especially missed because it was a forum for students' questions and it served a purpose to encourage students' attendance, limit drug use, and motivate students to complete their education. This class helped the students make better choices by giving them correct information and by teaching them to be problem solvers and think for themselves. In the absence of this class, some students quit thinking about their futures and their school attendance plummeted. Within the first week of starting the prescribed review some students became truant and I guessed the additional work requirements could have spawned their absence.

Since Monkey's had only missed one day and he was doing well in my class, I began with him first. I said, "Orlando, how old will you be in the ninth grade if you pass?"

He reported, "I'll be fifteen and turn sixteen when I am a freshman."

I congratulated him, "It is good that you are not too far behind. Most students who turn seventeen in their freshman year think about quitting school because they get discouraged. You are a smart guy and I want you to realize your potential. You need to be here every day for our review. You don't want to stay another year in the eighth grade do you?"

Orlando said, "Thank you Mrs. G. I'm going to pass because I have to. I don't want to be in the eighth grade next year. I want to graduate college too." Orlando told me he would be the first in his family to graduate high school. His grades were average at his home school, he had not been working up to his capacity, but he was currently passing all of his subjects. He only had one hurdle; Orlando would have to pass the math portion on the state exam to go on to the ninth grade. I encouraged him to stay for math tutoring because that was his weakest subject. After talking to Orlando, I felt good about the education goals he had set for himself and I was fairly competent he would be successful.

That was not the case with Gypsy; he was coming to school showing off expensive new athletic shoes, more than one different pair, and he was laughing out loud in class about nothing. My heart sank as I realized he probably had crossed over and was now willingly participating in gang activity because he was sporting the fruits of his labor. However, it was Gypsy's glazed expression and effortless laughing at inappropriate times that convinced me he was using drugs. He was coming to school more often than Bear but he was arriving at school increasingly later every morning and he was truant two days his first week back. I joked with him one morning when Bear was not in attendance about the two boys taking turns coming to school. I postured, "Are you and Bear sharing one brain? Is that why you take turns coming to school? On one day you carry the brain and learn the lessons and the next day Bear brings it to school? I just thought I would ask because the two of you have not been in class together all this week."

Gypsy laughed and said, "No, Mrs. OG, we share other things but not a brain. Don't worry. I got this and you know I will pass. I'll be a freshman next year."

I told Gypsy I certainly prayed he would pass and that I was worried about a different kind of behavior I had seen in him. "You know drugs steal from the person who uses them. Drugs steal your intelligence, your future, and sometimes your freedom. You have already experienced the loss of freedom with the ankle band you wear. Don't let drugs steal your intelligence and your future because you are better than that. I want you to fulfill your destiny and be the person you are supposed to be not the person drugs make you become."

Gypsy looked down then gradually focused back up on my face as he said, "Thanks, Miss OG. I'll do my best."

Bear only came to school two days out of that first week and when he came he always wanted to sleep in class. I took his truancy as a sign he was using drugs more frequently and staying up late while partying with friends. Bear had been in our program three times over the last two years and he was steadily going downhill in his physical appearance and in his classroom performance. When I talked to him about his poor attendance he replied, "I always pass tests and I don't need to come to school." I explained to him that he could not pass my class based on his test scores and we did other things besides take the state test. He had missed clinical labs and the work we did in class counted as daily work grades. I told Bear he had transferred into our program with less than passing scores. He was not concerned and stated, "I will be passed on because I am older (he was turning sixteen) and I will pass the state test."

Bear was an enigma. In the past he had been successful taking tests for which he had not studied. I was curious and asked him to show me how he managed to get passing grades on a publisher's objective test that was a companion to our text book. I discovered, he was able to logically dissect questions and figure out what was really being asked. He showed me how he looked for clues in other questions on the exam. Objective test often asked for parts of the same information in different ways while simultaneously giving information which could help astute students get the correct answer on similar concept based questions. The state test had always been easy for Bear to pass because he had learned to compare questions and to contrast answers until he delineated the truth. Also, Bear had an excellent auditory memory and paying attention to his teacher's lectures was enough stimuli for him to learn. I tried to explain to bear that his drug use could compromise his natural abilities and that he needed to get clean and sober so he could pass the test. Bear just laughed and said, "It doesn't matter. I'm going to get my GED and work with my uncle in construction. My parents want me to quit school now and they don't understand why I have to go. In Mexico, I could have quit after the sixth grade."

After conferencing with Bear, I determined he would probably not pass the state exam this year. He was not as sharp as he once had been and his mind appeared sluggish while he sought words to explain to me in English how he could guess the correct answers on a test. In addition, his classroom performance had deteriorated, his transfer grades were failing, and I could not convince him to put in any extra time after school to review the material. I tried to see if peer pressure would work and I asked Gypsy to bring Bear with him to tutoring. Bear did come one time…and he was high on drugs, he could barely stay awake during the class, and I had to repeat instructions to him over and over again. I was unsuccessful communicating the risk Bear was taking with his education and he would not acknowledge the possibility of his imminent failure. I decided I could not let Bear's situation get me down because I had offered him help which he politely refused. However, I continued to tell Bear he was missed when he came back from being truant and that he needed to review so he could pass the state exam.

I continued tutoring other students during my planning period, before and after school, and I worked non-stop to help my students pass the state exam. The annual test should not have meant a lot to me because I didn't feel the full weight of responsibility for students' academic performances. However, I knew the test results were important for many of my learners. Students who had failing report card grades in science could be considered for promotion if they passed the science portion of the state exam. When I previewed my students' transfer records from their home schools, I realized many of them could fall into that category. Since, failing the eighth grade a second time could determine whether or not some of these students ever made it to high school, helping them pass became my focus. If they failed they would increase their risks for dropping out of high school in their freshman year.

Finally, when the time came, I administered the test without even considering the results. I was exhausted and I was just glad it was over! I did not give my students' scores a single thought until the last day of school. Right before I turned off and unplugged my computer, I pulled up class statistics and I looked at each section's performance. Sixty-seven percent of my students in the traditional eighth grade section passed the state exam which really delighted me and it was my circus trio's period that performed well. However, Bear did not pass the test and I am sure he was shocked to find himself assigned to the eighth grade again the next year.

One other group performed fairly well. Half of the students in that section were sent to us because they were getting high at school by inhaling the paint thinner they called Tally and I knew that many in this group were still abusing the substance. I marveled that these students scored as well as they did because their daily use of a foul smelling chemical had deteriorated their memories and they did not perform consistently in class. My other two student sections were comprised of mostly learning disabled students and neither group came close to a passing percentage I could be proud of. I knew their scores reflected their poor attendance and I mused, "I can't teach them if they don't come to school." I guessed that I would receive a teacher incentive based on the percentage of students in my two of my groups that met the grant criteria.

However, it was no longer important for me; the students' outcome was set and I had done my best to help all of them. I smiled seeing that both, Monkey and Gypsy had passed the yearly exam and they would be freshmen in high school the next academic year. I spoke out loud, "Dumb and Dumber wised up and became smarter. However, what conjugation comes after dumbest because Bear got ...?"

Discussion

Incentive programs for teachers may be created because individuals may believe teachers need motivated to do their jobs well. There is a danger in offering money awards which are linked to student performance. Incentives can be prejudiced against certain groups of teachers like our alternative educators who taught some of the poorest performing students in our district in disapportionate numbers compared to other educators. In addition, teacher incentives may often be restricted from educators who teach certain subjects like English and social studies because student performance in math, science, or special education may be valued above other subjects taught. Therefore, teacher incentives offered to some staff and not others could create a hostile working environment by devaluing select teachers' job assignment.

In addition, rewarding teachers based on their students' performances does not make sense. Student achievement is not totally dependent upon a teacher's competency. Students' abilities, school attendance, home life, role models, and drug use all play a part in learning. For this reason, teacher awards based on student performance are not scientific. Individual variables in students' lives and abilities cannot be made uniform nor can they be isolated for testing. Students cannot be made equal; they are individuals who have varied abilities and life circumstances. Competent teacher does not always equal good student performance and incompetent teacher does not always equal poor student performance. However, teachers could use more money because the level of education now desired by most school districts is the masters' level and the amount teachers' owe in student loans may be increasing for that reason. **Explain how teacher incentive programs could be made fair and could be attainable for all educators.**

One thing is true; teachers will put the curriculum aside to teach a test when additional pressure is applied by their school district. Again, I cannot speak for others but bullying attitudes prevailed when stakes were high for one school district I worked and that district's drive to obtain state recognition overshadowed the supportive atmosphere of past years. Every teacher training and meeting became focused on what had to be done for the district to obtain the highest status on the state test and threats were reportedly made, "Heads are going to roll and people are going to lose their jobs if this isn't done." It appeared that administrators may have been bullied, I really don't know but the stress was definitely rolling down hill to incorporate all staff.

At one particular meeting when I had enough of the workplace threats I commented, "I come to work every day to do a good job. I don't get up in the morning and say today I'm going to do a bad job and see how much work I can get out of doing. I do my best everyday and I do it for the students. I resent being threatened by my employer because I am an educated person and I know that there are basically two responses to that type of supervision. One is to comply and take abuse because threats can foster co-dependency and fear. The other response is to stand up and say take your best shot, do what you are going to do, and I will do what I am going to do. I am one of those who would do the latter. I would, as our students say, go gangster! Your see, baby gangsters can educate their teachers about some things too! Where is the love? We made recognized status for three years in a row without threats. Why can't we make the next higher level the same way?" The reply I received is that some people may respond to that type of supervision, affirmed my suspicions about our school district's intent and it felt hostile.

However, in defense of the administrators in that district, a new tone developed, threats ceased, and intimidations were no long used for motivation. I believe other people like me broke ranks with the philosophy being propagated and I saw a return of our familiar team spirit. We almost lost the opportunity to improve our academic standing because we came close to caving under the pressure and initially, we lost our supervisors' support. Like herding cattle, our administrators were snapping whips and yelling at the tops of their voices warning the herd of the coming storm, the state test. However, when the storm approached, teachers were already overdriven and many were tempted to just stop, back up in a circle, and let the wind blow. I for one ignored the rush and kept plotting along while doing what I did every day for the good of our students. I believe I had the best test results that were possible to obtain considering the abilities and life circumstances of the groups I taught. It wasn't lack of teacher effort or teacher incompetency that caused my students to fail. **How do supervising methods affect teacher performance? What would your ideal teaching work environment look like?**

Topics for Research

What is an objective test? How do objective test measure academic growth and student potential? What ethnic, socio-economic, or race groups perform best on standardized test? Why aren't test results used to assign students an instruction level instead of being used to fail students and judge teachers?

Things to Do

Attend school board meetings to find out how teachers are paid and oppose teacher incentive proposals which are tied to student achievement. Test results should measure students' academic growth not a teacher's performance. Principals are supervisors and they should evaluate their employees and award merit pay based on teachers' all over job performances like all other employers do. A Principal knows if a teacher implements and uses best education practices in the classroom, comes to work and leaves work on time, and is a valued asset to the school district. Insist supervisors receive better training because they should follow federal employment laws when evaluating their employees. Teachers need to oppose, through their professional organizations or other means, incentive plans which do not take into account the full measure of a teacher's job responsibility. Hostile work environments should not exist in our schools.

14. Nurture Learning in Middle School

According to one ERIC Clearinghouse article on students' motivation to learn, "... Natural motivation will survive only in schools where the curriculum is worth learning; where students focus on learning (not on competition or grades); and where students feel valued...." (Student Motivation: Cultivating a Love of Learning). This article tells us students want to make the connection between what they are being asked to learn and how it will be useful to them in their future, this is called relevancy. The second principle states the focus of education should be on learning not on grades or competition; student growth should be measured and grades should not be assigned. The third element necessary for nurturing is that students should be valued as individuals who have unique education goals. Our current public school model does not do any of these things. We do not consider students' academic interests when we prescribe a universal curriculum that lacks relevancy to the learner. We fail students by whole grade levels and we do not celebrate their academic gains in increments. We do not value our students because we do not allow them to set unique education goals. We are doing the complete opposite of nurturing learning in the United States; we are killing our students' natural interests and desires for education. Cumulative exams, like the end of the year state test told about in this story, example the very thing wrong with our education model. Students could pass or fail a whole grade level based on their performance on one test.

The first thing we need to address in education reform is relevancy because today's young people are distracted from learning by the wealth of things they are required to study. Much of this forced knowledge will serve no useful purpose in their futures. Our ever expanding curriculum may be causing some students to suffer from adult like stress because they end up feeling there is too much to do and too little time to do it. Just like their parents, our students find themselves in demanding situations and may want to prioritize the relevancy of each task as it applies to their future life goals. Relevancy is important to students because they will often question their teachers in middle school or high school about why they have to study a certain topic. Motivation to learn can be diminished in some students because there is too much to learn and the material they are being asked to learn will have little effect on their functioning as an adult in our society. Our students are smart enough to realize that their presence in school represents taking up space for school funding reasons and wasting their own time.

An analogy which might help us understand our students' current dilemma is a comparison to shopping in a mom and pop grocery store contrasted to visiting a mega superstore to purchase an item. You could easily find what you need on the store shelves in the first scenario or mom and pop would help you locate it. In the second situation, you might become overwhelmed looking for the item because there is just too much stuff, what you need is not easily found, and your pleas for direction are ignored. In the last situation, you might think about the importance of the item and if you can live without it for a while, then you just might walk out of the store without making a purchase. Students could be exiting our education system because they have become overwhelmed with required studies, we are not helping them find what they need, and they decide they can live without what we are offering.

One student, a fifteen year old young man attending our alternative program, serves as an example of what can happen when a child believes something is worth learning. From the beginning Jack was disinterested in what we were studying and he was content to zone out while other students actively participated. Getting him to comply with the structure and discipline in the classroom was not a problem but he was not engaged in learning. Then, Jack surprised me one day in science class by taking an interest in our lab activity. We were learning how to use the triple beam scale to find the mass of an object. I demonstrated three different methods and the third method, finding mass by addition, sparked his attention. During this lab activity, students found the mass of a small paper container and then added 2 grams of measurement to the total sum on the beam. When the scale went out of balance, their task was to put small amounts of a granulated solid substance into the paper container to make the scale come back into balance. When the scale balanced perfectly, they would know that they had exactly two grams of the substance in the paper container. Of course, the granulated substance we used was harmless table sugar but Jack pretended it was cocaine. It appeared Jack had aspirations to be a drug dealer.

He actually said, "Finally, something that's useful to learn!" Although I corrected his reference to drugs, his motivation to learn how to measure mass with the scale continued and he scored the highest grade in class on our lab assignment. Once he was engaged in learning, I made this young man my lab helper because he was accurate, very careful with the lab equipment, and he enjoyed teaching other students how to use the scale. In turn, I believe this student felt valued. Before long, Jack was gaining other lab skills and took pride in assisting during lab demonstrations and activities. As a teacher, I had made the decision to value the value this student placed on being able to find the mass of a quantity of a dry substance regardless of his reference to drugs. I suppose I could have set him out of class for inappropriately referring to the sugar as cocaine but Jack would not have learned how to use the scale correctly, one of his learning objectives, and surely he would have caused discipline problems on his return to class.

The story about Jack, though his ultimate goal for learning was a perversion of our educational objective, demonstrates why curriculum should to be relevant to students' future ambitions. According to the theory of cognitive development purposed by Piaget, middle school aged children around the average age of twelve years develop the ability to think formally. When the formal operational state arrives students begin to consider the outcomes of their actions and the emergence of this type of thinking is important and empowers students to set long-term education goals. (Formal Operational Stage of Cognitive Development). In reference to Piaget's theory, Jack's motivation to learn came from him being able to think about his desired life outcome, becoming a drug dealer, and his ability to recognize that performing the activity in lab could help him achieve that goal. Teachers have long been told that they need to show students' the relevancy of material covered so students can value the things we are mandated to teach. When we do this we completely ignore what experts like Piaget have taught us and we are forcing learning.

When we nurture learning we appeal to students' values and those values sustain students' learning. One authority states, "Students who seem to truly embrace their work and take genuine interest in it are intrinsically motivated" (Motivating Students, Karin Kirk). Personal values are intrinsic substances which cannot be seen but are often expressed in words and deeds by our students. Many of our economically challenged, inner city students, like Jack, are intrinsically motivated to earn lots of money and may openly state they are going to be a drug dealer when they grow up for this reason. Drug dealers may be the only role models they know which have huge amounts of disposable cash. Somehow we have got to tap into our students' desire for elevated incomes, what they value, and show them there are other ways, educational pursuits, to obtain their goal. In addition, students recognize getting an education is hard work while anyone can become a drug dealer with little effort. For these reasons, education needs to appear effortless and the rewards of education must be recognized as substantial.

Effortless learning may appear at first glance to be an oxymoron. However, learning only needs to appear effortless; it doesn't really have to be easy. Anything that students enjoy doing in class can change their perception about the actual work being done and the highest compliment ever paid me as a teacher, was when students said I knew how to make learning fun. Today, technology has the potential to make learning fun for all students. The majority of youth today enjoy using computers and to most students, work may hardly seem like work at all when computer time is assigned. In addition, feedback can be enhanced on computer based education programs so students' efforts are immediately rewarded. Students are not distracted by classroom competitions for grades when placed solo at a computer because they only compete with themselves to improve their own performance. Students could see, in real time, what concepts they master and make decisions about completing additional assignments to raise their competence level on CBTs (Computer Based Training programs). We have already discussed using technology in a previous strategy to maximize the proficiency of a new individualized education model I proposed. But now, we can see how the use of technology could enhance student motivation because using computers to learn may appear effortless while making learning fun. The ability of students to choose their curriculum based on their individual educational goal, relevancy, and the use of technology to accomplish those goals can be immediately gratifying and easily accomplished.

However, we know our current factory-model does not allow middle school students to choose curriculum relevant to their education long-term goals. In fact, middle school students do not set long-term educational goals at all, which Piaget theorizes they are most capable of doing. Instead, we dictate curriculum to middle school students as if they are still in grammar school when these learners need more choices and less directives. At a critical stage of student cognitive development, we may be alienating instead of nurturing their learning experiences. One source supports the rationale for nurturing student learning through making curriculum relevant this way, "We must take into account that not every child will need or want to do the same thing. A curriculum must therefore be individualized" (Engines for Education).

As an example, migrant worker or immigrant children from the Southwestern United States whose families are not familiar with our educational system may not have the same educational goals as the curriculum dictates. Honest hard work is valued by many in this culture and learning to read and do math at a sixth grade level, enough to gain employment, may be thought a sufficient goal for some students. Many of these students already could have adult responsibilities and may work part time jobs while attending middle school (self). Adding to our difference of opinion about education goals, students who are from Mexico and their parents, may assume that a sixth grade level of education is all that is necessary due to their past experiences in their country of origin. One source, the Encyclopedia of Nations, reported that compulsory school attendance does not exist in Mexico for students. The individual states are compelled to provide free public education through grade six. This report emphasizes that Mexico's education system is improving but the fact remains children are not compelled by law to attend school and parents have to pay for their children's education after the sixth grade because it is not funded by the government. Therefore, Mexican immigrants may not understand our compulsory system (Mexico-Education). This cultural difference is something to consider in large city school districts with large Hispanic populations.

On the other hand, our country's education system does not value some of our Hispanic students' values nor do we nurture their learning because we mandate curriculum which is not pragmatic for them. When we insist our immigrant middle school population study algebra, literature, or physics and students' goals are to own and operate their own business, we may be hastening Hispanic student drop-out rates which are already higher than other groups nationally. One report from the National Center for Education Statistics states, 44.2% of Hispanic young adults born outside of the United States were high school dropouts and young Hispanic adults born in the United States are still more likely to have dropped out of high school than any other group of students (Dropout Rates in the United States). Our educational system needs changed to recognize students have other goals besides attending college and we need to nurture learning in all culturally diverse student groups by valuing their pragmatic needs for specific types of education.

We cannot wait until students begin high school to address goal setting for future careers or wait to give students specific curriculum choices. Middle school students need to perceive their studies as being relevant to their unique goals. When students languish in middle school they certainly will increase their risk for dropping out of high school. In fact, they may be close to the legal age which allows them to leave school when they enter high school. Decreasing student dropout rates in our student populations which live in our inner city, toxic neighborhoods is an attainable goal for education reform and establishing individualized tracks of education in middle school is how we may attain that objective.

One source agrees with this precept and states that "Education ought to be about building learners abilities to do useful things" (Engines for Education). Our current education model which prescribes a broad range curriculum limits teachers' ability to respond to the specific needs students have for learning detailed information, in their expressed areas of interest, and may actually handicap the education process for some students. The first question the designers of curriculum should ask themselves might be, "Do all students need to know this information or is this information relevant only for students who are going to seek advanced degrees in a specific subject area?"

Since education standards and testing decisions may be totally determined at a state level, state reforms in this one area is needed. Approving new textbooks alone to meet educational guidelines will not change our system. Textbooks only reflect what educated persons think the rest of the world needs to know about their subject. Textbooks may not reflect what the rest of the world needs to know about a specific subject to work, live, and be productive citizens. Therefore, our current textbooks may only serve to taut the goals well educated academies perceive are needed and may not be useful for the general population at all. We have to be careful not to junk up education with useless bits of information which some deem important simply because it is significant to them.

In fact, middle school students' motivation wanes when thick textbooks are presented to them and states may be wasting valuable education dollars by adopting new text books. Due to the explosion of the information age, our written sources can become outdated before going to print. Our knowledge base is increasing exponentially and I predict we will reach a limit on the amount of information we can require the masses to proficient. No doubt, when that happens educators will become overwhelmed along with their students and our state governments may find a need to scrap the textbooks containing infinite curriculum mandates. These are already next to impossible to cover in our current academic school year. Individual academic goal setting for students will make sense at that juncture because one mind cannot hold all the information we are gaining and proficiency in all areas will be impossible. Relevancy will take on an entirely new meaning and hopefully, it will be prized as a tool for learning because it does inspire students to learn. Quality learning verses quantity exposure should become our new aim. Our massive curriculum mandates do not nurture student learning and specific instruction is more relevant for our times.

In addition to narrowing curriculum mandates to increase relevant learning for students, our grading system needs eliminated. Grades act as extrinsic motivators for student learning but they are not a sustainable force because as soon as the grade is given, students may feel free to forget the information. That could be why many students perform poorly on comprehensive exams. Kohlberg's theory of moral development, "Individualism and Exchange" explains some of the other things that can happen when grading is used as a primary motivator (About.com, Psychology). In simple terms, cheating, lying, and other human frailties may be exposed when personal interests are challenged. Dysfunction result as students try to circumvent the structure to get their individual needs met for passing grades and grade promotion. Moral development is not determined by chronological age and even educators have been found cheating when students' performances on tests determine promotions or job retentions. Too much power is being relegated to the results of an annual performance test. Power corrupts and there is some evidence that recording untrue tests results and cheating episodes on state level tests occur every year in varied school districts across the United States. The evidence is complete and shows we may have created dysfunctional school environments by using these yearly examines to determine the fate of educators and their students, and that children may be worse educated now than what they were before we began using this method (CBS News).

According to Kohlberg, this human response is to be expected when much is at stake. Grading systems have the potential to cause some students to cheat, fail, and not retain the concepts taught. In addition, they unfairly judge teachers incompetent when students fail. These things, our grading system and state comprehensive exams which have the potential to damage both the student and teacher need abolished because they do not nurture learning.

Another reason grading systems are ineffective with specific populations is that they rely on a person's desire to avoid negative consequences. In my teaching position, a failing grade appeared to be of little consequence to my baby gangsters. These students could raise a shirt and show you where they had been knifed or raise a pant leg and show you where they had been shot. My students knew they had the capacity to survive worse things than a bad grade. Since I could not "Blast a cap in their a_ _"… Oh well, you get the idea. Our grading system is ineffective with this population and we should scrap our current grading ritual in favor of creating a positive learning environment.

Three things were identified by this article which nurtures students' learning, curriculum relevancy was the first, focus on learning was second, and valuing students was third. Relevancy is the key to student motivation and it accomplishes the third nurturing strategy as well. When students are given choices and they choose curriculum which is relevant for them then students are being valued as individuals and their individual needs are met. The second thing identified was the need to focus on learning; measuring student gains instead of student failures nurtures learning in students. When we nurture people we cheer them on to accomplishment and celebrate their winnings not their failures. Poor grades do little to highlight a six month student growth in learning when we are focused on students' failure to meet the entire curriculum requirement for the year.

Teachers are trapped in this web of educational woes with their students while their hands are bound behind their back. They are simultaneously being told if they can't save the children they will be eaten first because it is their fault the children are there. Who tied the teachers' hands with curriculum mandates and timelines which disregard students' intrinsic motivation to learn things which are relevant? Who insisted that teachers pass to the next grade level students who lacked competence? Who instituted a system which tells students they are dumb and that they are failures? Who said teachers have to hold back the gifted students so schools can continue to receive funding for them all twelve years? It certainly wasn't teachers who did this. They didn't tie their own hands and they are tired of being chewed on. Let's just fix the system so we can nurture student learning!

References and Resources

"Dropout Rates in the United States," nces.ed.gov/fastfacts/display.asp?id=16 ·

"Formal Operational Stage of Cognitive Development," Piaget's Stages of Cognitive Development, psychology.about.com/od/piagetstheory/p/formaloperation.htm

"Georgia schools tighten test rules after cheat audit," Dorie Turner; Ledger-enquirer.com

"Kohlberg's Theory of Moral Development," psychology.about.com/od/developmental psychology/a/Kohlberg.htm

"Mexico-Education," Encyclopedia of the Nations, nationsencyclopedia.com/Americas/Mexico-EDUCATION.html

"Motivating students," Alan Haskvitz, reacheverychild.com/feature/motivate.htm

"Student Motivations and Attitudes: The Role of the Affective Domain in Geoscience Learning," Motivating Students," Karin Kirk, SERC, serc.carleton.edu/NAGTWWorkshops/affective/motivation.html

"Student Motivation: Cultivating a Love of Learning," Limsden, Linda S, ERIC Clearinghouse on Educational Management, scholarsbank.uoregon.edu/xmlui/bitstream/handle/1794/3294/student_motivation.pdf?...

"Teachers Caught Cheating," Francie Grace; CBS News, cbsnews.com/stories/2003/10/28/national/main5803555.shtml

"A Tripartite of Motivation for Achievement: Attitude/Drive/Strategy," Bruce W. Tuckerman, The Ohio State University, dennislearningcenter.osu.edu/all-tour/apa99paper.htm

"What a Curriculum Should Contain," Engines for Education, engines4ed.org/hyperbook/nodes/NODE-72-pg.html

15. Baby Daddy

Our seventh grade class was studying genetics when Toni arrived. He was a handsome young man with curly black hair and a nice smile. He was average size for a seventh grade student; about five foot six in height and of normal weight. However, his appearance was not totally healthy due to his skin color that often looked pallor and was sometimes tinged with yellow. There were other things that bothered me about this student's physical appearance. On some days Toni's normally wavy hair would turn into ringlets that were wet with perspiration and he would barely be able to hold his eyes open. On those days his eyes showed weary and tired he complained of a headache and he seemed powerless to lift his chin which he propped on his hands. Toni's mouth would hang open forming a permanent gap as he struggled to stay awake. Some days Toni was only bodily present in class while his mind was completely absent from instruction.

When Toni was present with both his body and mind he paid attention and he made suitable attempts to do his work. He showed a measure of interest in everything we studied until the day I presented a slide show of birth defects, some were human and others were pictures of animals. The slides were not particularly offensive nor were they inappropriate for seventh grade students to view. Obtaining knowledge of certain human birth defects was required by our state learning objectives. Down syndrome (Tri-some 21), Sickle Cell Anemia, Cystic Fibrous and other common anomalies were discussed because students would be tested on their knowledge of those genetic differences in human beings.

Usually students demonstrated a high interest in viewing the slides and most students were already familiar with some human birth defects. Students would ask questions about dwarfism because many of my students watched a TV show, "Little People Big World." Other students may have checked out library books that contained information, searched a web site, or had visited the Rippley's Believe it or Not Museum in our geographical area. Therefore our study of genetics required me to use few motivational strategies because students had a natural curiosity about the subject.

I was surprised during the presentation and accompanying lecture when Toni looked away from the monitor, put his head down, or covered his eyes. Toni was so visibly upset at one point in the presentation, I halted the lesson and repeated my beginning instructions by saying, "Class, remember that I have given you permission not to look at the slides if you find them upsetting and you can just listen to the lecture." At first, I thought Toni was just a real sensitive child because he even looked away when I presented a picture of a two headed frog. Other students begged to look at specific slides more than once or asked me to display the imagines longer. I was taken back by Toni's reaction.

Toni averted his gaze through most the presentation and he raised his hand requesting permission to stand in the hall until the slide presentation was over. Instead, I cut the presentation short and told the class that we could resume our activity later that afternoon. After getting the rest of the students started on their processing activity, I invited Toni to come into the hall with me so I could talk to him without other students overhearing our conversation. Since Toni demonstrated signs of extreme stress, I wanted to find out if he was just super sensitive or if he had a problem. While students began their learning reinforcement worksheets, I observed the class through the upper glass portion of my door and I quizzed Toni, "I could not help but notice the information we covered this morning about birth defects and human anomalies was upsetting you. Do you want to ask any questions about the material covered or do you need to talk about anything that might have bothered you during our lesson?"

Toni shrugged his shoulders and said, "My girl friend is going to have a baby soon. I am worried because I use drugs and I drink lots of alcohol. Do you think my baby is going to be alright?"

I was use to fielding these types of questions; Toni was not the first one to bring up human anomalies which could be the result of prenatal alcohol and drug use. Many of my students were using alcohol/drugs and were sexually active so pregnancy was always a concern. Once they learned about human genetic defects, students generated lots of questions. However, I had never seen a student before this incident, show physical signs of stress regarding the subject. Most students were detached or might say crass statements like, "If my son looked like that I would kill him and then I would kill my girlfriend for having him. I would not want a retard for a kid." When students reacted this way or made comments showing they lacked understanding and tolerance, I thought it was my job as an educator to help them gain a better understanding. Therefore, our study of genetics and human birth defects allowed me to teach tolerance in science class and I liked having that opportunity. Tolerance was one issue I anticipated and addressed with baby gangsters during genetics instruction. However, Toni presented a sharp contrast to usual attitude I experienced and his deep concern touched my spirit.

"There are lots of different variables that go into making a human being, Toni. Scientist cannot say for sure what causes every birth defect. Parents can do everything right and still have a baby born with genetic anomalies. Other times, parents do everything wrong and they have a perfectly normal child. However, you are correct that exposing a developing infant to alcohol and drugs is not a good thing to do and there is a specific birth defect that results from a mother drinking alcohol while pregnant. Does your baby's mother drink and do drugs?"

Toni said his girlfriend had stopped using alcohol but she still smoked a little marijuana. He had very specific questions about drug and alcohol use and their effects on the developing fetus. I gave him some resources and promised him that later in the week during a learning power class I would schedule the computer lab so he could research the topic. As we concluded our brief talk, Toni informed me his baby's mother was sixteen, he was fourteen, and they both wanted the baby very much. In fact, Toni said, "I can't wait to hold my little baby in my arms. I want to be a good dad." His face had become animated with true joy when he said this and I could not help but smile at him. When Toni told me that his family and the baby's mother's family were planning a wedding in the spring I was not surprised. Since these two young people were from a different culture and I knew their culture valued family, an upcoming wedding and the young couple living together in the infants' grandparents' house would be customary.

I was still thinking about Toni that afternoon on my way home from work because the joy expressed on his small face left a lasting impression in my heart. He wanted his baby and he wanted his baby to be healthy. I would not have been surprised to find out that Toni's girlfriend became pregnant when one or both teens were under the influence. I was sad to hear that the baby's mother still might be using drugs and I knew Toni had a serious problem as well. His complaints of morning headaches, pallor skin color, and profuse sweating were all clues to his trouble. Toni's weary, yellow tinged eyes and his constant complaints of headaches led me to believe Toni did not just drink alcohol at weekend parties like some of my students. Instead, I suspected Toni drank during the school week and was often hung-over in class. Toni had reported he drank a lot so he knew he consumed more alcohol than what he should.

Many young people I taught functioned like adults outside of school and they earned the privilege of using adult substances like alcohol through their contributions to the family's welfare. They worked jobs and they helped pay family bills along with their parents. I regretted these students losing their youth in favor of earned income but I knew it could not be avoided in most instances. These families were often under educated according to our country's standards and they were lucky to earn minimum wages. In his culture, Toni might be viewed as a grown man and for that reason he was at high risk for dropping out of school. Unplanned pregnancy could function as the official announcement of his maturity and becoming parents might cause both Toni and his girlfriend to abandon their educations. These students could end up living in poverty and raising their child in poverty.

I reminded myself that Toni was not the first middle school parent I had in class over the last five years. There was Bertha, a thirteen year old African American student who came to school while still lactating and wet her blouse in the front. She started a fight when one of the boys in class kept staring at her chest and she tore up one of my science books pushing it at him across the table. Bertha had been an incest victim and her child, like her sister's, had been conceived by her stepfather. This thirteen year old student was too young to be placed in a district program for teen moms, so she was assigned middle school attendance at our alternative school. Bertha was in a donut hole of our teen parent education program. She might have been able to receive some services but she was not eligible to attend the school for teen moms because she was not in high school and she was too young!

Bertha was intelligent and learned so quickly that she amazed me but she was frequently truant. I didn't understand her absence because Bertha's mother was being paid by the state to provide childcare so Bertha could attend school. When I asked this student about her childcare arrangement she reported her mother worked nights, slept during the day, and she wanted Bertha to stay home and take care of the baby so she could sleep. Without access to a teen parent child care program, Bertha was destined to be truant. Bertha knew her mother would sleep and not attend to the child when she was at school. Bertha would have to pass middle school to gain a placement into a teen parent program and her truancy record would go against her passing seventh grade. Bertha's child would be three years old before she would be eligible and by that time she could be pregnant again. I was sure Bertha would drop out of school.

Then, there was the fifteen year old Jimmy who was in the eighth grade and having a third child by a third girlfriend. He was a real charmer! I could see where his life was going because he said his goal was to be a gigolo. Jimmy was a drug dealer and he saw no need to get an education because he was living the high life. He had money, girls, and access to all the drugs he wanted. He was so blinded by all he had that he could not see what he was missing. He definitely was missing his opportunity to get an education. Eventually, Jimmy was apprehended and had to serve time in jail. Hopefully, he obtained an education while he was placed there.

Momentarily, I saddened while thinking of one little girl that touched my heart more than all the others. This eighth grade student had been raped when she was just twelve years old. While attending a party with a sixteen year old friend she tried alcohol and drugs for the first time. At the urging of her new found mentor, Crystal became drunk and high and she was raped by someone at the party. Later Crystal found out the girl had tricked her into coming and sold her for payment of a debt to a drug dealer. Now Crystal had a one year old baby and her parents did not let her out of their sight. Crystal was not allowed to participate in after school activities and she was not allowed to date until she graduated high school or left her parents home. She had to work after school for a relative at a small Mexican restaurant and use the money she earned to buy formula and diapers for her baby. Crystal told everyone her story because she did not want other kids to be deceived like she was by an older teen they trusted. This little doll learned the hard way how kids prey on other kids when they have drug addiction problems.

Most of my middle school parents lost out on their childhoods and the normal experiences they should have had as teenagers. They talked about how hard it was to be a parent and go to school or work. Any number of them wished they could have taken back their decisions that led to an unplanned pregnancy. However, Toni was an enigma to me because he was a child who really wanted to be a parent and he expressed joy at the possibility. I had only had one other male student who expressed a similar sentiment and I began racking my brain while trying to remember his name...Duck.

Duck was not a biological parent but the baby belonged to his sister. Hannah and Duck were from a family of ten children and their mother was a crack addict. The children had been removed and put into foster care more than once while they cycled in and out of our alternative program over a period of two years. The children were always returned to their mother when she got clean and sober. I was frustrated with the child welfare system because these students were not permanently moved but I guessed ten children from one family overwhelmed the system to the point the workers wanted the kids to go home. Thinking about the logistics of sibling visits made me dizzy because all of those children could not have been placed in the same foster home. Duck was a sweet kid and had academic ability.

One day when other students began tormenting Duck about living with a foster parent and he was feeling down about his situation. I informed students that I had been a foster parent and asked them what was wrong with foster parents. Then, I had several students ask me in class what they they would have to do in order to come live with my family. After that, living with foster parents was not necessarily seen as being negative by Duck's classmates and he bragged about the nice home he lived in and the privileges he was given. Duck's grades were good when his home life was stable. However, these unfortunate kids, Duck and Hannah, had real unstable lives. When they were returned to their mother, Duck and Hannah came dressed in dirty clothes and they lost weight. These students were always asking teachers for something to eat.

One morning, Duck was upset because Hannah had not come with him to school. Some of the other students reported Hannah met a man on the train that morning and told Duck she was going with this guy because she was hungry. The students said Hannah yelled at Duck when he tried to stop her, "I'm going to get money so I can eat." I cut Duck a lot of slack that morning and allowed him to do a coloring project for me instead of doing his scheduled class work. Duck was on the edge that day worrying about his sister.

Hannah ended up pregnant and since she was already sixteen in the eighth grade, she was lucky enough to get into the education program our district created for pregnant moms. Hannah was able to complete her high school requirements through this service. However, Duck only completed his eighth grade year before giving up his education to stay home and take care of his nephew. He stopped coming to school because he did not trust his mother to provide proper care for the infant. Duck began using drugs while at home with his mother; he was surrounded by other people who were using and the temptation was just too great.

When Hannah finished school, Duck resumed his education in high school but often came to class under the influence. One day I saw him stagger down the hall mumbling nonsense words and I knew he was really high. I notified the tenth grade math teacher who thought Duck was just messing around. If you didn't know some of the kids it was really difficult to tell because most of our students acted goofy at one time or another. I made a point to tell the new teacher, "I know this kid and he is really high. You should send him out for an evaluation." After that, whenever I saw Duck he was some degree wasted.

For a short time, after Hannah's baby was born, Duck had really matured and stepped up to become the man in his family. He loved his nephew and his carried pictures to show off Hannah's child. Now, two years later, Duck could not even take care of himself. It was amazing how one quick decision made by Hannah impacted her brother's life. Duck was the only other guy I encountered in middle school who genuinely wanted to parent. Now, my thoughts came back to Toni and I was afraid that substance abuse would interfere with his ability to be a parent just like it had with Duck.

I made a decision to present a lesson on alcohol abuse the very next day during learning power class and hoped it would benefit Toni. During my planning period I rushed to set up my demonstration table and my overhead presentation for the class. I justified the lesson change by reviewing the district's learning objectives for the seventh grade and discovered there was one objective that fit regarding students' knowledge of alcohol and drug use. My new lesson would allow me to teach human body functions, chemistry, and substance abuse issues at the same time.

I marked the side of four different glasses with ounce markings and I colored three different containers of water. After I filled the glasses to the specific levels I needed, I set them aside on the display table. All would represent liquor; one would be hard liquor like whiskey or tequila, one would be wine, and the other beer. Students filed in and sat down and looked immediately to the display table. As soon as the students walked in one student asked, "What's that Mrs. G.?"

I answered, "That is our part of our lesson for the day. This glass is hard liquor, like Tequila. The next glass is wine or a wine cooler, and the last two glasses are beer." Then I asked, "Which one of these drinks contains the most alcohol?"

Most students thought that the beer contained the most alcohol because there was more of it. Once I explained they all contained the same amount of alcohol I asked, "Which one of these drinks, if you drank too much of it, could cause you to get alcohol poisoning and die?"

One student said, "Mrs. G you just got done tell'n us they are the same. If one causes poisoning then they all do."

I replied, "That's true but one will get you quicker than the others."

Toni raised his hand. "Yes, Toni. Do you think you know?"

Toni postured, "I believe that the hard liquor would get you first because there is not much in that glass and I have never seen anyone drink that little Tequila."

The students laughed, and I replied, "That's right!"

"My ole man drinks it out of the bottle until it's gone," piped in one young man.

I addressed Toni, "You are right, Toni. Some people use a tall drinking glass or drink it straight from the bottle. How many drinks of alcohol would this whole glass equal?"

Another student who was good in math said that would be about six drinks of alcohol!

How many drinks does it take to make a person drunk? I let the students make various guesses then I passed out the diagram of the brain that matched the one I had on the overhead. For the next twenty minutes we looked at the diagram labels that showed how much of the brain was put to sleep by adding drinks of alcohol. Finally when we got to the tenth drink in one hour, I explained to the students that the person drinking is now in danger of dying. I said in a very quiet voice as they listened intently, the most protected part of the brain which is responsible for our breathing and heartbeat would now go to sleep and forget to keep us alive. The students were often silent when I got to this part of the lesson.

Toni was the first one to raise his hand, "Mrs. G., am I in danger of dying when I do shots with my mom?"

"How much do you drink?" I asked.

"I have been drinking with my mom every Friday night since I was ten years old. She said she knew kids tried drinking and she would teach me at home. I thought it would be fun and I thought my mom was cool for teaching me. We lined up shot glasses like the amount you showed us for hard liquor and we had a contest. The first time we did it I passed out at thirty-three and as my head hit the floor I heard my mom cheer and say she won. I have been trying every since to beat her...but I always pass out first! Now I drink two or three times a week and I drink a lot. I'm afraid I am an alcoholic."

The other students in class were amazed as I was by Toni's story and waited quietly to hear my answer. "A lot of parents think it is better to teach their kids at home about alcohol and drugs by letting them use in their presence." I paused and carefully began again, "Raise your hand if you know parents sometimes make mistakes." All the hands went up. I continued, "Scientific research has concluded that people should not drink alcohol until they are over eighteen years old. If you start drinking at thirteen or fourteen your risk factor for becoming an alcoholic is fifty percent. To put that in perspective, there are twelve students in our room and if you all drank alcohol before starting high school then six of you could end up being an alcoholic. However, if you wait until you are fifteen, sixteen or older your risk decreases. Only ten percent or about one student in our class out of twelve would become an alcoholic if you all waited until you were all eighteen years old to use alcohol for the first time."

"Is that why there is a law regarding minors drinking?" One student posed.

"That is an excellent question. How many of you think the law about minors not using alcohol is a good law?" Only about half of the students raised their hands. I shuttered thinking I still had more work to do. I let the students argue their positions about minors using alcohol until everyone had their say then I directed the class back to Toni's question.

Looking at Toni I repeated his question. "Were you in danger of dying when you passed out? Yes, if your mother would have put you to bed and you threw up after passing out then your vomit could have gone into your lungs and stopped you from breathing. That is what happens to college kids when they drink large amounts of alcohol while going through a hazing at college and that is why most colleges have banned students from doing those kinds of rituals. Drinking too much alcohol at one time can cause death.

The diagram of the brain we just looked at showed us that drinking ten shots of hard liquor within one hour could stop a heart from beating and could stop a person breathing. Remember, parts of the brain that guard certain body functions go to sleep in an ascending order of importance and the less important functions are sacrificed first to keep the body alive. That's why people experience blurred vision, cannot walk a straight line, or speak well when they get drunk or before they pass out. Some brain functions get sacrificed and they are shut down to keep the heart beating and the person breathing. Alcohol is poison to the human body and people do die of alcohol poisoning. In addition, people die from poor decisions they make while under the influence of alcohol like driving while drunk. They also kill other people when they get into car accidents while they are under the influence. "

One girl raised her hand slowly, and said, "Mrs. Gifford, are you saying that nobody should drink alcohol?"

"Everyone has to make their own decision regarding their health habits. I cannot tell you it's alright to drink alcohol given the health risk associated with using that drug but you have the right to choose. However, I can tell you the truth about alcohol's effects on the human body and show you the statistics which tell us it is better to wait until you are older to take your first drink. Also, I can ask you never to drink and drive or ride in a car with someone who has been drinking. The risks are just too great. I do want all of you to grow up drug free, alcohol is a drug, and using alcohol carries health risks."

I allowed a five more minutes for comments and questions. Many of the children wanted to talk about family members or friends who had died because someone had been driving drunk. I let them vent then redirected the class to the physical effects of alcohol on the body. A couple of students said they didn't care about the physical risks because they could always get organ transplants, new kidneys or a liver.

However, when we discussed choosing recipients for organs transplants, the students unanimously said people who are drug addicted should not be given transplants because they would just ruin those new organs. As class ended the students said they were sorry to leave because they still had more questions and wanted to keep talking. As Toni went out the door he said, "Mrs. G., I am really sorry I messed up and got sent here, but I am glad because I got to meet you."

I quietly responded, "Thank you," to this sensitive and sincere young man and I offered him a referral to our school counselor to talk about his concern. He politely declined and said I had given him the information he needed and he knew what he was going to do. Two weeks later I found out his plan. As my last class of students lined up to leave my room on Friday, I was surprised to see Toni entering my room. He walked up to me and hurriedly gave me a hug, "Mrs. OG, I'm going! I saw my probation officer after the lesson we did on alcohol and I told him I want to get clean and sober because I'm going to be a dad. He is picking me up when I get home from school today. I'm going to a treatment program so I won't be here anymore. I just wanted you to know!"

After I wished Toni good luck, I closed my classroom door overcome with emotions. I prayed that Toni would be successful in the program, he would stay clean and sober, and I prayed his baby would be born healthy. I prayed that Toni would find a desire and a way to complete his education. I knew Toni would make a great dad if he could overcome his addiction. This young teen dad who loved his unborn child and wanted to be good father brought tears to my eyes.

Discussion: Parents are their children's first teachers. They teach their children about making choices which may affect their health like smoking, drinking, or using drugs. Even, when parents tell their children "Do as I say and don't do as I do" there is research which shows children will follow their parents' examples before they follow their parents' words. When parents do directly teach their children, like Toni's mother, their children usually do not question the parent's intentions and may believe that their parents know best. When Toni's mother taught him how to drink alcohol it was presented to him like a game. Being a ten year old child, Toni wanted to play. **Why do parents involve their children in their alcohol or drug use?**

Topics for Research

What percentage of unplanned teen pregnancies are consequences of youth drinking alcohol or using drugs? What additional health risks do teen moms face compared to mothers in their mid twenties? Should parents allow young teens like Toni, 14 years old, and his girlfriend, 16 years old, to get married? Should a teen boy be given custody of his child if the mother wants to adopt the child out?

Things to Do

Explain the connection between drug/alcohol use and date rape to girls. Do this before middle school age if you suspect your child may use these substances early. Health risk for young mothers and their babies should be discussed. Don't let teens think that it is acceptable for them to have babies while they are still living in your home and dependent upon you for support. Don't hesitate to tell your teen you think it would be unfair for them to expect you to support their children. Advise them of the consequences that they might personally face if a teen pregnancy occurs. Parents should communicate with their teens about these issues before pregnancy occurs.

16. Teen Parents

Teen pregnancy rates may vary from state to state, region to region, and they change year to year. Currently, the United States still remains at the top of a world list of births per thousand to teen age girls in developed countries. Our rate is 52.1 % per thousand births and our closest competitor is the United Kingdom with a rate of 30.8% (People Statistics, Nation Master. com). In addition, recent national statistics for teen pregnancy has shown an increase of 3% as reported on the NBC nightly news (January 26th, 2010). This new rate of teen pregnancies after periods of decline could have many explanations but the possible outcomes for public education are always the same, an increased need for teen parent education programs and an increased student dropout rate if teen parent programs are not provided for this student population.

In my preceding story I told stories about several teens and most were not eligible for parent programs because they were too young. Others were male who have not traditionally received the same education services as their female teen parent counterparts. Both age and sex criteria for teen parent program enrollment may eliminate some younger students participating and their ineligibility may increase truancy rates or hasten students dropping out of school. One source states, "Less than one third of teens who have children before the age of eighteen ever get their high school diploma" (National Campaign to Prevent Teen Pregnancy).

The trend today is to keep pregnant students in their home school environment due to lack of funding for special programs. After all, pregnancy is not catching and it is not a disability which mandates schools by federal law to provide special services. For this reason, students who are teen parents may be considered just another segment of the general school population. Teen parents may be supported by a range of public school services including: counseling, career guidance, vocational training, home instruction, referrals for medical care and child care, parenting classes, and bus transportation. One such public funded program in Carrollton, Texas may serve as a model for helping high school pregnant teens and teen parents. However, middle school teen parents receive limited services at their home school through this program (Mary Grimes Education Center).

There is some evidence that younger students are becoming parents and one US city, Houston, has the highest percentage in the nation of girls giving birth under the age of fifteen years old. Houston has maintained a "Tough balancing act" taking care not to approve of teen pregnancy while providing services to teen parents. Their overall goal is to prevent dropouts and their services to teen parents include: free daycare, flexible school hours, night classes, and online courses (Erika Mellon; Houston Chronicle).

Middle school students need teen parent programs too. We may not want to signal approval to these pregnant youth by publishing program availability but we do need to institute a plan to keep them engaged in their education. Educational reform in this one area could take more than one direction. One school district having the highest pregnancy rate in the United States has been urged by its parents to conduct sex education classes for teens. Although their teen pregnancy rates are extremely high at 64.4 for every one thousand girls aged 15 -19, pregnancy is not the only concern voiced by parents in the DC school district. One in every one-hundred young people between the ages of 13 to 24 is believed to be HIV positive and DC's AIDS rate is believed to be ten times the national average. This activist group reported that along with teenage pregnancy, STD rates are steadily increasing and have grown over 200% between 2003 and 2007. This information tells us that even when youth aren't getting pregnant they are having unprotected sex which leads to contracting STDs and possibly AIDS. It is no wonder that DC parents support comprehensive sex education in their schools and want that instruction taught to children before they become sexually active (DC Healthy Youth Coalition).

There are other school districts which have similar statistics. North Texas is in the middle of the Bible belt and has its own issues with teen pregnancy and venereal diseases. Its pregnancy rate is second only to DC. North Texas' fastest rate of growth for new HIV positive cases is found in the same 13 to

24 year old age group as DC's (People Statistics, Nation Master.com). The geography of these similar statistics should cause national concern because they show us teen pregnancy and venereal disease is not a city, district, or regional problem; it is a national concern.

Teen pregnancy impacts all of our citizens through raising the need for additional welfare, health, and education dollars. At a time when we need to be conservative to pay off national dept we may be confronted with expanding services to a new generation of drug affected or developmentally delayed infants. Children born to teen moms are at high risk for being born premature and having health problems.

Premature birth due to the mother's lack of physical maturity and lack of early prenatal care is an especially troubling outcome of teen pregnancy. Preterm infants born to teen mothers have amplified risks for having under developed lungs and bleeds in the brain. Both of these conditions are life threatening and expensive to treat. Bleeds in the brain can cause a child to have life-long physical and mental disabilities and a diagnosis of cerebral palsy which is ten times more common in preterm infants (Merck Manual Home Health Edition). According to this source, cerebral palsy cannot be cured and children born afflicted may require extensive intervention services including special education throughout their school years.

In addition, certain genetic defects, like Down's syndrome, may be as common in children born to young teen mothers as they are in children born to women over thirty-five years old. Down syndrome is a genetic defect which cannot be cured and children born with this disability definitely require special education services. Recent trends show older mothers are birthing more children born with Down syndrome but researches state this statistic is related to women delaying pregnancy in favor of career pursuits (WebMD). Researchers once believed egg maturation levels were responsible for the phenomenon in both groups of high-risk mothers, teens and older mothers. Experts believe female gametes may be breaking down in older mothers and could be the cause of the genetic mutation while it was theorized teen women's eggs may have been immature at conception which could be the cause of Down's syndrome in their children. However, no current research has proven that theory and I think there might be a more plausible explanation. Teen mothers could be at risk for having children born with Down syndrome and other genetic defects because they may be experimenting with alcohol and drugs. Alcohol, marijuana, and many other substances teens experiment with, contain chemicals called teratogens, substances found in the environment which may cause birth defects (MedicineNet.com). Teen mothers simultaneously experimenting with drugs/alcohol and having sex might be reflected in a higher portion of infants born with birth defects to these young women.

Alcohol is known to cause a specific birth defect, Fetal Alcohol Syndrome. It has been identified as the leading cause of mental retardation in the United States (Fetal Alcohol Syndrome..., Morrissette). The added risks of alcohol and drug use while pregnant by young, teen mothers may overwhelm their infants' chance at normal physical and mental development. Since these young girls are already at a high risk for delivering their babies early and premature infants are often born with physical and mental disabilities, teen mothers' use of illicit substances may place their infants at risk for all types of birth defects.

We have already learned in a previous strategy there has been a 233% increase in learning disabled students attending public schools in recent years. For this reason, we should consider funding teen parent programs which educate young parents about taking care of themselves and their developing fetuses because these types of programs may lessen the need for increased special education funding in the future. Not to mention, theses service might prevent needless human suffering for the infants born too soon with life-time disabilities. As many as one million infants are born to teen parents each year and approximately three-fourths of those are born to unwed mothers. These teens are at risk for becoming long-term dependent upon welfare assistance and their children are at risk for having poor health, education, and life outcomes (aspe.hhs.gov...). Therefore, some schools that have higher than the national average teen pregnancy rates may want to consider prevention initiatives along with adding more services for younger teen parents. If these programs are not expanded or pregnancy prevention education is not provided then the school districts may be confronted with higher costs in the future educating teen parents' special needs offspring.

Public education can only do so much because we are limited by our parents' wishes and many parents do not want their children to be taught sex education at school. My concern is that many parents are not informed themselves about current teen sexual behaviors and some might be too embarrassed to take on a comprehensive discussion with their children when faced with their inquiries. One source I found recommends parents need to talk to their kids about sex: to provide accurate information because what they learn elsewhere may not be true, to reflect personal and moral values parents want their children to follow, to help children understand the consequences of becoming sexually active with special attention focusing on pregnancy and sexually transmitted diseases, and to avoid children being emotionally hurt (WebMD). This site list topics parents should be familiar with and should incorporate in their discussion with their children.

Some parents might become more comfortable talking to their children about sex if trainings were offered by school districts which informed parents of current youth sex trends and taught them how to talk to their children about these topics. Parents could choose to attend this type of training or their children could be required to attend comprehensive sex education classes at school without parent permission. This one district policy change could be supported by local teen pregnancy rates and health statistics on venereal disease and HIV among teens. This reform is needed now because there is not enough funding available to take care of our current special needs population in schools and we lose education dollars when pregnant teens drop out of school. National support could be gained if the Department of Health and Human Services provided public service messages to parents that they need to have that birds and bees talk with their children. There are many things we can do that don't involve teaching children sex education directly if parents will accept our help. However, if parents won't work with us to limit teen pregnancy then we need to teach the students directly. This reform is necessary for our time.

References and Resources

"People Statistics; Teen birth rate (most recent) by country," Nation Master. com; nationmaster.com/graph/peo_tee_bir_rat-people-teenage-birth-rate

"Teen Pregnancy Rates Increase," NBC nightly news January 26th, 2010

"School-Age Parenting Program," Mary Grimes Education Center; cfbstaff. cfbisd.edu/marygrimes/new/sapp.htm

National Campaign to Prevent Teen and Unplanned Pregnancy; thenationalcampaign.org

"Cerebral Palsy (CP)," Merck Manual Home Health Edition; merck.com/ mmhe/sec23/ch284/ch284a.html

"Talking to Your Kids About Sex," WebMD; webmd.com/sex-relationships/ guide/talking-to-your-kids-about-sex

"Definition of Teratogen," MedicineNet.com; medterms.com/script/main/ art.asp?articlekey=11315

"Fetal Alcohol Syndrome: Parental experiences and the Roleof Family Counselors," Patrick J. Morrissette; nova.edu/ssss/QR6-2/morrissette. html

"Moving Teenage Parents Into Self-Sufficiency: Lessons from Recent Demonstrations," Health and Human Services report; aspe.hhs.gov/hsp/ isp/tpd/synthes/summary.htm

"New Poll Shows DC Parents Overwhelmingly Support HIV and Sex Education," DC Healthy Youth Coalition; metroteenaids.org

"Parenting between classes," Erika Mellon; Houston Chronicle; chron. com/disp/story.mpl/metropolitan/6606083.html

17. Doctor Sandy

Sandy was barely thirteen years old but her face reflected the look of a hardened thirty year old street vagrant. Her nails were short, chewed and chipped and they were painted black. When I first saw her fingernails I thought she might be a "Goth" and I wondered if Sandy might be portraying a dark, weird figure for social reasons. Goth students were considered genuinely strange by all other students' standards at our school and they were avoided. However, Goths were not frequent victims of torment or hate crimes because of their weirdness. According to some students, Goths were just too creepy to mess with. Sandy's dark slacks, black fingernails, and raven colored hair certainly added to the illusion she might be part of this one bizarre student group. However, after observing this student I decided she probable was not a Goth and that her greasy hair, unhealthy looking skin, and dirt spotted slacks indicated she just did not have good hygiene.

Sandy did have fine delicate bones in her face which revealed Spanish decent and she could have looked quite lovely if she would have cleaned up a little. Her eyes were exceptional dark jewels encased in darker circles. When I looked at Sandy's eyes, they reminded me of underwater caves. Hiding deep within the darkness, her eyes darted quickly from side to side like a sea creature lying in wait and surveying its surroundings for prey. As I observed Sandy, her eyes came to rest on my teacher's station and her visual interest in the objects on top of my desk led me to believe Sandy was casing her new classroom environment while looking for things to steal. I knew the look because I had students in the past who had stolen things from me and I guessed what sort of games Sandy might play with me in order to get at the stuff she targeted. I knew better than to keep anything of real value in my room but value did not matter to some students.

It was the thrill of seeing a shocked expression on their teachers' faces when they realized something was missing that inspired some students to steal. Other students took pleasure in disrupting the learning environment by moving or hiding the papers their teachers needed to present a lesson. A few students would be bold enough to sabotage or hide equipment to confound their instructors. These kids' behaviors were born out of a desire to gain control of the learning environment. Many who acted this way wanted to prove their gangster abilities to their classmates and they thought it was fun to mess with their teachers' minds.

However, at our school there could be other darker motives for taking ordinary, desk-top teacher supplies. Some things like paper clips could be shaped into types of weapons that could be hurled across a room at another student. These sharp pointed darts with paper wings could be found hanging in the soft ceiling tile if intercepted and tossed upward by the intended victim. Ink pens were prized for their graffiti carving abilities on the metal stall doors in student restrooms. A stapler could be fired in rapid succession like a machine gun toward another student's eyes. In fact, students could fashion a weapon out of practically everything we used in our science lab. Much of what they needed was displayed openly on shelves along one wall for quick lab access. This science equipment often drew students' curiosity because some of it could have a street value. Therefore, I had to stringently enforce my classroom rule that students could never be out of their seat without permission.

Sandy did not like my rule and she began to walk out of her way, when allowed to get out of her seat, to gain access to other parts of the room which drew her attention. Sandy noticed I had her under surveillance when she did this and I believe her frustration started to mount due to my close supervision. I caught Sandy trying to sneak out of her seat many times that first week and she would go out of her way to walk around my desk on the way back from sharpening her pencil. For this reason, I flipped Sandy seating arrangement and placed her next to my classroom entry door and farther away from my desk.

In addition to Sandy trying to roam the classroom with malicious intent, she seemed desperate to get attention from the boys in class and she interfered with learning when she attempted to gain their notice during instruction time. Frankly, the boys found her behavior irritating and said her personal appearance "Creeped" them out. In order to keep the peace,

I had to move Sandy again and I sat her in the back of the room with a row of empty seats between her and her nearest classmate. I told the male students in class if they turned around to respond to Sandy's calls they would stay after school for detention. After that, the boys found it easy to ignore Sandy and she quit trying to engage them while in my room. Sandy was pretty much segregated in class because she now sat at the outside corner closest to the exit door, in the back, with a row of seats between her and her nearest classmates and no one sat across from her on either side.

I told Sandy she must go straight to her seat when she entered my room, I walked with her in a direct path to make sure she understood my directions the first time, and I had her reenter my room and walk the path I had shown her correctly while I observed. From that day forward, Sandy was not allowed to ever get out of her seat in my room; she could not even get up to sharpen her own pencil. When Sandy began breaking the pencils as soon as I sharpened them for her, I handed her a manual sharpener to use at her desk which had to be returned to me at the end of each period. I told Sandy if she forgot and left class with the sharpener, I would put her on the detention list for the day because she would have stolen a piece of my classroom equipment. This only happened once and Sandy got the idea I would not be played nor would I relent her restrictions. By the end of that first week, Sandy became compliant with our classroom rules and she adapted quickly to my classroom routines. When Sandy began focusing on her work I discovered a very intelligent seventh grade student who was capable of completing her learning objectives in the time allotted during each class period. Once her preoccupation with taking things and her attention seeking behaviors that bothered the boys in my room were controlled, Sandy surprised me by being a good student.

Then Sandy began a new annoying habit; she started whining for additional restroom breaks during class periods. One middle school teacher set a precedent by giving into Sandy's request and the rest of us became plagued by Sandy's whining for this special privilege every day. I recognized it was a huge mistake to give Sandy unrestricted time in the restroom because I suspected she was using drugs due to her unhealthy appearance. I was sure her attempts to steal were related to her need for money to buy drugs and I knew private restroom time would afford her the opportunity to use.

Sandy could be very convincing; the physical distress witnessed when she requested an emergency break did not appear faked, even to me. I began to wonder if something might be physically wrong with Sandy but I was handling the situation with caution because she had proven untrustworthy. The very first time Sandy pleaded to use the restroom, I redirected and said, "You know when my own children didn't want to take no for an answer they received discipline. You are not going to wear me out and I am not going to change my mind. Therefore, you may not ask again or you will have a detention after school. However, if you think you might have a physical problem that causes you to need the restroom more often than other students and you would like to talk to the nurse, I can give you a referral during your PE class. Tell me now if you want to go to the nurse… because if you ask one more time to go to the restroom in this class, you will be staying after school. Sandy said she wanted to see the nurse and I made her wait until the end of science because I did not make it a practice to release students from my core class.

When other students went to PE, Sandy and I walked down the hall to the nurse's station. Sandy reported that she thought she had started her period and needed a sanitary product. I explained to her that the nurse dispensed those products to the girls and Sandy would need to go to the office whenever she needed one. I told her it would be better if she brought her own supplies in the morning and gave them to the nurse because the school used generics and she might not feel comfortable wearing those. Sandy thanked me for taking her to see the nurse and I felt a little guilty about making her wait the entire class period after what she told me.

As I turned Sandy over to the nurse, I instructed Miss Watson that Sandy needed to go straight to the gym for PE when finished. I expected that Sandy would be escorted to the gym because all the staff knew our school rules required constant supervision of students. However, that is not what happened and I was forced to deal with Sandy a second time that day over her seeking additional time in the girl's restroom. When this happened I realized in spite of what Sandy had told me, she lied to me and there was more to her situation than what she had portrayed.

I was in my room laying out supplies for my next class when I heard a student's feet in the hall. I hurried to my door to see Sandy walking out of the girls' restroom. I quickly reasoned there was not a good excuse for Sandy to be down our hall; the school nurse had a restroom attached to her examining room and she let girls use that private space when they had a need. I thought Sandy had manipulated the office staff into letting her goes to the gym by herself or she had slipped out when they were busy. Whatever the reason, I knew I had to tighten the reigns and inform others of Sandy's games.

I quickly escorted Sandy to PE and told her I would report her unusual behavior to the school principal. I reminded Sandy that she did not have to stay at our school if she could not follow our rules. After leaving Sandy with the PE teacher, I conference with our office staff and told them I had found Sandy unsupervised in the restroom. I requested their help and told them we all needed to confirm Sandy's whereabouts when she left our custody. When I explained it was a health issue and Sandy could be using her time alone to do drugs, the staff understood my concern and I felt confident that they would not let Sandy leave without an escort again. I reported Sandy's peculiar behavior to my middle school team and they all agreed to deny Sandy individual restroom breaks even if they could supervise. We followed through with our decision and Sandy intensified her pleadings.

The very next week Sandy raised her hand and said, "Mrs. G., I have to see the nurse because I am having my period." I was surprised Sandy was not embarrassed to speak out loud or in front of the boys in our room about something that was so personal. Since she was not embarrassed to share this information in front of the class, I decided to answer her forthrightly.

"Sandy, you cannot be having your period today because you went to the nurse last week while having your period," I replied. The boys all laughed because they knew that Sandy had forgotten the referral I had granted the week before and they became interested in Sandy's response to me.

"Well, something must be wrong with me because I'm having it again!" Sandy dramatically answered.

In a highly irritated voice I answered, "Sandy, you know my rules. You may not leave science class to see the nurse. If you really need to go, I will walk you down when the other students go to PE. For now, do not ask me again or you will be kept after school for a detention." Sandy did not reply but she fidgeted in her seat and banged her books around a little until I called her name and gave her the "I'm over your behavior look." At the end of class, I walked Sandy down to the nurse again and decided to use the second opportunity to conference with the nurse. I was hoping the nurse could help me find out what caused Sandy's frequent restroom request. I made Sandy sit in the front office waiting room while I went in first.

"Miss Watson, Sandy continues to ask to use the restroom in all her classes and with all her teachers. She told me today that she is having her period. Last week when I brought Sandy to you she said the same thing. Since we know that should not be happening so soon, I think Sandy is just looking for an excuse to get out of class to use the restroom for some other purpose. She does not appear very healthy and I am concerned she might be using some type of drug. She could use it in the privacy of the restroom when no one is around to see and tell on her. If you could look for signs of substance abuse I would appreciate it. I have not been able to reach her mother by phone do you think you could try to reach her and see if Sandy has any unreported medical concerns? She might have a bladder infection if she is sexually active. I really don't know what is wrong and I think we should first make sure that Sandy doesn't have any documented medical problems. I have been worried about Sandy because she looks so ghastly!

I have not been able to reach her mother by phone. Do you think you could try to reach her and see if Sandy has any unreported medical concerns?"

Miss Watson replied, "She might have a bladder infection if she is sexually active." I hadn't thought of that possibility.

"Sandy is supposed to go to PE next but if you have any concerns for her health we could put her in the ISS room until you reach her mother by phone. I want to make sure that Sandy is alright but I do feel she is just seeking attention or wanting to go to the bathroom for some other reason. I would appreciate any help you could give."

I took a deep breath and continued, "Last week Sandy came down our hall instead of going to PE class. I don't know how that happened because students are not suppose to go anywhere in the school unsupervised. When I caught her she was coming out of the restroom and I know you let her use the private bathroom off your office. Something is not right with Sandy's behavior. Do you understand my concern?" Ms. Watson said she understood because Sandy had used her bathroom prior to being released for PE and an office staff person had escorted Sandy to her next class. Ms. Watson promised to personally escort Sandy to her next class and to call Sandy's mother to find out if she had a legitimate excuse for needing additional breaks. I left the nurse's station feeling that we would soon have an answer to Sandy's problematic behavior.

I returned to my room and started to print student progress reports that were due the next day. While shuffling papers, I heard feet again in the hall. Quickly, I moved to my door and arrived just in time to see Sandy run into the restroom. So, I followed her in. She was already in a stall with the door shut so I let her know I was outside waiting for her. As soon as she walked out, I reminded her to wash her hands and we proceeded into the hall where I halted her walk. With great tension in my voice said, "Where are you supposed to be right now?"

Sandy answered that Coach let her out of PE to use the restroom.

I responded, "Why would he do that? Coach does not let students out of class to roam the building unattended."

Sandy didn't answer my question but walked toward the fountain to get a drink of water and said, "I'm going back. I just need to get a drink of water." I let Sandy get her drink because I wanted to observe to see if she had something in her mouth and needed water to swallow it. I watched carefully but I could not tell for sure.

On our way back to the gym I informed Sandy, "Congratulations, you have earned a new rule. When I or any of the other school staff see you by yourself then you will receive a referral to the principal. I have already talked to him about your sneaky behavior and I will let him know today how you continue to break our rules. This is serious, Sandy. You did not have to come to our school; you could have been retained in youth detention. As long as you are here you are going to follow our rules or we will kick you back to the juvenile justice system. This is your one chance to do the right thing. Don't mess it up. We do have a waiting list of students who would rather be attending school here than where they are right now. Other students might fit into our program better. I'm afraid that you are going to find yourself in more trouble than what you want if you continue to try and circumvent our rules."

Now standing in front of the gym door I said, "Repeat to me what I told you." Sandy said, "I can't walk around the building by myself."

I quizzed, "What happens if you break the rule?"

Sandy started slowly, "You will make a referral to the principal?"

I corrected, "Yes and what else?" Sandy acted like she didn't remember so I gave her a starter, "JJAEP?"

Then she remembered and said, "The principal can send me to the juvenile justice system."

I opened the gym door and shooed Sandy in to join her group then stood waiting until Coach noticed me. "Sandy keeps sneaking down our hall and getting out of class to use the restroom. I wanted to tell you because I know you can't leave the other students unsupervised to watch her and you have no way of asking the office for assistance when you are down here alone without a phone. Sandy is up to something and I need your help to stop her. I think she is using drugs so you might want to watch her close during PE. You know I am always concerned one of our kids is going to die in PE class because they dropped acid, or snorted cocaine, or have done something else stupid before running and exercising."

Coach informed me he had not seen Sandy come into class and he never gave her permission to leave. Coach went on to say that sometimes staff members just walked a student to the gym door and once the kid was inside they left. If Coach was busy with other students at the opposite end of the gym he might not even recognize a new student was joining the group. An opportunistic, sneaky student like Sandy could have easily disappeared before Coach turned around to notice her. Now I understood how Sandy was getting away and walking freely through the halls. If school staff did not bother to get Coach's attention then the new student could slip back out the door and be gone before anyone knew it. Coach kept one eye on his students playing basketball as we talked and we agreed quickly that everyone needed to be advised about his situation. I said, "Thanks, Coach. Now, I understand what is happening!" Coach flashed his famous thumbs up sign and turned to supervise his motley crew.

As I walked back to my room I decided Sandy's drug of choice was in pill form because she was determined to have her drink of water before we went to PE class. As I raked my mind for new teen drug trends, I thought about Jimmy. He almost died while using "Four bars" at school. Four bars was a street name given to the drug Xanax, a psychotropic medication used to treat anxiety. When students were caught with this drug, they bragged about being able to purchase it and other drugs over the internet without a prescription. I shivered with fear remembering how close we came to losing the life of one twelve year old boy.

Jimmy weighed only about ninety-five pounds; he was muscular but of slight built. He appeared healthy but he was one of the shortest male students we had ever had at our middle school. To his credit, he was always neat and clean and he was a cute kid with a great smile. As I remembered it, he was never fully compliant with our school rules and he was emotionally immature. Managing Jimmy's behavior was difficult for all the middle school teachers including me. I had a theory about students like Jimmy. I believed the cute students who make other students and teachers laugh may get away with more disobedience in the classroom. In the beginning, Jimmy had been one of those students which caused me to constantly be on guard so that would not happen.

My discipline plan began with students learning to take responsibility for their actions by issuing an apology while stating what they had done wrong. I informed Jimmy the first time I disciplined him this way that apologizing was an act of repentance and his apology meant that he was going to change his behavior. Jimmy would apologize but his repentance was never genuine and he would resume his previous transgressions as if he had never been disciplined. As his behavior worsened middle school teachers decided that a uniform front had to be presented this student. We planned a student-teacher conference and decided to enact our own version of "Jumping a kid into our program." With all the middle school teachers present in the room and Jimmy by himself, we took turns extolling him for the positives things we had seen regarding his abilities. Then we informed Jimmy of the behavior changes he needed to make to be successful in our program. This was the ultimate discipline tool used by our team and when we presented a unified front student's often corrected their misbehaviors. Parents were notified by phone and if they objected they could be present for the meeting. Often we were unable to reach parents or they delayed calling back after receiving a message and the meeting went on without them.

However, during the jumping in ceremony with jimmy our principal interrupted and told us we had to release the student immediately. After Jimmy left we were informed of a sticky situation with his parent. Jimmy's father was an attorney who threatened to sue our district when his child was suspected of being under the influence of drugs at school. The father refused to let his son be drug tested. Negotiations between the district and his father caused Jimmy to be placed at our alternative school. The father agreed to send Jimmy to our alternative program for thirty days instead of the police being called to arrest Jimmy. The administration was afraid to brooch the subject again with his parent and we were plainly told teachers were not to call Jimmy's parents and any discipline used had to be cleared through our administrator. It seemed teachers were expected to suspend discipline with Jimmy that we would have normally applied to other students.

The middle school teachers knew we would be tormented by this child's behavior but we feared personal consequences if we tried to correct Jimmy. Unless teachers performed discipline together and kept excellent documentation, this twelve year old kid could possibly cause a highly qualified teacher to lose her job. Way too much power was given to this student and he used his power maliciously to interfere with other students' rights to get an education. Jimmy came back to school the next day with a sense of entitlement and his behavior worsened. Most teachers were just documenting his behaviors, setting him out in the hall, and trying to forget he was there. When this happened he would run door to door and disrupt everyone's class.

Some days it did not appear that Jimmy even recognized he was in school and he would completely ignore his teachers and their classroom rules. This was one student who could have been a poster child for the phrase "Crazier than a road lizard" in his actions. This four foot nothing child thought he ran our school because we were not allowed to discipline him or report his behavior to his parents. I felt truly limited in what I could use to manage this student's behavior. Jimmy no longer appeared cute to me nor was he funny; he was a torment. I turned his desk to the wall when his behavior became outlandish and Jimmy would pout then go to sleep. Jimmy wasn't learning in my class because I was unable to discipline him properly so I could not teach him. I was afraid I would reach my limit with this student and do an insane thing like call his father and tell him how his actions were destroying his son's chance to get an education. But I was wrong because something else happened before I reached that point.

About ten thirty one morning, I recognized Jimmy's normal joking behavior had been replaced by darker deeds. He was verbally and physically aggressive toward other students; he used offensive language in class to a girl and he began to pound on another male in class. I happened to see the RSO officer walk past my door, hailed him, and asked if he could escort a student up front for me who had committed sexual harassment, hit another student, and who I thought might be under the influence of a drug. After I told the officer what Jimmy had said and done, he requested that I send Jimmy out into the hall. The RSO disappeared with Jimmy as I wrote out my first office referral on this student.

The nurse phoned within minutes and asked me if I knew what drug Jimmy had used. I honestly answered that I did not know and I reported that his behaviors were more like a person who was drunk. I suspected he had taken some type of drug which suppressed central nervous system function. The nurse requested that I identify the physical symptoms which alerted me to Jimmy's suspected drug use on the referral form and bring it to her because the principal was sitting in her office. I thought, "Great, even the nurse doesn't want to take responsibility for saying this kid is under the influence of a drug at school and the principal is sitting next to her waiting her opinion."

I asked the teacher across the hall to watch my class while I carried the completed form to the front office. I knew the principal would need the information I documented when Jimmy's parents were called and I had been careful not to be inflammatory in my comments. I just reported my observations. When I dropped off the form, Jimmy sat glaring at me while I read the report to the principal. I had put Jimmy's words in quotation marks that he had spoken to a girl in class and I emphasized sexual harassment. I reported he had hit another student and disrupted learning for the entire class by his behaviors. I gave the principal a way out; he could address sexually harassment and assault instead of drug use if he preferred.

I headed back to my class with a mission. Drug use at our school almost always came in multiples. I sensed someone in class would inquire what happened to Jimmy and I would get an opening to go fishing for information and I was right. As soon as the other teacher left the room, one boy asked, "Are you mad at Jimmy, Miss OG? I ain't ever seen you put a student out before."

"I am upset," I responded. "But... maybe not for the reason you think. Jimmy is very small for his age, we don't know what drug he used, and I am afraid that he might accidently overdose on the drug due to his size. I don't want to ever read in the paper or hear on the news that one of my students died due to drug over dose. I would be really sad if any of my students did not live to grow up and fulfill their destinies. It would be such a waste of human potential. You know there is no one else that will ever be born in this world that is just like you? That is true and that is science. So every person born is really special. No one knows what they will be when they grow up or what they might do with their life. Our whole society could suffer from the lost."

One girl looked puzzled as she asked, "What do you mean Miss OG? Ain't nobody going to miss that lil'ole boy. He's a pain."

I explained, "What would have happened if Thomas Edison had overdosed on drugs and died?"

One of the students shouted out, "We wouldn't have electricity!"

I asked again, "What would happen if Sir Isaac Newton died as a teenager?"

That one was harder and there was a slight pause before one girl raised her hand at the front of the room and said, "We would not have been able to fly to the moon."

I transitioned flawlessly right into the lesson, "Which law of motion did Newton discover that had to do with rockets?" We continued working until the last five minutes of class and as students completed their participation sheets, the boy who started our discussion raised his hand timidly. After looking around the room to make sure no one was watching, he handed me a note with two words on it. It said "Four bars."

Quietly I said, "Jimmy?" He nodded yes and I mouthed thank you. Nobody had raised their heads from their papers and I was sure that the boy who shared information with me was undetected. This young man's actions gave me hope because he witnessed to me he cared what happened to Jimmy even though he didn't necessarily like him. How this boy knew Jimmy was using four-bar would give me pause to think later. For now, I had a clue and I pursued it.

"If I just knew what four-bar was…?" I said silently as I racked my brain trying to match the street name to the real drug. I was familiar with many drugs' street names due to working in social services and with substance abusers but there were new drugs today which I was not familiar. I was stumped after my computer research because my internet resource did not have a reference for the name four bars. As I puzzled what to do I thought, "Sometimes I can trick the students into telling me the information I need to know." However, I knew I should not single out the young man who slipped me the paper because other students would finger him as the snitch if I pulled him out of class to interrogate him.

Besides, I didn't have time to play "Mess with the students' brains" game. Jimmy was really high and I was worried for his safety. In the past, I would just act like I knew something when I didn't and students would become careless by sharing information they thought I already knew. I had learned to feign understanding in a lot of situations just to gain more information about student drug activities. However... if I really needed to know something and I didn't have the time to play the game then I had to find a student who would tell me what I wanted to know. Since I had been employed long enough at the alternative school to have a relationship with high school kids who were former students of mine, I decided to cruise the high school hall and try to pick up an informant. I found Anthony passing to his next class in the hall and greeted him with a head side jerk and a "Wuz up?"

He answered me, "What up with you Miss OG?" Next, he gave me the shoulder to shoulder, bro greeting that is usually reserved for guys. I said, "I have got a real big problem and I was hoping you could help me." Anthony replied he would do anything for me because I was his favorite teacher in middle school. I told him the little kids in middle school were using a pill to get high and they were calling it four-bars.

He immediately anticipated what I needed and said, "It is Xanax, Mrs. G. and you can get it off the internet."

I thanked Anthony and said, "You know I have got to keep fresh or the little kids will get over on me. Stop by my room and tell me what you have been doing. I like visiting with my former students." Anthony promised he would do just that and I did look forward to hearing about his life plans and his education goals. I had high hopes for Anthony but I was sorry to see he was back at our alternative school. I theorized, knowing him, he probably was not doing his school work and was socializing instead. Of course, there was an issue of his marijuana use. When I taught Anthony's class I could not convince him marijuana use could hurt his brain and his ability to remember. Marijuana was part of his neighborhood culture and his family life. According to Anthony, he started smoking marijuana at the age of ten so he had now been smoking for about six years. I did some quick calculations and realized Anthony would be turning seventeen this year and was in danger of becoming a drop out. I needed to talk to him about the Districts' Evolution program because I knew things weren't going well at his home school or he would not be here again. I promised myself that I would talk to Anthony later and encourage him to stick it out to get his education. "For now," I reminded myself... "I have to concentrate on Jimmy."

Now, I knew the name of the drug that Jimmy was using and I was really worried. Depending upon the dosage in milligrams he could be in serious trouble. One pill that was an adult dosage would be too much for his small body. Also, I was concerned for our other middle school students because we never found just one child using something like this. I was sure more than one kid in the middle school was "Poppin' four-bar" and I could probably identify them by the behavior changes I witnessed over the last couple of weeks. Secretly, I suspected at least five other students.

I amazed myself with the depth of anger I felt as I spoke out loud, "Kids now days will use anything without knowing what it is or how it might affect them. It would be a full time job teaching students how drugs hurt their bodies. They have no concept of how medication like Xanax is prescribed and what it legitimately used for. These students could all be in danger of dying any minute!" This pill use was something new at our school and I knew the types of pills students had access to might be limitless. They could get them from grandparents' or parent's medicine cabinets and they could talk other students who took psychotropic medications into selling or giving their medicine to them. But the source Anthony shared with me had not even crossed my mind. Students could get pills off the internet with their parent's credit card number. I acknowledged that it made sense pills could become the drug form of choice at our school. Pills would be easier to hide during our morning check-in procedure. All our staff needed to be alerted to this new situation.

After talking to Anthony, I had to return to teach my other classes but I went to tell the nurse and resource officer what I had discovered at the end of the day. I was surprised to find out Jimmy was allowed to leave the building with other students. I had assumed Jimmy's parents would be notified of his condition and that intervention would be provided by them to ensure his safety. What happened next should have never been and it is every parent's worst nightmare. Jimmy was almost run over and hit by a city bus as he staggered aimlessly around and under the influence of a drug. I did not understand how this could have happened. Jimmy was clearly wasted at 10:30 in the morning when I referred him to the office; if he was still high at 3:30 in the afternoon then either he took additional drugs during the day or he had taken enough of the drug to mess him up for five hours! I was later told that Jimmy's parents gave instructions to put him on the bus at the end of the day. Their decision almost cost their son's life and it may have caused one teacher to lose his job.

When the students were dismissed they lined up on the edge of the parking lot and on the boulevard that ran along our main street to wait for the bus. One of the people who supervised the students' departure this day was a gentle giant who was careful about observing our students and their actions. If it had not been for his quick reflexes Jimmy would have been hit by the city bus because this man retrieved Jimmy by his collar just in the nick of time. A split second too late and Jimmy would have been dead. Of course, the supervising teacher could tell something was not right with this student. Out of his concern for the boy, our hero continued to watch Jimmy as he meandered down the street. Since some of our students had to walk to the train station and take the rail to get home it was not unusual that Jimmy should head that way.

However, this man suspected Jimmy was not functioning normally and he was unnerved by the earlier incident. As soon as the other children were safely dispersed, the self appointed guardian drove his car along until he saw Jimmy being escorted out of a business and he watched him as he walked into another shop. Having good intentions the man parked and walked into the shop after Jimmy. That is when the Good Samaritan saw our student acting like he was going to steal something and he said, "What are you doing, man?" The shop owner noticed and angrily shouted, take your kid and get out of here before I call the police. The guardian caught Jimmy by the arm and ushered him out of the building. The teacher decided he was not going to let this kid wander the street in his kind of a condition and that is how the protector made a well intentioned mistake.

211

He knew that a teacher should never put a student in his own personal car and take a kid anywhere. However, his car was there and the guardian had an urgent personal commitment that made him feel conflicted. He did not have time to go back to the school and wait for a parent to come and he didn't know if any other staff would be available to wait with the boy. It was just easier to put the kid in his car and deliver the student to his home on his way to his scheduled appointment. The problem with his choice was that the Guardian did not know where Jimmy lived and he trusted Jimmy to tell him the correct address.

Jimmy did not get taken home. He was taken to the address he gave but it was the wrong address. However, our gentle giant watched Jimmy until he walked in the door and he was sure Jimmy was safe inside. Our teacher went on his way thinking the kid was safe when in fact he may have delivered him to another source of drugs. Jimmy definitely knew the people who lived there because the teacher was waved on by an adult. When Jimmy did not arrive home at his appointed time all kinds of chaos was initiated as Jimmy's frantic mother sought his whereabouts.

The mother called the school superintendent and all the board members wanting to know where her twelve year old son was. Initially threatened with a law suit if they tried to identify Jimmy's drug use at school, the administrators were now threatened with another legal action if Jimmy was injured on his way home from school. The child's need for safety had been carelessly ignored by his parents who may have been more concerned about their community image rather than the safety of their child and the school district may have been more concerned about the parents' threats than about Jimmy's safety. Jimmy was at risk for physical harm because of both of them! Sad to say, it was our guardian teacher who tried to help Jimmy that was blamed, reprimanded, and left our school district at the end of that year. We all assumed that this good man was not offered a renewed teaching contract due to this incident.

It was eleven o'clock at night when Jimmy returned home. Of course, he blamed the Good Samaritan teacher whom had tried to help him. Jimmy said he had to make many bus changes to find his way home, he did not know how to make those changes, and that is why it took him so long to get there. The truth is that Jimmy probably took some more drugs which delayed his return. I sighed to myself; "Drug users are devious whether they are children or adults. They know how to turn stories around and blame other people."

After this incident, Jimmy was withdrawn from our school by his parents and they cited the reason for his transfer as the teachers. According to them, we were all against their son and he had not done anything wrong and we had jeopardized his safety. I felt the real reason had more to do with the parents being notified Jimmy could to be sent to the juvenile justice system for chronic classroom disruption, assault on another student, and sexual harassment at an alternative school. I was sure that Jimmy's father was informed of his son's possible trouble with the law and he moved his family into another school district while trying to save his professional reputation.

When comparing Jimmy's behavior to Sandy's, I had determined the drug used was not the same because the two students' behaviors were completely different. Sandy did not seem high and she had more of an unhealthy appearance. She had raccoon eyes similar to narcotic users but she did not appear disorientated or drunk. Whereas, Jimmy appeared to be under the influence Sandy just appeared ill. However, I was sure Sandy was taking some type of drug in a pill form just like Jimmy. Sandy's health continued to be a concern to me and I prayed that we would find the answer soon for her sake.

I received four new students in Sandy's class section the next week and one, Martha, didn't seem to mind Sandy's appearance or her annoying manners. Martha befriended Sandy and I was glad for the friendship because all the other students in middle school had isolated Sandy; they tolerated her presence but they would not talk to her. Martha was tall and had the thick, muscular body type of an athlete; she played basketball at her home school. She was always groomed well and I hoped she would influence Sandy to take better care of her appearance. Martha was obviously resentful of her placement at our alternative school and she was concerned about missing out on playing her favorite sport. I explained to her that once placed with us she could not return to her school for sport events or any other school activity. She would be arrested for being on her home campus if she violated that rule. I told her, "Relax, you are a smart young lady and you will do well here. Just follow the rules and you will be out of here before you know it. The only thing you will miss is some basketball practice at your home school. You will be back in time for the beginning of the season and you could play if you keep your grades up."

Then Martha reported, "My grades aren't good and Coach told me I had to bring them up if I was going to play."

I replied, "Don't worry about your grades in science as long as you are here every day and you do your work then you will pass. The biggest reasons why students fail at their home schools are they don't have good attendance and they don't do their assignments. You will pay attention in my class and you will do all your work. If you don't come to school then you will not earn your thirty good days and you will not get sent back in time to play basketball. The only other element is tutoring and all the teachers at our school will tutor you if you want their help. However, once you get into trouble here and you start getting disciplined, you will start losing time and that will delay you from getting back to play basketball. Do you understand how it works?"

Martha nodded and said, "Yes." I walked away thinking this child is going to do alright, she has a goal. After conferencing with Martha, I sat her directly across from Sandy in the classroom. Sandy would now have a lab partner and Martha would have a mentor that would help her adjust to our classroom routine. The two girls were told they could work together as long as they did not disrupt the rest of the class. Sandy enjoyed her new role and she kept Martha on track recording daily goals and completing assignments. Martha's adjusted well with Sandy's help and she was doing all of her own work without complaining by the end of that week.

The following morning while taking the eighth grade class into my room, I saw Sandy's seventh grade group exchange money in their restroom lineup and in the presence of their teacher. When I heard one teacher say, "Put your money away," I stepped out of my room quickly and into the hall to see seventh graders counting out one dollar bills between them. I knew then the seventh grade students were dealing for some type of drug in the hallway, in front of God and everybody, because they thought teachers were oblivious to their business. While waiting for their turns to use the restroom, these students were paying for the drugs they would pick up during their morning comfort stop. Since the going price for pills was less than other drugs I expected the students were buying pills. With one leg in my classroom and one in the hall I whirled to ask my eighth graders "What is the going price of candy?"

One student laughed and said, "Mrs. OG you should have been a cop. Man, you are all over us and know everything we are doing. Those seventh graders are careless and they don't know how close you listen. Now you are gonna spoil their fun!"

I replied, "So hate me because I care. People can't drive cars while drunk without killing other people and students can't learn at school when they are using drugs. They kill their chance for an education. It's my job to help you show the world how smart you are, drug use is making you all dumb, and you all make me look like I am a bad teacher when you don't learn. Therefore, I will keep on watching for drug use. Are you guys in the seventh graders Kool-Aid?"

"No, those little kids are stupid. We got real drugs and don't need their pretend stuff. I just think it's funny they are out in the hall passing money in front of the OG," replied the student who spoke earlier. After this comment I thought … If the seventh grade was not using real drugs then what were they using? I called over the teacher who naively told the students to put their money away and I informed her, "Those students are dealing for something that they are passing in the restroom." The teacher looked at me in disbelief and said her mind didn't work that way and she hadn't even considered money being exchanged in the hallway as a sign drugs were being sold. I asked her to watch the way students acted in class because I was trying to figure out what they were using. Later she reported the students were always goofy so she could not tell if their behaviors were different. I agreed with her about the goofy part and said, "We both know that is why many teachers are unwilling to teach middle school."

When that same seventh grade group came to me I was eager to observe them. Originally, the clinical lab I had planned would have permitted the students to work in groups and I would have been rotating between those groups. However, after seeing these students exchange money in the hall, I purposely switched the group's assignment. Now, I would take these kids to the computer lab because they would be much easier to supervise. The students would sit in one direction facing their monitors and I would have an optimal position; I would watch the students from behind. I flipped the schedule just to confound students that morning and I was waiting for someone to get overconfident.

Once in the computer lab, I decided to sit Martha and Sandy apart; I wanted to make sure the students were not helping each other and I needed to complete Martha's program entrance evaluation. I was distracted momentarily as the computer teacher called my attention and asked me to cover her students in the lab so she could use the restroom. As I nodded yes, I saw a flash of movement out of the corner of my right eye and I turned in time to see Sandy jump back into her chair. In Sandy's hurry she knocked the chair over. Sandy quickly sat her chair upright and slipped back into it while flashing me a guilty look. I thought I had seen something passed between the two girls and I knew this situation should be checked out quickly. I walked toward the lab door and peered out to catch the attention of someone from the office. I wasn't disappointed because our counselor, Miss Lopez stepped around the corner and I stepped outside closing the door while viewing my students through the window.

"Miss Lopez I need someone to take a couple of girls out. I'm not sure but I think I just saw drugs passed from one to the other." I hated to involve Martha in this but I had to find out what Sandy was sharing. I knew it was a long shot because the girls could have been passing gum or candy but my gut feeling was that something else was passed. Miss Lopez inquired which one passed and which one received. I pondered, because I interrupted the deal but as far as I could tell Sandy passed to Martha.

The counselor decided to take Martha first and she called her out. After searching and interviewing both girls they were returned to my class. The report I received was the girls stripped to their bras and underwear in the presence of the nurse and nothing was found. The counselor said, "Of course we could not ask them to strip naked and something could have been hidden in their bras. Martha told me she doesn't use drugs because she plays basketball but she knows someone is bringing stuff into the school. She said the kids talk about how easy it is to sneak drugs in." The information the counselor received from Martha was as close as she got to a confirmation that Sandy might be dealing. I thanked Miss Lopez and thought it was time to impress upon my team teachers the seriousness of our drug situation.

I advised my friends to be on high alert concerning Sandy's behavior and I told them I was sure Sandy would feel over confident and become bolder because she had not been caught this time. I felt she would get careless and slip up. The next day, our English teacher was working at her desk and students were doing seat work. She noticed Sandy reaching into a plastic baggie that she was holding between her thighs. The clear plastic bag was almost invisible under the desk where Sandy had squeezed her thighs tightly together around it. The English teacher did not relent in her demands as Sandy tried to tell her that she was just eating candy; the teacher demanded Sandy turn over her cache which revealed pills. The police officer was called, the drugs were confiscated, and Sandy was escorted to the ISS room across from my classroom.

I did not know what was going on until the officer returned and handcuffed Sandy a few moments later. She was arrested and removed from our school. Now we would find out what Sandy had been taking and maybe dealing to other students. At my lunch break, I anxiously set out to find our counselor. As I rounded the corner to the office, I came face to face with Miss Lopez, "Good work, Mrs. Gifford! I guess you heard? After you alerted the English teacher, she caught Sandy in her class room using and maybe dispensing pills. The pills were medications prescribed for high blood pressure and other medical conditions. Sandy would not tell us where she got the medicine so the police will have to find that out. She will be gone for a few days to JJAEP (juvenile justice system) but you know she will be back. Keep up the good work!"

I had a sudden revelation and now I knew why Sandy wanted to use the restroom so often. Medicine which lowers blood pressure could act as a diuretic causing them to lose water from their body. Now, I understood why Sandy was so dark under her eyes; Sandy was probably dehydrated! In addition, the medication probably made Sandy feel dizzy or light headed and she thought she was getting high due to that feeling. However, Doctor Sandy did not have any idea of the seriousness of her actions when she self-prescribed and took medication which lowered her blood pressure. Low blood pressure can be a serious illness.

Discussion

Today children have easy access to prescription drugs because almost every home has some in their medicine cabinets. Recently, realtors in my area were telling their clients, when they had an open house scheduled, to take their prescription drugs with them when they left their homes. People were coming to view open houses and raiding medicine cabinets! I know it sounds crazy that someone would want your prescription drugs or that a child would take a medicine prescribed for an adult family member, but it does happen. Pills are easy to conceal and easy to take at school. Students may not worry about being found in the possession of prescription drugs verses illegal drugs and they may think prescription drugs are safe to use.

Teachers and parents need to maintain a constant vigil for this kind of drug use. In addition to children not understanding the danger of self-prescribing their own dosage, there are two other frightening aspects involved in kids using pills to get high. The first, students do not just use one kind of pill at one time. Often, students make a pill cocktail; it is sort of like playing suicide by mixing drinks. The synergistic effects of combining pills are very unpredictable. Putting two things together does not mean you will get double the effects. Instead the combination could be fifty or even one hundred times stronger and cause serious injury or even death. That is why people who are taking a lot of prescribed medication should purchase all of it at the same drug store and inform each of their doctors about other medications and even over the counter things they are taking. Often, a pharmacist is needed to cross reference the medications against each other to make sure they are not creating a death dealing concoction.

The second concern is alcohol used in combination with pill taking. Like pills, students have easy access to alcohol. It is in students' homes or in their friends' homes. Alcohol is a depressant and it is poison to the human body. In small amounts, one to two drinks, the worst thing that happens is that the worrier in our brain gets put to sleep and we relax. Our liver will process the alcohol and rid our body of the poison. However, drinking alcohol in combination with taking pills could kill because the body will focus on getting rid of the alcohol first. Since alcohol is more toxic to our bodies than other types of drugs, the brain prioritizes the need to process and eliminate alcohol first; so the pills kill the person. This is how most accidental overdoses that result in death occur. If a kid uses pills then drinks alcohol it places them at risk for death. **Why may some students think using prescription drugs to get high is safe?**

I deviated in my story to talk about another student, Danny. His situation epitomizes what is wrong with public education. Like teachers, administrators are subject to school politics and may fear losing their jobs. Our administrator had been warned not to rock the boat or cause any trouble with Danny's father and he promptly warned us of the same thing. If teachers had not stood together to discipline this child and documented his behaviors then our administrator could have been subject to dismissal. Knowing this, I addressed Danny's inappropriate comment to a girl in class and called his behavior sexual harassment, which it was, and I only hinted Danny's behavior was drug induced. I was able to remove Danny from my classroom so I could teach and the principal did not have to call his parents alleging substance abuse. Therefore, I may have had some culpability in what almost happened to Danny. I gave my principal a way out because I had empathy for his situation; I felt he was being bullied into making special accommodations for this student. **What role do school principals play in educating students?**

Topics for Research

What are the current drug trends in your school district? Are there any laws that prohibit or regulate certain drug sales on the internet? How could parents be involved in creating school policies to identify drug use in students?

Things to do

If you are a parent you must educate your children about the dangers of taking any kind of medication, mixing drugs, or mixing drugs and alcohol. Watch your credit card account on line and follow up on charges that may be related to web purchases. Be aware, children can use your card to purchase drugs via the internet. Set a good example and do not use or exchange medicines in the family prescribed for someone else.

If you are a teacher, be vigilant and persistent in identifying children like Sandy who want to operate outside the rules and who want to have special privileges. The old standard once thought about children just wanting special attention may not be true; they may want a special circumstance that allows them to use drugs.

18. Teen Drug Trends

Although it may not be listed in a teacher's job description, learning to be a drug detective may be necessary. Current statistics for 2009 provided by NIDA show there is a steady increase in drug use among tenth and twelfth grade students and almost twenty-five percent of our high school seniors have used an illicit drug in the last month. In addition, marijuana use has increased in the same two groups to show 15.9 through 20.6 percent of our tenth and twelfth graders have smoked marijuana in the last month (drugabuse.gov/infofacts). Although marijuana use increases may initially appear stalled for the last five years, there was an increase in monthly use when compared to previous reported years, 2007 and 2008. These statistics show teachers need to be concerned that up to one-fourth of their students may be coming to school under the influence of drugs. Large city school districts which draw students from drug and gang infested neighborhoods may experience higher than national averages due to the populations they serve. Therefore, educators who are teaching high risk students should make every effort to stay informed of current teen drug use trends.

In my story, Doctor Sandy was abusing high blood pressure medication which precipitated her need to use the restroom and caused her to have raccoon, dehydrated, looking eyes. Sandy participated in one of the latest forms of drug abuse gaining popularity among young teens. Prescription drugs are easy to obtain and they are easy to hide; the use of these substances may be hard to detect. Students call drug dealers who dispense pills a candy man. According to one former prescription pill addict, he could find anything he wanted by simply roving school hallways to find a candy man. When interviewed by ABC NEWs, Doctor Jason Powers, chief medical officer for Right Step who specializes in drug treatment stated, "It's scary because kids nowadays are using heavy prescription drugs which are just as dangerous if not more so than street drugs...."(ABC NEWS/Health).

According to this interview article, parents and school personnel should all be aware how very easy it is for students to obtain pills and be aware of the games teens are playing with pills.

Students may attend "Pharm parties" where teens drop pills into a common container and pass it around calling it "Trail mix." Teens who use pills this way may call the party experience "Grazing." The above terms: candy man, grazing, trail mix, and "Pharm" parties are terms used by kids to hide their drug use from unsuspecting adults. When school staff is not aware of coded drug expressions students can support each others' use at school. Students may perceive they are putting it over on adults and their teachers are dumb because they are uninformed. Therefore, students will often talk openly using terms unfamiliar to their educators. If teachers are too focused on learning objectives and completing student activities they could easily miss student conversations in passing.

However, it's not only conversational clues that are missed. Students pass drugs and money right under the noses of school personnel if staff is uninformed and focused on schedules instead of student activities. Our students, seventh graders, not only exchanged money in the hall for drugs they became bold enough to pass drugs in the hall. After Sandy was apprehended our prescription medicine problem may have decreased because students knew we would be watching for that form of drug use. That is when I begin to notice students in the lunch room fashioning bubbles out of their plastic lunch wrap. Students would pop these loudly in their mouths and laugh. At first, staff would just tell the students to stop playing and eat their lunches. However, students began to carry bubbles in their pockets outside the lunchroom and that made me suspicious. When I saw a student pop a bubble in his mouth and immediately stop for a drink of water in the hall on the way to class, I suspected the bubble was treated with a chemical like PCP that could have had a bitter taste. I realized students had switched the choice of drugs to avoid detection and I watched closer for proof. That afternoon during my planning time I heard the seventh grade class in the hall and I stepped out in time to see our police officer was escorting the boys to the restroom. I observed while he left them momentarily to check the restroom before allowing them to go in. That's when students openly exchanged bubbles and money in the hall and in front of cameras.

As soon as the officer walked out of the restroom the bubbles were concealed. I hailed the officer, walked down the hall to stand in front of the boys and demanded they empty their pockets of their bubbles. When they did this I handed over the cache to the officer and he looked puzzled. He just scolded the students for acting like babies and later threw them away without drug testing them. Although I did not get the action I expected from the resource officer, student drug use was confronted and the look on students' faces was priceless when he took their stuff. However, when our RSO officer failed to drug test the bubbles I realized that teachers are not the only ones who may be naive about student drug use. In absence of proof I simply told the students that the whole staff had been made aware that their bubble inventions could contain a liquid drug and any student found in possession of a bubble could face serious consequences. Students quit making bubbles.

I continued to notify all my classes that I was watching for students who might be bringing drugs to school and every time we discovered our students were using a different way to get high I assigned my students research on their drug of choice. They needed to know what the effects were on their bodies and minds. This strategy agrees with NIDA's (National Institute on Drug Abuse), second prevention principle which calls for addressing all forms of drug abuse. Prevention education has to be ongoing with students and target community trends to be effective. (drugabuse. gov/). The steps I took constitute a deterrent strategy which used direct confrontation to limit student drug use at school. Basically, this strategy works because students become aware school personnel are observing their behaviors, listening to what they are saying, and identifying the drugs students are using.

Many schools may need to formulate a new drug-deterrent policy in their schools, one that requires all school staff to become responsible for identifying student drug use. It could read something like this: Since it is our job to keep students safe and students are currently risking their health, safety, and their education to use drugs, we are seeking to eliminate drug use from our schools. We are <u>not</u> going to search students' persons or possessions for drugs but will use student behaviors and classroom performance as our indicators. If students are: failing school, having poor attendance, wanting to sleep in class or are being hyper in class, causing classroom disruptions, behaving in disrespectful ways toward themselves, fellow students, or school staff, and they are not following our school rules then students will be suspect and they will be asked to take a drug test.

(Student identification and consequences have been discussed in an earlier strategy. These could be listed in school policy handouts). All our educators are required to take substance abuse prevention training and all personnel will be watching for signs of student drug use.

This prevention effort which confronts student drug use based on class room performances and behaviors coupled with a "No refusal" policy discussed in an earlier strategy would allow educators to refer all students for drug testing who manifest indicators and all students would become aware they could be suspect. I believe that students' behavior and grades would improve and drug use could be eliminated from our schools. On the other hand, as long as students think teachers and administrators are unaware of their drug use at school, it will continue and they will get bolder in their displays of use. An example of this boldness was seen in my story where our seventh grade students openly passed money in front of hallway cameras and in the presence of their teachers.

Let's review what we have discovered about teachers keeping fresh on student drug use. Teachers need to: keep informed about current drug trends, they need to listen closely for unfamiliar words or terms that students use, they need to share information pertinent to student drug use with all staff, they need to watch for common school materials used by students in different ways (plastic lunch-wrap bubbles), they need to report unusual student behaviors in the classrooms and hallways, and teachers need to anticipate that students will change their drug choice when they are discovered because when deterred from one kind of drug activity students will just "Switch up" to use something else. Most important, every teacher should assume some students are going to be coming to school under the influence and some students, even in an alternative education program, will be using drugs while at school. Educators who are teaching at inner city schools may need to be more aware than other educators because their student populations may reflect higher incident rates of substance abuse. Teachers need to confront students about their drug use and they need to stay informed.

Every school district needs to hire a community liaison, drug prevention educator. The ability of teachers and administrators to e-mail or pick up the phone and contact a district person to ask information about student drug use would be helpful. A community liaison would coordinate prevention efforts with the police department and other agencies, widen and initiate substance abuse education training for district personnel, and could supervise all substance abuse initiatives like drug counseling and referrals for treatment. This position could possibly be grant funded by several sources and the right person in this job could close the gap between research and our prevention efforts. This disparity between research and practice has been identified as problematic by the Education Development Center (edc.org/newsroom/articles/).

We need to get serious about eliminating drugs from our schools and we need resources to do that. Every large school district should have a substance abuse community liaison director to act as a resource for teachers and administrators. Most teachers may not even consider that drug dealing and drug using is going on in their schools or in their classrooms. I would have been totally unaware of students' drug activities if I had not worked in other social service fields before returning to teaching. Like the teacher in the hall I might have said, "Why you all got your money out? Put your money away." This teacher was blind to students purchasing drugs in the hallway right under her nose.

Today, our public school teachers may be blind to student drug use because educators' minds do not work that way. Teachers can be so focused on preparing lessons and teaching the state objectives that we may forget our efforts could be in vain if students have diminished consciousness in the class room. Let's be honest, ever since Helen Keller was taught how to read, teachers have been burdened with the miracle worker expectation and the public at large is still expecting miracles from us. We are expected to teach some students who are not capable of learning because of their drug impairments and we are often punished by public opinion when these same kids don't learn.

As educators, our job today is to teach students academics even when they have limited mental awareness of their surroundings or purpose in the classroom. We need a miracle to do this! In a perfect world we would get drugs out of our schools but if we can't then we need to limit their influence by implementing deterrent strategies. Our teachers need trained to identify student drug use and they need the latitude to refer any student who demonstrates behaviors which disrupt learning for drug testing. Teachers need help doing this and school districts can help by initiating new student drug identification policies, by providing the training and support teachers need, and by employing a community drug prevention liaison to coordinate the services for the entire district.

References and Resources

"Popping Pills Latest Trend in Teen drug Abuse," ABC NEWS; abcnews. go.com/Health/story?id=4273683&page=2

"Preventing drug Abuse among Children and Adolescents, Prevention Principles' and "Applying Prevention Principles to Drug Abuse Prevention Programs," and "High School and Youth Trends," National Institute on drug Abuse; drugabuse.gov/

"Deterring alcohol and drug use among middle school and high school students," Education Development Center; edc.org/newsroom/articles/ deterring_alcohol_and_drug_use_among_middle_a...

19. Devil Woman

Maria was a twelve year old, chubby-cheeked cherub in the seventh grade. She had beautiful bronze toned, creamy soft skin, heavily-lashed, large expressive eyes, and amazing straight, gleaming-white teeth …that I saw often. She was always talking! The first day this student spent in my class was an exasperating experience for me. Not only did I halt class instruction twice to give Maria correction but I also had to place her in the hall so the other students could hear what I was saying! On her first offense, I had Maria stand and apologize to both myself and her classmates. As I pointed to the class discipline poster on the wall, I informed Maria if she did not apologize and stop talking during instruction time she would be removed from the class and she would have to stay after school. She did a decent job apologizing after I assured her, students were allowed to talk softly during their seat work time. However, while I was directing students to start their practice activity Maria tried to initiate conversations with students around her once again and began loudly laughing and talking. This time I informed Maria she would be staying with me after school and she began a tirade accompanied by angry looks and Spanish swear words. At that point, I informed Maria that she had to go stand in the hall but she responded by placing her arms across her chest and by sticking out her lip in a pouty baby fashion. Her actions indicated to me, Maria was reluctant to follow my instruction or to go into the hall.

So, I walked to her desk and made her uncomfortable with my close proximity until she relented. As she bounded toward the hallway, she halted momentarily and gazed over her shoulder with a proud look. Maria had succeeded in getting set out of class on her first day of attendance and I had the distinct feeling she had wanted that to happen. Her victory expression reminded me of fox who had been chased from the hen house still carrying a squawking victim in its mouth and though retreating, stopped at a semi-safe distance to lift its leg and mark its territory. That overconfident appearance caused me to initiate a hot pursuit. Maria had stolen some of my class instruction time and she was not going to get away with it. Once in the hall, I showed Maria where to stand so I could observe her for the next two to three minutes while I gave instructions to the other students. I told Maria when her classmates began their seat work activity I would call her back into the room and I would work individually with her. I warned her not to wander or peek in other rooms on our hall because other teachers would view that behavior as disruptive and she could possibly receive more discipline from them.

After separating Maria, I turned my attention to the class; I gave directions, divided my remaining students into work groups, and passed out homework. True to my word it only took about three minutes. However, during that short time, Maria had taunted me in the hall by pretending she was going to leave the area. She would lead a little with one foot like she was preparing to flee then she would hop back in place and laugh. Her antics continued until she became bored with her game. Then, she boldly proceeded to press her face up against the door glass of an adjoining classroom while making a pig-nosed face at an unsuspecting teacher. Of course, the classroom was disrupted when students burst into laughter and they gave away Maria's position. Maria's became aware her target for mischief was not amused as the teacher flew out of her door and backed Maria toward the opposite wall assaulting her with stern words of warning. I almost felt sorry for the wide-eyed Maria until I realized she had just discovered which teacher might have a short fuse today. Maria confirmed my suspicion by bending over and emitting loud squeals of laughter while holding her sides until her face reddened. The dismayed teacher looked puzzled and flashed me a, "What do we do now" look. I gave a discreet head side-jerk and rolled my eyes in Maria's direction letting her know our new student would be challenging. After assuring my co-worker that our jovial seventh grader, Maria, would be duly punished I had a sobering thought, "What if Maria does not fear consequences?" Then I answered myself, "She would be a teacher's worst nightmare." As I returned my wayward student into the classroom I hoped my insight was not prophetic.

From the actions this student demonstrated on her very first day, I could tell Maria was determined not only to wrestle away teachers' classroom control but she also planned to make fun of her educators while tormenting them. The fact that Maria had not demonstrated any remorse for her behavior when confronted by my fellow teacher and had instead, laughed in her face evidenced Maria's lack of respect for adults. The only thing that I had seen work so far with Maria was proximity control; she had left my room when I moved close to her desk and she had backed across the hall when the other teacher approached her. From the experience I had already gained teaching baby gangsters I knew that approaching a student too quickly and getting too close could evoke an undesired physical response. However, Maria had backed away quickly like she expected to be hit and seeing her do that made me think I should not use that approach again.

Once back in my room, I offered Maria a reward and I told her if we finished the science class orientation within the next ten minutes then she would be able to join a group, work on her daily processing activity with other students, and she would be able to go with her classmates to the next period. As I gained her attention, I assumed this strategy worked because Maria highly desired the attention of other students. Next, I set Maria off to the side of my desk with her back to the rest of the students and her face toward the discipline and rewards posters. I could tell Maria was uncomfortable with a face off and noticed that her body tensed, her fingers made a fist, and she looked angry. I moved my chair a little farther away from Maria to retrieve an orientation guide and stretched to hand it back to her. I left my chair in its farthest away position in an effort to make her more comfortable. I began by asking Maria what her favorite subject was in school. She just shrugged her shoulders. Then I asked her if she remembered what she last studied in science and she replied, "Nothing" and "I have been in lock up."

I told Maria that we had a lot of catching up to do before she transferred back to her home school and since she was staying this afternoon, we could begin today. Maria whined and said she couldn't stay after school because her mother was picking her up and she would be mad at her if she was made to wait. She broadened her tale to include a mandatory meeting with her probation officer that would cause her to go back to jail if missed. Of course I had heard it all before. Maria's expression changed from "I'm playing you and enjoying it" to "Au-oh you got me" when I informed her that I would be calling her mother to verify the appointment. I assured my new student that if she did have an appointment with her probation officer then I could call that person as well and explain that Maria had to stay after school for discipline reasons.

My last statement was met with, "Please, Miss, please ... I will do anything you say." Now that I knew what motivated Maria, a call to her probation officer, the trick would be transferring her compliance to rules which might be born out of her desire to avoid negatives to her willing participation based on her desire to receive positive reinforcements. The methods that I knew worked best with students like Maria were building a relationship based on mutual respect and creating a safe and predictable learning environment. For the next ten minutes, I began building a relationship with Maria while I explained my classroom behavior expectations, classroom structure, and the academic requirements. Acquiescence to our middle school program and my classroom expectations would help Maria feel safe. Her environment should become more predictable as she watched me implement the same classroom structure every day and as she watched me discipline all my students in the same way.

While I talked to my new student, an occasional whisper could be heard by other students in their study groups as they tried to help each other with their assigned seat work. I congratulated myself on the audible exchanges because the students were focused on their assignment that morning and I did not hear one illicit drug related comment. The absence of street talk made me realize how far this particular group of students had come in the past few weeks and I was thankful they had passed through the program adjustment period because I was sure these kids would set a good example for Maria. I heaved myself up from the desk chair realizing I would find out soon enough as I sent Maria to a well engaged study group.

When Maria tried to distract other students from their activity they kept their eyes on their papers and one of the students said, "We have to use this time to finish our work. I want to win the Good Apple Award." He looked up at me and said, "Isn't that right Miss OG? I can win it this week?"

I replied, "Yes, you are eligible for the award this week. You have been doing good work in science class."

He replied, "Man, I can't believe it! I ain't never had no good grade in science before."

The other students didn't notice or mind his grammatical errors and I chose not to correct him. Somehow it just seemed wrong to give Billy a negative when his esteem was just beginning to increase. So, I chose to model correct grammar, as best I could, and leave grammatical corrections to the English teacher. Hopefully, if we both did our jobs right, the students would learn to speak good English and discover an ability to do science. Besides, this little guy was working his head off for me and his enthusiasm was contagious to other less performance-orientated students. Sometimes all it took was one student who other students thought was dumb, to start making good grades and receiving awards, to shame them into a classroom competition. I admired this little guy's determination because once Billy was encouraged and met with a little success he didn't quit or manifest the "I've done that and been there" attitude which can halt some students' progress. Billy was dedicated to being the top student in my class, and he was not going to let Maria or anyone else stand in his way. Maria would have to do her work in his group.

As class ended, I announced that it was time for the students to write down something they had learned today on their self-evaluation forms and they needed to check off the work they completed on their daily assignment sheet. I reminded the students that both of these forms showed me the amount of learning they accomplished and that both had to be filled out fully to get a good daily grade. As soon as students finished their paper work, I had them line up in single file to transition to the next class. However, I noticed after I made the students ready that Maria had moved in line to stand behind a boy who was delicate looking and small for this age. I pulled her out of her preferred location and returned Maria to the first position I had chosen for her as I instructed, "New students always walk at the front of the line."

When coach arrived he commented about having a new student, I introduced him to Maria, and I quickly added, "She will be staying with me after school today." My clue gave Coach a heads up and emphasized his need to watch our new fledgling closely. Coach signified he got my hint by winking one eye, making a clicking sound with his tongue, posting a raised thumb. I watched as Maria followed coach doggedly down the hall and I hoped he would have better luck with this young lady than I had that morning. However, our new student began to harass Coach no more than twenty yards from my door. Maria slowed the line down when she strained to see the whereabouts of her new interest behind her, Lonnie, and all the students piled up against one another during these unscheduled halts. Twice Coach stopped the procession and probably realized his efforts where futile because he next placed Maria on the opposite side of the hall, to walk by herself, in front of him. Later that same morning, Maria was set out of PE because she had been caught inappropriately touching Lonnie and may have hurt him when she grabbed and squeezed his private parts.

She was put out of school for the rest of the day, her mother picked her up early, and I did not get to keep Maria after school as I had promised. I wrote myself a note, "Don't forget! Maria owes you time and call her mother," at the top of my 'To do list' for the next day. First thing in the morning, Maria was sent to the ISS (In School Suspension) room when she walked into the building. Her assignment to ISS for three days was part of the discipline she received for her misdeed the day before. Our staff reacted quickly to correct student misbehaviors that mirrored sexual harassment in the adult world and inappropriate or sexual touching was not allowed. All of the staff knew our middle school students were highly sexualized and some were already parents. Teaching these children how to respect their own bodies and appropriately interact with other students was an awesome task. While mulling over Maria's actions on the previous day, I decided that other students would need some additional instruction on this matter; her deed reminded me I had yet not covered that issue with my current groups of students.

I often walked a dangerous tightrope in our personal and social responsibility class teaching on such topics. Unofficially, our administration approved of the teachers talking to students about risk factors like becoming parents to soon, sexual harassment, and the physical effects of drugs on the human reproduction systems. However, all the staff knew which subjects were dangerous to discuss with students and which ones could lead to a teacher being disciplined or even fired. For this reason, some teachers avoided these subjects all together. However, as a science teacher who was teaching human anatomy I decided what my students needed to know about their bodies went beyond form and function to include personal responsibilities and consequences. I always consulted with our school administrators or counselors when a topic was a particularly delicate one and I made student handouts available for review.

Sometimes, it was difficult managing discussions because most students knew only street language and wanted to talk about things using the slang terms with which they were familiar but I insisted that students use acceptable scientific words when asking questions. For this reason, I had created a question box for those students who either did not know the scientific terms or who were too shy to ask questions. I told the students, if I feel it would be inappropriate for me to answer your question in the classroom then I will refer you to the school nurse. I shuddered while thinking about the questions Maria might ask in class just to get attention and what gross things she might say just to make the other students laugh. I reasoned if she was bold enough to touch inappropriately she would be bold enough to ask inappropriate questions in class. I shook off the foreboding feeling and headed for the ISS room with Maria's work for the day.

Maria smiled broadly when she saw me walk in and reminded me that she didn't have to stay after school with me because she had been sent home. I replied, "Yes, but don't worry, dear, you can stay this afternoon. I have already called your mother and she knows to pick you up later."

Maria pushed out her bottom lip like she was going to cry and then suddenly tilted back her head and rewarded me with her now familiar loud cackle. "Alright Miss OG. See you then."

I winked at Maria on the way out of the room and thought to myself, "That went well and she even used the name the other students have given me." Apparently, Maria had been talking to her class mates and she had received an unofficial orientation about her teachers. I sighed, "Hopefully, they had informed Maria that I ran my classroom and that the students would never be in charge." I was thankful for the percentage of students in my charge that liked studying science and the unofficial communication between students seemed to always work in my favor. Even difficult students had shaped up in my class to become decent science students so I had hope for Maria.

Off and on for the next two weeks, Maria was kept after school by every other middle school teacher at least once and she spent a couple of more days in ISS for various misdeeds. However, she was showing signs of adjusting to my classroom structure and she had made fast friends with the boy, Lonnie, whom she had molested on her first day. I was a little afraid of this new friendship because Lonnie had been an A student in science, was respectful, and had excellent behavior in class. I theorized it could go either way; he could pull Maria up or she could pull his class room performance down. The good news was that Lonnie was at the end of his stay and could be leaving soon. I would be relieved when that happened because I did not want this new found friendship to lessen his interest and performance in school.

I was pleasantly surprised at the end of the second week of Maria's stay when I passed back learning packets to the students for the previous week's work. When I looked again at Maria's weekly grade average I thought, "Maybe this type of school just might work for Maria." I had placed a red apple stamp in the right hand corner on her learning packet and she had received a grade of 86%. To my amazement Maria was following instructions, completing most of her work, and responding positively to my classroom management style. However, the ability to make good grades did not seem to impress Maria. There was absolutely no recognizable expression on her face or emotional reaction generated when Maria received her graded work. I had looked up Maria's grades from her home school and they had been very low. For this reason, I didn't understand why Maria had not let out a holler of excitement; she was loud every other time over things that were not nearly as important.

I puzzled to myself, "One of the most important things I do for my students is to show them their own true abilities and help them gain confidence so they can succeed academically when they return to their home schools. Usually, my students act totally surprised and will get more than a little excited about their good grades they receive in science for the first time." I was truly amazed by the apparent disinterest Maria demonstrated because students usually reacted strongly to their own achievements and to my classroom rewards system. That is when I realized Maria did not fully understand the reward system we talked about on her first day. Today she would find out more and if I was lucky then she would be motivated to continue her good work.

I continued to pass out other students' work around Maria while observing her behavior. Several kids were buzzing back and forth while sharing their earned grades. Maria finally seemed to notice the excitement and asked, "What does the apple mean?" I started to explain but stopped because Billy jumped in with great excitement to share what he knew with Maria. I decided to listen to my student's explanation.

"If you get two red apples you're eligible for the Good Apple Award. Your name goes on the tree in the hall and you earn one extra good day. It means you get out of alternative school one day sooner. I forgot what the yellow apple means," the perplexed student offered as he looked to me for an explanation.

I hurriedly replied, "Don't forget one apple on the tree represents two weeks of good grades and classroom behavior and... you can only earn an apple on the tree if your other middle school teachers have recommend you for the award. That means you must be passing their classes and have good behavior for them too. The yellow apple signifies the Golden Apple Award and it means that you have had good behavior and an average of 85% for four weeks in row in science. When that happens, I send a good news message to our student counselor notifying her of your stellar accomplishment. Every Monday the principal and counselor meet to discuss which students are eligible for release. They know the Golden Apple Award is very special and it shows that students are doing well in our program.

Maria groused, "Grades don't matter. My mommy doesn't love me. She says I am bad and the devil has me. She doesn't care if I get good grades."

My heart began stinging as if a literal arrow had plunged deep within the muscle. I replied, "Maria grades should matter the most to you. You are a very smart girl and if you get an education you will have a good life when you grow up."

Looking down at her desk Maria responded, "What's the use? I'm going to die soon." She flopped her head down dramatically on the desk then quickly jerked up it up again to look me directly in the eyes and said, "Ms. Gifford do you love me?"

There was a slight awkward silence but I quickly found my voice and answered, "I love all my students. Of course, I love you."

She continued, "You would be sad and cry when I die? That is good. Someone will cry for me." The other students were intently listening and I wanted to redirect the conversation but I needed to make sure Maria was not planning to hurt herself. I had never seen this melancholy attitude in her before now and I sort of wished the old ornery Maria I knew would come back. Maria's dark mood modified once again and this time she became highly animated while galloping the fingers of both her hands across the top of her desk saying, "Oh! Miss OG, I run from the bus to my apartment." Then Maria proclaimed as she shook her head from side to side and looked down, "I'm soooooo...scared!"

I asked, "What are you afraid of Maria?"

"That they'll shoot me or rape me," she vehemently declared while nodding her head up and down verifying the truth of her statement by her actions. Now her words tumbled out like waters breaking through a dam and she continued, "I think about dying all the time. I dream about dying. It makes me nervous and I shake." Maria held out her hands and they were visibly shaking. Next, Maria demonstrated with great flair an effort to control her shaking limbs as she growled "Ohhhh....," and folded her arms across her chest while promptly tucking one hand under each of her arm pits. Maria gazed upward and while looking at the ceiling she seemed to regain control. She clammed up sharing her private information just as quickly as she had released it. Again ... there was an awkward silence.

Everyone had been intensely listening for what Maria might say next but she didn't offer anything and the class was left hanging until a male student at the back of the room said, "Where you stay, girl?" Maria gave the name of her apartment complex and he proclaimed, "I'd run too if I lived there, Miss OG. Hey, you know ....? He got shot over there. He got a bullet scar on his leg; it look nasty."

I had to get the students back to learning science but now I was a little shaken because I knew the student that had been wounded. He had been in my class the previous year and it was the first I had heard of the unfortunate event. I was thankful the boy lived because some of our other students had not been so lucky. Every Friday, every holiday and at the end of each school year I would always remind the students to be smart when they were out on the streets and not to take chances which could result in them being injured. I worried and I prayed for the safety of my inner city, baby gangsters because they were just children who were surviving their drug and crime infested neighborhoods the best way they could.

Momentarily, I was lost in deep thought until I realized my face reflected my heartfelt sadness. My mind brought me back to the classroom and the tasks at hand but the reality of my students' living situations continued to weigh heavy on my heart. Even though witnessing violence was a normal occurrence for inner city children I thought my young students should never have to experience being a victim of violence themselves. Now, not only were they victims but it appeared they anticipated being victimized to the point of incessant worry. Maria's testimony had initiated my insight into the lives of all my students and had witnessed the hidden fears with which many of them lived daily. Even though I realized fear could help these kids survive on the streets if it caused them to be cautious and street smart, I knew those same fears could cripple my students' hope for a future. Experiencing daily fear could cause some of these kids to develop anxiety disorders and could lead to serious mental health issues. Now, I was afraid Maria might be one of those students whose fragile mental health was cracking because she witnessed her anxiety in a dramatic, uncensored way.

I needed to address this situation with my students but I could not do it during core instruction so I pulled my thoughts together and redirected the group, "Class we can talk more about his subject during our elective class this afternoon. Remind me what we were talking about when you come in and I will allow time to discuss things we can do to help us feel safe in our neighborhoods. For now, let's turn our attention to our assignment sheets and begin working. Some of you are getting very close to earning that Golden Apple Award."

Immediately, the rest of the students prepared for instruction. Maria was quiet for a while during my lecture time but as soon as seat work began she tried to draw other students off task. I asked her to step out in the hall with me and explained, "You are not in trouble this time; I just wanted to talk to you a minute." With the door open and one eye on the class I spoke softly to Maria and told her I was concerned about what she had shared in class and I wanted her to talk to Miss Lopez, our counselor. Maria said she already saw a counselor due to her probation orders. I assured Maria that our counselor was someone she could talk to more often at school and she would not have to wait for a weekly appointment. I finished by telling Maria, "It seems like something is bothering you today. I do not want you to feel sad and I want you to earn a good day so I will send the counselor to you and you can decide if you want to talk to her about anything." Maria nodded and said ok, maybe she would talk.

As soon as class ended, I called the counselor and told her Maria just went to PE and it would be a good time to pull her in for an initial evaluation. I repeated the comments Maria had made in my classroom and asked the counselor to assess Maria for possible suicide expressions. Since, I had worked as a therapist in the past I was alerted to Maria's need for additional support by the statements she made in class. Maria was showing signs of depression and anxiety and it sounded like she did not have a good relationship with her mother. However, I knew sometimes young people were just over dramatic, would fabricate information to gain attention, and that Maria might just be one of those kids. Whatever her problems were I was glad I did not have to figure it out by myself and that I had the support of a school counselor. Maintaining control of the classroom and teaching Maria were enough of a challenge and I needed the professional help of our other staff to ensure her safety. I was concerned about this twelve year old child's possible suicide expression.

I remembered a student suicide my second year teaching at the alternative school. The young man was fourteen and he had only been in my class twice. Due to his lack of attendance, I had never really gotten to know Jay. Several of the students went to his funeral and told me he had hung himself because his girlfriend dumped him for another guy. The next week after Jay's death students wanted to talk about his suicide in our personal issues class so we talked about other choices Jay could have made. I asked, "What would have been another choice for Jay?"

One of the boys replied, "Go find another girl! No one should kill themselves over a girl."

I asked the students if they thought drug or alcohol use might have influenced their friend's decision and they said Jay was a heavy pot user and sometimes smoking can make you feel sad and tired. I invited the students to tell about other negative consequences they knew which might have resulted from a decision they or someone else had made while under the influence. Then, I asked my students to promise me the next time they were getting ready to make an important decision and they had been using alcohol or some other drug they would ask themselves, am I making the decision or is alcohol or the drug choosing for me? After that discussion, I promised myself that I would ever be vigilant in identifying students who expressed low self worth and demonstrated unpredictable changes in their mood that might come from drug use.

Now, I was beginning to wonder if Maria was using drugs because I had never seen her act so melancholy before that day. I was glad that Maria felt safe enough in my classroom to share her feelings but I knew her security was not due to just the classroom structure I provided or due to the relationship I was building with her. Instead, it was due to the other students sharing fear as a common denominator. That afternoon, when I let students vent about their feeling of being unsafe in their neighborhoods, I learned more than I what really wanted to know about the lives of my students. The class had a simple format and I initiated the discussion by sharing an incident about a time when I felt unsafe and let the students tell me what they would have done in my situation. Next, students shared their neighborhood experiences and we discussed choices they could make which might keep them safe. I learned enough that day in our elective class to make my prayers extra long that night and every night thereafter for the physical safety of my seventh grade, twelve to fourteen year old students.

In the following week concerns for Maria's physical safety and mental health turned to apprehensions about her ability to sustain academic success in my room. While Lonnie's classroom performance remained stable Maria's started slipping. Maria was still working in my class but she was making a minimal effort and I knew permission to talk during work group time was the only positive motivator she was responding to in class. So, I integrated another positive and allowed Maria to become a classroom helper. This gave her an opportunity to use her big muscles and seemed to alleviate some of the nervous movements she demonstrated when she was sitting. In addition, I thought being a classroom helper would serve as a bonding mechanism; if Maria felt like she belonged and was an important member of the class then she might manage her own behavior better.

At that point, Maria was only mildly interfering with other student's learning but I saw signs that some were beginning to see Maria's presence as an annoyance in class. This group of students wanted good grades and recognition for their accomplishments and they did not always have patience with Maria when she attempted to clown. They began to distance themselves from Maria by openly requesting she not be assigned to their work groups. I did not want the other kids to push Maria away because it appeared she had rejection issues already with the adults in her life and peer relationships might be her only emotional stabilizing influence. However, I knew if Maria wanted to be accepted by the other students she would have to respect their rights to get an education. I reasoned, "If Maria performed her class chores well then her peers might perceive she was helping them and they might be a little more tolerant of her behavior."

Maria did intensely care about the other students. She did not make fun of other kids or pick fights with them and she had befriended a non-English speaking girl who other classmates totally rejected. To her credit, Maria allowed herself to be Sue's target and thought it was funny when Sue did sneaky things to her. Sue would pinch her, steal her pencils, and hide her worksheets. Maria laughed at her and said Sue was just a little loco and she liked her for that reason. I knew Sue's mischievousness was probably due to her boredom because she knew very little English and I knew very little Spanish. Maria spoke both languages and although I was apprehensive about Maria's trustworthiness, she became a classroom translator for this student because none of the other kids liked Sue and did not want to help her.

Now Maria had two new tasks, classroom helper and translator, and I had a good reason not to assign her to other groups which made other students in class happy. Maria always partnered with Sue and things really calmed down as Maria was given a reason to talk in class to another student. For about one week, Maria hardly noticed her grades were improving again and I dreaded the day when she became aware. I feared Maria's self-defeating behaviors would return when her grades improved. It was evident that Maria had the potential to be a leader and she began to really bond with our class. Then Sue went back to Mexico and Maria received another better than 85% weekly average which made her eligible for the red apple award. What I suspected was true; Maria was not happy about her grades or Sue's leaving and her behavior worsened.

My relationship with Maria was better on some days than others; she continued to ask me several times if I loved her and each time I would reply I love all of my students and of course I love you. However, I knew Maria's need to hear a verbal expression of my affection could have professionally embarrassed me. I was sure my current supervisor would think I was too soft on the students and acting unprofessional when I responded to Maria the way I did. Maria was much older than most students who needed that kind of reassurance; usually twelve year olds do not ask their teachers if they love them. There was an unexpected side effect to Maria's attention seeking behavior in my class I had not anticipated. Two or three more students began walking in my class, even one eighth boy did this, and after saying good morning said, "I love you, Mrs. Gifford."

I had discovered that many of our students were emotionally immature and often needed to regress in their teacher-student relationships before they could go forward and act age appropriate. So, I understood what was happening but my work assignment in a secular school gave me pause. I felt like I was coming awfully close to teetering off that tightrope I walked daily as a teacher at the alternative school. My students were not even supposed to like me... let alone love me! In all honesty, I did love my students and I could have taken anyone of them home and raised them as my own. They were just kids who needed to feel safe so they could grow up, get an education, and make something useful out of their lives. Yes, in spite of the crimes they committed, the drugs they took, and the sexual relationships they had, most of our students were just little children and not teenagers at all.

It never ceased to amaze me how thirteen or fourteen year old hardened gangland soldiers who were sporting ankle monitors for felony like crimes they committed, dissolved into baby talking five year olds when I presented them with a coloring page as a reward for a job well done. I learned that all my students whether they were obnoxious, pugnacious, or gangland rebels needed the reassurance of safety in the classroom before they could concentrate on learning. It became evident to me their safety was dependent upon receiving reassurance from me that I truly cared for them and their motivation to learn resulted from the relationship I built with them. As I reflected on student achievement, I realized I had a problem developing a teacher-student relationship with Maria. I could not sustain her good classroom performance because she demonstrated inconsistency in her needs. She would seek attention from me then push me away through her bad behavior. I thought her relationship with her mother was hindering Maria's relationship with her teachers and that Maria wanted to fail because she was familiar with failure and rejection.

Other middle school teachers complained they were over her behavior and they were confronted with an obnoxious Maria in their classrooms. She played games with these teachers to see if she could rustle control of their environments. Teachers complained Maria's behavior was out of control and she was leading other students astray. I thought Maria knew exactly she was doing and she was not out of control; she had actually gained control by getting other student's attention and by disrupting learning. When Maria was in one of those moods, I expected her to yell "Boots and saddles" as she began herding other students in class toward a climatic cliff of disobedience and classroom disruption.

Some days I could hear her all the way down the hall cursing or talking back to staff. I saw Maria less often in my class as her behavior worsened because she ended up being assigned to the ISS room in the morning before reaching my class later in the day. Maria seemed to be almost in a panic state as she gained more control through terrorizing our school staff and I reasoned that she no longer felt safe because adults did not appear to be in control. I thought Maria was wildly modulating between wanting to control things so she could get her attention fix from other students and wanting the adults to be in control so she would feel safe. I'm not sure that Maria knew what she wanted; I reasoned her home environment must have been chaotic because she seemed most comfortable in chaos.

Other students had told me Maria's mother was a drug dealer and certainly that would support my chaotic life style theory. The information students shared with me made me think Maria could be using drugs because she might have easy access to the stuff. I began to investigate a little about Maria's home life and I conference with our assistant principal and counselor while trying to figure out if any adult might know what our students were saying was true. During one of my conferences with other staff members I found out that Maria had been sent to the juvenile justice system prior to coming to our school for physically fighting with her mom and that the altercation was the result of Maria stealing her mother's money. I reasoned if Maria was trying to reproduce a family pattern of interaction between herself and her female teachers then we all needed to be concerned. Family violence was an ingredient that had not yet been poured into the mix but Maria had threatened to hit one teacher. I began to process this student's quick mood shifts and anxious behavior seeking to discover a drug induced behavior pattern. I worried that Maria's use of drugs could blur her boundaries enough and cause her to assault one of us.

Her relationships with the other teachers seemed to be deteriorating and I often saw Maria standing in the common hall where she had been set out of class because she could not be sent to the ISS room every day. However, the general consensus was that middle school teachers could not teach and manage the behaviors of other students unless Maria, one lone student, was absent from the classroom. I did sympathize because my progress managing her behavior had not been stellar. When interacting with her, I knew I could lose all the progress I had made within a twinkle of an eye or a sudden shift in her mood. My patience was running thin along with my energy reserves for the constant check and check-mate game we were playing in my classroom on those rare occasions when she was present. I had learned to place Maria's desk facing the wall for a few minutes and give her an opportunity to calm down before allowing her to rejoin the group. I would give her a chance to apologize and get her behavior under control before I took any other discipline measures because I wanted her to stop herself and manage her own behavior. If she was really bad then I would take away her PE time and send her to ISS just for that one period. I was consistent in my response to her and it seemed to help. Other teachers were trying to find methods in their classes that worked with this difficult student and I have to admit, they couldn't find many options.

I had seen Maria go into the bathroom unsupervised when other teachers had placed her outside their doors, even for short periods of time. Since the bathroom was a place where drugs could be hid and used by students I reasoned Maria's unscheduled bathroom breaks explained why her behavior became more outrageous as the day progressed. I thought she purposely was getting sent of class out so she could sneak into the bathroom unsupervised and use whatever drug she had stashed. Since I had other classes going on in my room, I could not supervise her; all I could do was report what I had seen to other teachers. Due to her unscheduled morning restroom breaks, afternoon was not a good time of day to have science class with Maria. She was frenzied by the time she got to my class. I guessed other teachers thought I had Maria's behavior under control because I did not place her in the hall but I was only being courteous to them because I did not want her to disrupt their classes.

One exasperated teacher asked me how I was managing Maria and I replied, "I have made Maria into a classroom helper. She passes out folders and picks up folders, sets up the video and does other things I find for her to do. She only gets to do these jobs and get out of her seat if her behavior during class has been good the day before. Also, she has to be quiet when I am giving instruction to gain talk time during group work at the end of class. I have explained to Maria that the group work is for processing what the teacher has taught during instruction time and if the students are interrupted by her behavior, they can't learn enough to do the group processing activities. Therefore, the students would have to stay in their seats to get individual help and work quietly alone. This seems to work somewhat for me. When she is having a bad day I remove her from the group by having her turn her desk to the wall. If she regains her composure and apologizes to the group she can have another opportunity to rejoin the class. I will not put her in hall because I cannot supervise her there and I have seen her wander into the restroom when sent out by other teachers. However, she is only doing minimum work and not as much as in the beginning. As long as she is not obstructing learning for the other children and is making a reasonable small effort to learn I am satisfied. She is a difficult student to motivate and she has erratic behaviors which lead me to wonder about drug use. The other students we have now do help keep her focused."

"They are a good group," my co-worker replied, "But those seventh graders will be leaving in another week. If we don't get a handle on Maria's behavior soon she will ruin our chances of teaching the next group coming in."

I agreed. Most students spent thirty school days with us or time equal to one six weeks grading period. However, if a student was placed in ISS (In School Suspension) their days did not count toward the total thirty days. Maria was one of the students who were spending a lot of time in ISS and her time in our alternative program was being extended due to her classroom behavior. I was not kidding myself; Maria's behavior in my classroom was being controlled as much by her peers' acquiescence to the program as by my classroom management techniques. Since gaining quick compliance to our program was important, it was imperative that the current students model appropriate behaviors for new students. Maria was not going to help us transition new students! If she continued to challenge our structure in front of new students coming next week then these transfers would think our program was a joke. We would lose control and metaphorically speaking, "The inmates would run the prison."

In an effort to gain better understanding of Maria's behaviors I began to make notes about the physical characteristics she exhibited: the way she moved, her moods, her shaking, her talkative manner, and her eyes which seemed to shine brighter on days when she was the most hyper. Something clicked for me and pointed toward a specific drug use. I began looking closer for any indication Maria was under the influence of drugs.

A child like Maria could also be suffering post traumatic stress from living daily in fear for her life or she could have an inherited mental illness like a bi-polar disorder. Any one of those things could have explained her moodiness, lack of ability to concentrate, and hyper behavior. If she was using drugs more than likely the drug was a stimulant, perhaps even cocaine. I originally questioned my own discernment when that thought came to the forefront of my mind and I argued with myself saying out loud "This is a twelve year old kid!" However, I had fifteen years experience working with populations that used all types of drugs and Maria's behaviors indicated cocaine was her logical drug use choice. Besides, I knew the drug was easily obtained by our kids.

A crack rock could be purchased for as little as five dollars and if Maria's mother was a drug dealer she might even have access to the powder which would be easy to sneak into school. I was especially concerned about our students using uppers like Cocaine because teenagers tend to be more physically active than adults and even healthy kids can have heart attacks while using cocaine and exercising. If Maria had been using cocaine then ran in PE class the results could be disastrous. I thought to myself, "Maybe it was a good thing I sent Maria to the ISS room instead of PE and denied her participation in that class on days she was especially hyper."

Now, I was beginning to have fewer times to interact with Maria; she was out of science class more than she was in it. In all I only had about three full weeks with her because she usually was in trouble with other teachers before she came to science and was either sent home or sent to ISS. I knew Maria would never be able to pass the state test because she was not getting enough instruction. I decided to pull her from the ISS room during my planning periods to give her individual tutoring but this became ineffective. Maria did not want individual instruction and would ask to go back to the in school suspension room. I determined she was extremely uncomfortable in an adult controlled environment and was only bold when she had an audience.

I conference with another teacher who was making an extra effort like me to help Maria during her planning period and she reported Maria was not doing much for her either. All the teachers were taking work to the ISS room and we were communicating through an interpreter to her mother. During one of these phone calls, Maria's mother made it plain that she was tired of dealing with her daughter and stated she would like for Maria to go back to jail. The interpreter assured us that Maria's mother wanted her twelve year old daughter out of her house and life. Her parent would get her wish not too long after making that statement.

Maria had not been in my class regularly for about two weeks when she bounded into class on a Monday afternoon announcing she was going to be good from now on. I asked her, "Why did you decide to change your behavior?"

She answered, "It's my birthday!"

"Today is your birthday?" I queried.

"Not today, this week, Friday," she replied. "I'm going to have a party. My sister had her fifteenth. She had a big party. Now, I will have a party too."

"Congratulations Maria, we are glad to have you back in class," I replied warmly. True to her word Maria had a good week but was absent on Friday. During the week Maria was self-motivated and she shared with me her goals for the future. Maria wanted to be a child care worker said she loved working with little kids; they were fun to play with and they made her happy. I could see Maria in that role with her nice smile and jovial personality. Maria's true passion was expressed and I had high hopes she would finally settle down in class after we talked about the educational goals she needed to focus on if she wanted to become a child care worker. I had a good four days with Maria and then was shocked to hear of her fate.

The next Monday came and some of the students who had attended Maria's self initiated birthday party informed me she had been taken to jail on the night of her party. Apparently, Maria had not received permission from her mother to have the fling, became loud and unruly because she had been drinking, and physically fought with her mother. The students reported Maria also had drugs at her party. So, Maria was hauled away and spent her thirteenth birthday in lockup. She was absent from school for several weeks after that and teachers almost forgot the misery she caused us until she returned.

We knew that Maria would come back to us; most of the juvenile offenders processed back to their home schools through our alternative program.

When Maria did come back, she was different. The first two to three days she was quiet but she would not make an effort to learn and she tried to extract sympathy from all her teachers. With great dramatic effort Maria said, "I spent my thirteenth birthday in jail!" She did this in every teacher's room along with complaining that her mother didn't love her and wanted her out of the house.

My response was, "I am sorry you were in jail on your birthday. Would you like to talk to Miss Lopez about it?" Maria would always reply no and I always would say, "It's your choice." Secretly, I knew Miss Lopez would be coming to see Maria whether I made a referral or not because she had been having sessions with Maria before she was taken to jail. Miss Lopez would not forget Maria's needed her help. Maria would have an opportunity to vent at her counseling sessions and by giving Maria a choice to see the counselor, I let her know we were not going to talk about her jail experience in class. My job was to get Maria back on track with learning science and that was a big enough job for one person. I felt like I had been pushed back to square one with Maria but I was hoping she would remember my classroom structure and would adapt quicker this time since it was her second enrollment within the year.

Other teachers predicted Maria's failure upon her return to our program, they were prepared to do battle with her as usual, and they were correct. By the middle of Maria's second week of attendance she was wilder than ever and started openly swearing in my class. She was not even making an attempt to control her behavior and she began every class period by being unruly. Also, Maria had returned from lock up with a new distraction. She would burst out singing "I kissed a girl and I liked it." This brought her attention because other students in class laughed at her pretentions. It seems Maria had picked up on the diversity in this new group of seventh grade students and she wanted to be part of the lesbian crowd. She was determined to prove to these girls she was one of them and bathroom antics began to dominate our days. Straight students were refusing to go into the restroom with the four or five girls who were self-proclaimed lesbians and they certainly did not want to be in the restroom with Maria who was bold enough to kiss them on the mouth or touch them inappropriately. The gay-girl club had not posed a problem until Maria pledged herself to their ranks. In response to this new problem, middle school teachers had to provide closer supervision in during break times.

Now, thanks to Maria, a teacher had to stand inside the restroom observing the girls entering and leaving their own stalls to make sure they were not physically touching each other. When the supervision requirements changed and one teacher could no longer stand in the middle of the hallway to supervise both groups entering and leaving the restrooms, our middle school routine changed. Now restroom duty required two teachers, one for girls and one for boys. This meant two different teachers had to bring their classes together at the same time for break and there were twice as many students in the hall as usual. This resulted in too many kids lined up along the wall to maintain silence or order in the hallways and our middle school groups began to disturb high school classes. Since we were at a point in our school year when teachers were reviewing with students the end of the year exam and some school staff was complaining middle school students were disturbing their reviews while using the restroom, we had to find a way to get the middle school under control.

That is when I asked our principal permission to deny any student a restroom break based on that student being loud and disturbing other classes in the hallway. My reasoning was simple, as long as students were allowed to use the restroom after they caused a disturbance, the situation would not get better. Our new policy was approved and the students were informed, "If you are not quiet in the hallway during bathroom break then you will not be allowed to use the restroom. If you wet your pants then your parents will be informed that you had an opportunity to use the restroom but you acted like a fool in the hall, disturbed other classes, and lost your privilege until the next scheduled break. Therefore, you didn't make it."

As luck would have it, the seventh graders were studying the renal body system the day Maria caused a problem and lost her restroom break. During science class, I displayed overhead diagrams of the kidneys and bladder and presented a ten minute lecture on the renal body system. Every time I said the words bladder, kidneys, or urine I made it a point to emphasize each of these vocabulary words and I looked directly at Maria. The other students in class recognized what I was doing and they started cheering me on. After the way Maria had tormented our staff I took full advantage of my chance to torment her and I have to admit... it was sweet! Once I denied Maria a bathroom break based on her behavior in the hallway she never caused another disturbance during break time. In addition, other students benefitted from Maria's experience because they knew their bathroom privileges would be revoked if they disturbed high school classes.

Then I had to address sexual harassment with my students and help them understand the seriousness of their behavior toward one another. I was not surprised to find out some of the girls were just playing gay, Maria was one of those, and only one of my students was a wife to an older girl. After the sexual harassment training, Amanda came to my room and asked for help. She said, "I'm really not gay. I want to be free of my partner and I told my mom and dad what she does to me but they told me I got myself into this mess and I would have to get myself out of it. They won't help me." After discussing her situation, I learned the older girl, who was eighteen, had been Amanda's babysitter, had started taking Amanda to her house to stay all night when she was only ten years old and had molested her. The parents were totally unaware and they encouraged the relationship because Amanda's special friend bought her new clothes, other expensive gifts, and seemed to dote on her. The parents simply thought the older girl was treating their child like she was her baby sister. After two years Amanda was living with the girl in an apartment and was officially a wife. Amanda was only thirteen and when she realized she was a victim she asked her parents for help but they would not help her get free from the older girl.

Complicating the situation was the abuser's membership in a gang and her access to weapons. However, the thing that bothered Amanda the most was this girl now wanted her to recruit her classmates into partying with them, doing drugs, and she was forcing drug use on Amanda. Even though Amanda wanted freedom, she was afraid to report her abuse fearing her lover and the gang, to which the girl belonged, would take vengeance on Amanda's family for her betrayal. She would not talk to the police officer but finally agreed to talk to our counselor. I told Amanda what happened to her was not her fault, she had to make some hard choices if she wanted her life to change, and Ms. Lopez could help her process those choices. If there was one good thing that came out of Maria's trouble making in the girl's restroom then it would have been, Amanda sharing her situation and asking for help.

Nevertheless, I could not be thankful for Maria's gay-girl club involvement for too long because her classroom disturbances were steadily escalating. Maria caused trouble as soon as she got to school in her very first class and was often sent to the ISS room before lunch. When we sent Maria to poor Miss Marsh, the ISS teacher, she had her all day and afternoon teachers were losing time with Maria. In support of Miss Marsh and in an effort to gain instruction time for core teachers we instituted a new set of behavior plans. We checked Maria's behavior hour by hour; if she misbehaved in one class and was sent to ISS it did not mean she would stay in ISS the next period. We would take her out and give her another chance. If she misbehaved again Maria would forfeit her physical education time. Teachers were still keeping Maria after school for poor behavior and we were keeping her after school for individual tutoring. We were back to rewarding Maria's misbehavior with negatives; Maria wanted negatives, she graved them, and she threw fits to get them.

The whole middle school was under stress because of one child, Maria. Even though she had some minor learning disabilities and may have had undiagnosed emotional problems or mental illness, she still had the potential to do well in school. I had witnessed her ability on two different occasions when she forgot her own self-destructive mandate and achieved better than an eighty-five percent weekly average in my class. I was convinced the disruptive behaviors Maria demonstrated at school were more closely linked to her environment and to the drugs she might be taking than to her lack of academic abilities. Maria's behavior was deteriorating daily and it appeared to me that she was fast approaching a climax. I did not see how she could continue in her frenzied state to gather negatives in her life. The toll it was taking on her spirit was beginning to show; Maria was no longer pulling pranks or laughing out loud in class like she had in the past. Instead, her personality had taken an angry and sinister turn; I feared she was more capable of committing violence against staff than ever before. Her drastic personality change signaled to me drug use and I was sure she needed a referral to a teen recovery program.

Maria's had an upcoming special education hearing and I wanted the hearing participants to consider drug abuse as the larger issue and not credit Maria's misbehavior to learning disabilities or mental illness. Certainly, there were elements of those conditions which needed explored but I was certain substance abuse was the primary concern. I needed proof Maria was using drugs but I could not get the information I wanted from Maria's mother because I was certain she was involved in dealing drugs herself. In addition, there was a language barrier; I was sure the interpreter would not want to ask the mother the questions for which I wanted answers like, "Where did Maria get the alcohol and drugs for her thirteenth birthday party?" Since Maria was sent to jail for the first time when she was twelve years old I knew something bad had to be going on at home, even if it was just bad parenting. The fact that Maria's mother physically fought with Maria could indicate the mother might misunderstand our inquiries and start a fight with her daughter. Maria did not need to be locked up again so I would not risk contacting her mother.

As luck would have it, Maria's older sister who was in the eighth grade was referred to our program at about the time I decided to try and identify Maria's substance abuse. I just prayed that Maria's sister was not as disturbed as she was and that she cared enough about her sister to talk to me and help me identify Maria's drug use for the upcoming hearing. I quizzed Evita and asked her why she was sent to the alternative school. Her reply was guarded at first and she reported she had been drinking at a school function but nothing else. Then, Evita asked me if I taught Maria and went on to say, "She's bad and my mom says the devil has her." This sister confirmed stories that Maria had shared and said Maria physically fought with the mother, would often sneak out of the house, and Maria had stolen the mother's cash. I became bold and asked the sister if her mother was a "Business woman" and told her Maria had told me she was. I assured Evita that I had no interest in turning her mother in to the police; I just was trying to figure out how to help Maria. Once I assured Evita I understood the economics of drugs in her community then it was not difficult to get her to expose the information I wanted.

The sister smiled slightly evidencing her understanding of my benevolent mission as she reported her mother made drugs to sell. "So, Maria was stealing your Mom's business money," I asked in a non-judgmental voice. "Now I know why your mother wanted Maria to go to jail." I wanted to find out more about the types of drugs Maria had access to but the sister would only state that Maria would try anything. I gained the information I was fishing for when Evita testified to her own situation and said, "I use to do cocaine but I got off that stuff and I only smoke now." I posed, "Marijuana?" Evita replied, "Yeah, but it is good for you because it is a natural plant. It is good for your eyes and it cures cancer. I smoke it for my health." I didn't bother correcting these statements. I would find a way of working this into a science elective lesson for eight graders. Evita believed Marijuana was good medicine so I was sure other students believed the same thing.

After thanking Evita for talking to me I assured her once again that I only was seeking to help Maria with the questions I asked and I walked down to our counselor's office. Now, I had the additional information I needed to confirm Maria's drug use. One of the drugs she was using was cocaine. My conclusion was based on Evita admission she had attended a teen treatment program for cocaine addiction. Maria might be using more than one kind of drug and this certainly could explain the bizarre changes in Maria's personality and the argumentive behaviors I had witnessed in her lately. Maria's sister had also confirmed her mother was a dealer.

When I explained to Ms. Lopez how I received the information she was amazed Maria's sister had shared so much with me. I explained to her that I had honestly asked for Evita's help and had told her that Maria's education and perhaps her life might be at stake if we didn't get her needs correctly identified. Ms. Lopez promised to keep confidential the information I shared about Maria's family's source of income. We discussed the value of a referral to the state Child Protective Agency and decided against it. We would have only caused both girls problems in their home and their community. Besides, protective services would never be able to prove the mother unfit because she was a drug dealer. No one would testify to Maria's mother's business in court because they would fear gang retaliation. Instead, we felt a referral for Maria to a teen substance abuse facility for an evaluation and her possible treatment would be more beneficial. We knew Maria's mother would probably approve because it would get Maria out of her house and out of her business. At the end of our conversation, Ms. Lopez told me the information I shared was timely and she promised to discretely share Maria's need for a drug evaluation. After the hearing, Maria was sent to a residential program where she lived and attended school away from home. I'm not sure how long she was assigned this placement but I hope she was able to get both substance abuse treatment and mental health counseling while staying there.

Discussion:

There is no doubt in my mind that Maria's parent was to blame for her daughter's situation and that she was too involved in her own gang-banging and drug-dealing lifestyle to be a good parent. She made drug use and violence seem normal to Maria and she set a poor role model of what a woman and a mother should be. Maria was a product of her community and home. Students like Maria needed constant reassurance that they were safe, they tested the system to see who was in charge, and they made decisions about who to trust based upon that person's ability to maintain control of the classroom. Driven by fear and feelings of impending death, Maria constructed a perverted bucket list and subconsciously she decided to sample all the adult pleasures that were modeled for her because she might not live to be an adult. She sought her mother's attention by imitating her life style and Maria purposely did things to gain her mother's wrath. Even if the physical attention she got from her mother was negative, it was physical attention. Adult role models in her family and community almost destroyed Maria. **How did Maria's community and family influence Maria's bucket-list choices?**

Maria was offered an education by caring concerned teachers who were professionally accredited and dedicated to helping the neediest students in the district. I know that Maria failed to get an education while she was with me and she could not pass minimum state proficiency requirements. Maria needed drug treatment, mental health services, and she needed a restricted educational environment that would limit her contact with her family and community. Our public school system and even our alternative program could not meet Maria's needs. As a teacher, I did the best I could but I failed to educate this student. **Is educating students only about teaching academics?**

Topics to Research

How many inner city students suffer from anxiety disorders or depression? How might a student diagnosed with anxiety or depression behave in the classroom? How often is substance abuse issues addressed when individualized education plans are created for sped students? What kinds of behaviors evidence that a student may be on a path of self destruction?

Things to Do

If you are a teacher, identify students who might need additional counseling support. Talk with other teachers who have the same student in their class to get their impressions of the child's needs and behavior problems. Whatever you do, don't let your interaction with the child become toxic by waiting until you dread to see that child walk into your classroom before you do something. Most important, if you have to put a child out of your class for chronic disruptions then hold your ground and don't let that student back in until the school district can furnish you evidence that the child is going to get the help they need. Once a child is put out, administrators cannot legally cause you to allow that child admittance again in many states. Find out your school policies and advocate for our troubled kids so they can get the help they need and you can teach others in your classroom.

Always report suicidal expressions, even if you think the child is just being dramatic, like Maria. Teachers are usually not trained as mental health workers and they should not act in that capacity. Teachers can help their school counselor by observing students destructive behaviors and by documenting the students' expressions which might indicate suicidal intentions. Alternative school teachers may have a higher proportion of students who need counseling services. Teachers and counselors in these teaching situations need to develop a seamless working relationship and support each others' efforts to help students.

If you are a parent whose child appears to be living a perverted bucket list or whose behavior appears to be self-destructive then seek help for your child. Investigate to find safer places you can live which do not have high gang and drug activity. More important, if you are a parent who is setting a bad example through drug use and illegal activity then you should examine your priorities and hopefully, you will seek out help for your problems.

20. Teen Mental Health

The National Institute of Mental Health conducted a study in which they discovered teens show less activity than adults in their brain regions which control decision making. The results of this study propose many teen behaviors which appear self-destructive are really not purposeful actions but are evidence of an immature brain. ("Neuropsychologia, online Jan. 23, 2007...") In addition, this varied brain function is not unique to some teens; it is normal for all teens and it relates to the way serotonin is used in an immature brain. For parents and educators this study confirms what we have known for a long time; teens need to seek guidance from adult brains before they make life altering decisions. However, because their brains are immature teens can't recognize the need for adult counsel and they may make irrational decisions which place them at risk for destroying their own lives and for failing to get an education. For this reason adults must learn to anticipate illogical behavior from teens, provide close supervision for teens, and intervene when it appears teens are trying to self-destruct.

Given the above information how can we tell if a teen's behavior is abnormal and poses extreme risk? One authority purposes three reasons for concern, teen depression, teen anxiety, and teen low self esteem (Focus Adolescent Services: Self-Injury). According to this source young people who evidence these conditions might be at higher risk for self-injury and may more often display self destructive behaviors than other teens. In addition there is some evidence that teen depression and anxiety left untreated can become forms of mental illness in adulthood. Over thirty-five million children in the United States were placed at risk for developing mental illness (anxiety and depression) and for becoming substance abusers by their parents who were using illegal drugs in 2005. According to Howard Markel, MD from Columbia University, as much as 50% of our nations' children could be affected this way due to their parents drug use (medscape.com). This comprehensive "White paper" that was released from the National Center on Addiction and Substance Abuse (CASA) documented substance abusing parents are three to four times more likely to be neglectful or abusive parents and their children are at increased risk for suffering academic failure along with physical and mental illness. From this report we can surmise children living with parents who use illegal drugs or abuse other substances like alcohol, may evidence abnormal tendencies toward self-injury or self-destruction and they are prone to academic failure.

Once again, if we take the time to review statistics from previous strategies we have covered we realize that large city schools' demographics ensure they will have more students attending who come from homes where substance abuse is an issue. Therefore, these districts may have more students who demonstrate abnormal self-destructive behaviors and who may have underlying mental health concerns. Without a responsible parent to nurture and guide these youth they are bound to make irrational decisions and many of them will turn to substance abuse to cope with their unpredictable environments. In fact, some of these teens will develop recognizable self-destructive patterns of behavior (How to Recognize Self-Destructive Behaviors).

In the preceding story, Maria demonstrated symptoms of a teen developing serious mental health issues which may have been the result of constant anxiety about her own physical safety and she began to establish a pattern of behaviors which were destructive. Maria may have used drugs to cope with anxiety or depression she experienced because that coping model was established in the home by her mother. However, according to self-injury experts, Maria's drug use could have caused her mental health state to worsen because the drugs she used could have interfered with serotonin uptake in her brain causing her to be more impulsive and aggressive (Teens First for Health). Maria was a child who needed removed from her family and community in order to survive her teen years. She needed to be placed in a residential treatment facility for her living and educational needs.

Research tells us, other students with similar home environments to Maria may not use drugs to cope with their life situations the same way as Maria, but they all have to find a method of coping to relieve their stress. Some students may self-harm in order to gain relief from psychological stress. These students are seeking to alter a mood state and they may gain relief through: cutting themselves, burning their skin, picking their skin, pulling out their hair, eating too much, having unprotected sex, or other destructive acts. According to one source, students who perform self-harm rituals are children who have not been validated; they have not been allowed to express certain feelings or thoughts and they have not had good role models for coping with life's stress. For these students self-harm could "Replace their jittery, panicky feeling with a clam, bad feeling" (Focus on Adolescent Services: Self-Injury). They get some type of relief from doing these self-harming rituals.

Of course, the ultimate self-hurt is suicide and teen suicides are the third leading cause of death for teens between the ages of 15 to 19 year olds in the United States. One source reported that the teen suicide rate increased by 100% from 1979 to 1998 and survey data gathered from high school students in 2005 showed that 17% of all high school students had thought about suicide (Suicide Warning Signs). Included in this report is information implying some teens may be predisposed to commit suicide and students who are predisposed for mental illness and using illicit drugs or alcohol may increase their risk for developing mental illness and for committing suicide because brain chemistry can be altered through drug abuse. The long-term effects drug and alcohol use have on the human brain is currently being studied by a specific group of researchers in a new field of interest named the neurochemistry of addiction.

These are just a few of the things that are currently known about teen substance abuse which have been confirmed by researchers: the human brain continues to grow through adolescence, the brain does not develop normally when teens abuse drugs or alcohol, abnormal development of the brain during the teen years leads to learning disabilities and early addiction, substance abuse can also damage the areas of the brain which promote emotional and psychological health and could contribute to teen mental illness, the dopamine areas of the brain are the most easily damaged, damage to the dopamine areas can lead to reduced motor skills and damaged verbal learning abilities, and damage to the brain for teens may be irreversible depending on the type of drugs used and the length of their use (NIDA). Teen brains are fragile and alcohol and drug use at this age can lead to permanent, negative life out-comes.

This information leads us to ask questions like: How can public schools provide all the services needed for students who may be simultaneously mentally ill, learning disabled, and abusing substances like drugs and alcohol? After reviewing the neurochemistry of addiction findings we might ask ourselves which condition came first and in view of earlier statistics shared which documented a 233% increase in special education services provided to a new classification of students in the United States, learning disabled, we also might ask ourselves if the root cause of the exponential growth of this one group of students is due to a higher percentage of teens now using drugs. Why aren't we asking students to accept responsibility for their choices to use drugs and why aren't we asking their parents to be held accountable for their lack of supervision of their offspring? These are hard questions because they force us to face the real issues: increased substance abuse among teens, toxic inner city neighborhoods which have been surrendered to drug and gang activities, and poor parenting!

Instead, public education is taking the fall and teachers are receiving the majority of the blame; union busting and firing teachers seem to be the only reform solutions being recommended to correct student failure rates. The extent of this kind of education reform talk can be compared to a grunt passed between cavemen who throw rocks at each other when confronted with beast of prey as they ignore the real problem. Education reform must address and redefine the limits of public education. Teachers should not be expected to act as trained mental health professionals, substance abuse treatment experts, and highly qualified educators at the same time. Public education was instituted to educate the masses and prepare them for citizenship not to babysit psychologically-impaired, learning-disabled, substance abusing children who disrupt learning for all other students.

I know that special education laws may seem to limit some choices we have when confronted with students who have dual or triple diagnoses. However, there can be only one choice when substance abuse is indicated, regardless of other pre-existing conditions, because substance abuse among teens can precipitate learning disabilities and mental illness. Our path should be obvious because it involves choice; students choose whether or not they will use drugs and schools should be able to choose to eliminate students who are using drugs from their school population. Educators have a difficult time teaching students who have diminished consciousness in the classroom due to their substance abuse but when that substance abuse is combined with mental illness, learning disabilities and poor parenting, public educators should not be subject to even trying. We only cause the learning environment of more capable students to be disrupted and we deprive these students of a quality education.

Educational reform should come up with ways to identify and quickly place these students in residential schools or treatment facilities and we need to find funding sources for these programs. Parents should pay. Even if parents are in the low income bracket their earned income tax credit could be withheld and they could receive a reduction in benefits when their child is placed in a treatment facility or residential school. Substance abusing parents will continue to be derelict in their parenting until a higher authority holds them responsible and intervenes on behalf of their children.

References and Resources

"Self-Destructive Behavior," Parenting Teens; parentingteensresourcenetwork. org/self-destructive-behavior/article.php?cat=8...

"Neuropsychologia," online Jan. 23, 2007..."

"What is SELF-INJURY?" Focus Adolescent Services; focusas.com/ SelfInjury.html

"Parents and Substance Abuse," medscape.com; Howard Markel, MD, PhD; medscape.com/viewarticle/503855

"How to Recognize Self-Destructive Behaviors," and "Long-Term Effects of Drug Abuse on the Brain," eHOW; ehow.com_2074163_recognize-selfdestructive-behavior.html

"Suicide Warning Signs," SAMHSA; family.samhsa.gov/get/suicidewarn. aspx

"Teen Brain Development," NIDA; nida.nih.gov

21. The Deceiver

At first, my other students seemed to know the young man who walked in our room. At least, I thought I detected recognition in their faces… but I was mistaken. The recognition was related to his sexual orientation and not who he was as a person. Steve was a pudgy guy who smelled of strong, flowery after shave, wore false eyelashes, had painted fingernails, and his secretly possessed lip gloss in his pocket. Steve would have carried a ladies purse from classroom to classroom if handbags would have been allowed at our school and he caused quite a scene the first day he arrived when his purse was taken. Steve had a deep voice but he broke into into a falsetto tirade and cried like a little girl with real tears running down his cheeks when he was informed he could not carry a handbag at the alternative school. In addition, our school staff never quite recovered from searching Steve's purse because the search revealed Steve was carrying around ladies sanitary supplies, tampons to be exact. When asked by staff why he possessed these feminine products he simply replied, "I keep them in case any of my girlfriends might need them."

Unfortunately, the staff person checking Steve had gone into shock with the discovery and he spoke louder than what he intended to, which brought attention to the contents of the Steve's handbag. Other students processing into school that morning were hysterical with laughter and started gossiping about our new student in the breakfast room before I ever met him. That is why the other students in my class knew who Steve was; they had been talking about his weirdness in the morning room while waiting to come to class. If Steve's unusual appearance was not enough to call attention to his diversity then that first morning's check-in procedure surely sealed his identity. The other students did not just make fun of Steve because he was gay; they rejected him because he was weird.

I had other gay students in my class before and for the most part, students at the alternative school accepted and treated diverse students as equals. Our kids were pretty much tolerant of everyone else because most of them had their own idiosyncrasies and at their home schools, many of them may have been treated as misfits. Rarely did I see a new student rejected by the other kids at our school. So, I was surprised when this new guy in class was immediately and totally ostracized by all the other boys on his very first day. They did not want to sit next to Steve or talk to him. In an effort to protect Steve from becoming a victim I seated him within a cluster of female students. Steve didn't mind his placement among the girls and they seemed to be more tolerant of Steve than the boys in class. In addition, one female student struck up an immediate friendship with Steve.

While the other females marginally accepted Steve's attempts at conversation, LuAnn became his confidante. We soon found out why LuAnn so readily engaged her new classmate. During one of our social skills lessons, LuAnn explained she had an uncle who was a homosexual and she told the class how her uncle had been the target of a hate crime. She asked the other students to be more tolerant of Steve when she told the class about the brutal crime committed against her relative. After this class, LuAnn set herself up to be Steve's protector and she was determined that no one would treat him with disrespect when she was around. That is when I began to notice that anytime LuAnn was involved in a discipline problem, the actions she performed to defend Steve were the source of her trouble. I had a strange suspicion that Steve might be initiating conflict on purpose to test LuAnn's friendship.

LuAnn was a tall lean girl with teeth that appeared too large for her mouth. I could not see any fat on her body; she really appeared to be no more than skin stretched-tight over bone. I became concerned for her health and I asked LuAnn about her diet. LuAnn reported she ate all the time because her granny lived with the family and liked to cook a lot. However, one day I saw LuAnn give up her lunch money to a less fortunate student. Then she asked me if I had any crackers she could eat so her stomach would not hurt. When I asked her why she gave away her lunch money she replied, "I can eat tonight because there is food in my house but that boy won't have nothing to eat when he gets home from school." LuAnn had a big heart, she was naïve, and she witnessed love for her friends by being a sensitive caretaker. LuAnn was empathetic to a fault and that is why she was so easily deceived by Steve.

The emotional betrayal LuAnn experienced began innocently enough with Steve initiating gossip about the boys in our school he thought were attractive. LuAnn performed the role of cupid by telling a boy that Steve thought he was good looking and she would try to get the boy to talk to him. In turn, LuAnn told Steve about the boys she liked and asked for his advice to help her gain her love match. There was one particular boy in our class that LuAnn was gaga over, I had picked up on her interest, and I sat her on the opposite side of the room from this young man because I did not want LuAnn to be distracted from her school work. LuAnn made the mistake of telling Steve about her interest in Tommy and that is what caused the next problem.

As a middle school teacher, I knew that love dramas could dominate students' thoughts and actions and they could paralyze students' learning processes while deteriorating relationships between students. Jealousy, anger, and revenge often resulted from love match attempts... so it was in my best interest to squelch any romantic activity in class. I was always watching for student exchanges which might indicate a new love drama was emerging. I found out about LuAnn and Steve's cupid agreement after I intercepted a first note in class between the two students. When I confiscated the note, I was especially disturbed by LuAnn's attempted interventions. She knew all the other boys in class were straight and she should have known that passing a note to one of these guys for Steve might precipitate violence against her friend. In retrospect, the first note was pretty harmless because it merely said Steve thought a certain boy was cute.

Since, I had retrieved the note from Steve's hand while he was attempting to pass it to LuAnn, I kept him after school and explained he could not write and pass notes in my class because note passing took the focus off of our lesson. I did warn him about possible violence that could erupt if the intended student felt offended by the contents of the note. I thought Steve understood my concerns because I made him repeat back to me what I told him about note passing in my class and why I wanted it to stop.

However, I intercepted a second note within that same week's time but it was in LuAnn's possession. So, I told LuAnn she would be staying after school. This second note's content was particularly disturbing because it contained sexually explicit language that was clearly directed toward a heterosexual male in class. I knew it was written by Steve and the boy for who the note was intended would probably not have appreciated Steve's unsolicited attention. If the note had reached its target, Steve could easily have been assaulted in my class.

At first, LuAnn protested staying after school and she said, "Mrs. G, I didn't write the note. Why should I have to stay?"

I replied, "LuAnn, you know my rule. Besides, the note is not signed. I have no way of knowing who wrote the note. You are the person I caught in possession of the note so you are the one staying." Of course, I knew that LuAnn had probably not even read the note and was just passing it for Steve but LuAnn had become an accomplice to sexual harassment and I wanted her to understand the seriousness of the situation. I was hoping once LuAnn read the note she would realize how Steve had duped her and she would quit playing cupid.

Reluctantly, LuAnn entered my room at the end of the school day and began, "Mrs. Gifford, please, do I have to stay? I promise I will never pass notes again in your class."

I handed the note to LuAnn and said. "Is this the note I took from you? I want you to look only at the outside for now."

LuAnn looked at the small folded piece of paper which had a heart drawn on the outside and said, "Yes, that's the note. I drew the heart on the outside with my purple pen."

I continued, "Now, read this to me if you can." Lu Ann began reading in a loud and agitated voice which broke suddenly into silence. Her eyes widened and an expression which combined shock and horror took possession of her face.

She dropped the note on top my desk and staggered into a sitting position in the student conference chair placed close by. "Mrs. Gifford, I don't know what to say. I hope you don't think I wrote that note!"

I started slowly, "I believe you, LuAnn, but I wanted you to see for yourself the disturbing content that is recorded on this paper. Now, what do you think would have happened in class if you had been successful in passing this message? Keep in mind there are no other gay students in our class… therefore, the young man for whom the note was intended could have been offended."

LuAnn did not hesitate, "There could have been a big fight and Steve would have got beaten up."

I could tell there was something else bothering LuAnn as she rocked back in her chair and assumed a trance like stare at the floor. I noticed her jaw was tightening and she was gripping the arms of the chair so tightly that her knuckles whitened. Then she practically burst forth like a geyser as she jumped to her feet and proclaimed, "How could he? Steve knew I liked Tommy and I thought he was writing a note for me to tell Tommy how I felt. The whole time Steve listened to me talk about this boy he was planning to get Tommy for himself. He played me, Mrs. Gifford!"

This was certainly not a twist I expected because I did not know for whom the note was intended but I remained calm in order to sooth my very disturbed student. "LuAnn, I am sorry that you were hurt and that Steve deceived you. However, the question remains about the note. We need to decide what to do with this piece of evidence which shows sexual harassment. Since the note is not signed I think you should witness to the principal or school counselor who wrote the note. This paper constitutes unsolicited sexual advances made by one student to another and it is against the law for students to treat each other this way. Personally, I was offended by the language content in the note and I believe you were as well. However, you are partially responsible for the offense because you were intending on passing the note. You need to make it right by talking to someone in the office so we can get this kind of communication stopped between students."

LuAnn agreed to talk to the counselor so we walked to the office. After LuAnn left the counselor's room, I talked to Ms. Lopez. The counselor reported, "That note was alarming! I did not know that any of our students could even have those kinds of thoughts. However, all we have is LuAnn's word and the note is not signed. You will need to just keep your eyes open for further evidence of sexual harassment." I was disappointed that the problem was shifted back to me but I understood the reason for the counselor's decision. I did request she share the note with the administrators at our school and I asked her if sexual harassment training would be provided for the students this year. The counselor did not know about whether or not a specific training would be offered to students on this subject and she referred me to our substance abuse educator who also did not know. I was still waiting for some type of direction concerning the needed sexual harassment education from our administration when the next incident occurred.

I lined the students up to go to the lunchroom and observed them as they filed down the hall on the opposite wall from me. When about half of the class passed me, I moved to begin walking with the group and I glanced to the rear of the line to let the students know they also were being observed. As the last student exited the classroom, I noticed it was the student for whom Steve's note was intended. Steve was directly in front of him and a red flag waved in my mind. Tommy was walking behind Steve and that should have been a safe position. However, when Tommy exited the room he was in deep thought walking along with his head up while glancing at posters placed high on our hall walls and he was not paying attention to the movement of the line.

That is when Steve seized an opportunity by dropping his pencil as he abruptly halted his walk. Tommy continued his mindless wandering and bumped into Steve's backside. Steve immediately gyrated on Tommy's front as the horrified Tommy turned a sickened white color and almost collapsed in the hall. Momentarily Tommy lost his voice and only moved his mouth in protest. Then Tommy made a weak attempt to talk, "Help me, Mrs. Gifford. Did you see what he did to me?"

I had seen the whole thing and as I looked directly at Steve he said, "What? I dropped my pencil. It was an accident."

I stopped the progress of the line, sat Steve down in a chair across from another teacher's door, and asked my co-worker to stand with the offending student while I accompanied the rest of my class to the lunchroom. As I walked beside Tommy I discretely said, "Don't worry. I saw everything and Steve will not be in our class after lunch."

Tommy nodded numbly without talking and cast his eyes downward toward the floor. I was uncomfortable too and I realized I was partially at fault. I should have predicted Steve's behavior toward Tommy because the contents of the note I had intercepted was very graphic. However, Tommy was walking in line behind Steve and it never occurred to me he could physically touch him from that position. I continued to argue with myself about my own culpability as I escorted students to the care of the lunchroom staff and as I returned down the hall to write an office referral. My mind was confused while I remembered past experiences with gay students who had attended our school. None of them had displayed such utter disrespect for themselves or their fellow classmates. All of the gay students I had taught up until now, were unassuming, quiet, and often needed a protector.

I had to admit my relationship with these diverse students had been that of a protector, just like LuAnn. I did this because I never wanted any of my students to become victims of a hate crime. Eventually, my assumed protector roll caused me to go farther than what any teacher should have gone and I had physically laid my hands on one young man. I had grabbed the student's belt from the back, placed my knee behind his making him off-balance while tipping him back like a refrigerator on a dolly, and I had hauled him quickly out of my classroom into the hall. This student had been out of his seat and on his way across my room to hit Gregg, when I intervened. I knew my action was risky because the student attempting violence had a bi-polar diagnosis, was taking more than one type of psychotropic medication, and had recently attempted assault on his special education teacher. I knew protocol mandated me to stand back after ringing the classroom call button and I probably should have waited for the principal or police officer to come to my room. However, I had a knee jerk reaction to the threat and I was out in the hall with the threatening student before I realized it.

Gregg could have been seriously hurt before anyone arrived and I would have felt personally responsible if that would have happened in my room. Thank God, I had used the element of surprise to effectively avoid physical violence between the two students and that I was not injured. I was still recovering from surgery when I acted physically to save my student and the consequences to me could have been unthinkable. While reflecting I became upset over Steve's behavior and I wondered if my memory of seeing Steve molest Tommy in the hall right in front of my eyes would forever taint my perception of gay students. I might not react as quickly the next time a student was in trouble because of what I saw Steve do that day in the hall. My eyes had been open to the fact that gay students, like straight students, could be perpetrators.

I could barely control my own anger as I completed the office referral and wrote sexual harassment in large red letters across the top of the form. I walked Steve down to the office and returned with only enough time to use the bathroom before my next class began. As soon as I returned to my classroom with my same group of students, the counselor walked up to my door with Steve and I prepared to do battle. As I walked out the door, I blocked Steve's entrance into the room. The counselor looked puzzled because staff usually talked in the hall while viewing the students through the window. I did not wait for her to start, "Steve cannot come back into my room. His victim is present in this group of students and letting Steve into the room would be adding to insult to injury. Literally, I could not ensure the safety of either boy."

The counselor started, "Steve said what happened was an accident and he dropped his pencil."

I interrupted, "I wrote what I personally witnessed on the form and that is what happened. Steve is lying and he committed a sexual crime against a male student. We actually could say he assaulted Tommy by moving on him the way he did. I will call Steve's parents and Tommy's parents to tell them what happened, what I did about it, and what the administration is doing about it as soon as I have my planning period."

The counselor swallowed hard when I answered her so forward but she saw I was committed to addressing the sexual harassment of my other student and she backed away from my door and said, "I will take Steve to the principal with your report." I curtly said, "Thank you" and rejoined my group.

However, when I went into the classroom I noticed Tommy had tears in his eyes and he said, "Mrs. Gifford, I need to leave because I'm going to hurt somebody... and I am on probation and I don't want to do it."

I replied, "Steve is not coming back into my classroom so you don't have to worry about him."

Tommy jerked his head in the direction of the back of the room and with a shaky voice replied, "It's them, not Steve that's bothering me now. They said I liked it and I asked for it."

One of the other boys jumped in, "If you didn't like it bro, you should have beat him up. I would have. It's because you didn't do anything and we are just saying... you must have liked it."

The whole class laughed after the boy's statement and I had to react quickly. I moved to Tommy's side and led him to the hall and said, "Stand here and if any one comes by tell them you are not in trouble that you are just waiting for me." Then I returned full of furry to address the class.

I called the rude student's name and chastised him, "Who do you think you are and what gives you the right to make fun of someone who has been victimized? If your mother or your sister were sexually harassed or worse, maybe raped, would you make fun of them? What happened to Tommy was like being raped because he didn't want it and he did not participate. This is something someone did to him and it is illegal. The crime is called sexual harassment and it really is assault because Steve touched Tommy's person. As far as Tommy not beating Steve up, I think Tommy did the right thing because now only Steve will get into trouble and Tommy will not. Are you on probation? Have you ever been locked up?"

The student said he was not on probation and he had never been arrested. I told him not to judge Tommy until he had those experiences. I continued, "Tommy does not want to be locked up again and he is trying to do the right thing. I am going to bring Tommy back in to the room and you, all of you, are going to apologize to him. Do you understand? If one more negative word is said to Tommy about this incident then I am going to write that person up for sexual harassment too."

I bought Tommy back into the room and told him his class mates had something to say. I started with the particularly rude student first, who said, "I'm sorry, man. I ain't ever been locked up and I might not want to get in trouble if I was on probation. I know why you didn't fight. I'm going to take care of Steve for you!"

I immediately hushed the student by putting my fingers into my ears and by singing "La…la…la…la." The other students understood my actions and quieted the student committing the indiscretion. Then they took turns saying they were sorry for their behaviors. Ghetto handshakes pursued Tommy around the room as I breathed a silent, "Thank you, Lord." I praised the class for acting like true gentlemen and ladies and I told them I hoped they would always remember today because they had learned a lesson in compassion. I told my students to ask themselves this question, "If this had happened to me how would I want other people to treat me?"

Then, the boys began to talk about other incidents with Steve in the lunchroom. According to them, Steve had been harassing all the male students with obscene gestures while eating his food. The students said they tried to report Steve but the lunch room staff was oblivious to his conduct and thought the other boys were probably lying on Steve because he was gay. In an effort to teach tolerance, the lunchroom staff lectured the straight boys sitting at the same table with Steve so the offended students did not think it would do any good to report the disturbing incidents to other teachers. After hearing my students' testimonies I realized that most of our staff were probably playing protector roles and were focused on the safety of our gay students, just like I had been.

After our classroom confrontation, I did feel relieved about Tommy's outcome and the other students in his class seemed to understand better what had happened to him. I knew no one else in Tommy's class section would say anything about the incident but I worried about the rest of the middle school students knowing and continuing to cause Tommy embarrassment. Rumors traveled fast among this age group of children and since some of Tommy's classmates had been openly harassing him in the lunch room, other students could have a warped idea of what had transpired between him and Steve. By now, the whole middle school would be putting their spin on the story. During my last class of the day, my assumptions about middle school students proved true and I had another confrontation with a jerky little boy who thought Tommy's torment was funny.

The seventh and eighth grade groups had PE together that day and one of the seventh grade students began teasing Tommy during this joint class. The eighth grade boys threatened Darren and told him not to talk to Tommy about the incident which he overheard in the lunch room. Even though Darren was afraid of the older boys and stopped his behavior during PE class, he wasn't over his interest and he thought he could bring his entertainment for the day into my classroom. Like most ill informed gossips he did not know all the facts or suspect that I was the teacher present during the incident. Darren began, "Mrs. Gifford, did you hear… ha…ha…ha, about Tommy and Steve being caught while they were doing some homosexual stuff?"

I glared at this little trouble maker while calmly replying, "Since I was the teacher present when this happened I imagine I know more than you think you know." The other students became quiet and I knew they intended to pump me for information. However, if I did not address this group and the two other groups I taught, then Tommy would continue to be made miserable by other students at our middle school. "Class, I want to tell you a story and I want you all to listen carefully because there will be questions afterwards. Once there was a group of first grade students; they would all be about six years old. They came in from playing recess outside and they were hot, sweaty and thirsty. When the children lined up to use the water fountain one little girl took a long time getting a drink of water and the little boy behind her patted her on her backside and said 'Hurry up. I'm thirsty too.'

Now, the little girl went home and told her parents that a boy touched her on a private part of her body and the parents came to school demanding to meet with the principal and the boy's parents. The school explained what happened to the irate parents but chose not to hold a meeting because the school officials thought the little girl's parents were over reacting. Since the school personnel did not take the parents' complaint seriously, the little girl's parents sued the school district for allowing the boy to sexually harass their daughter at school.

Now, after hearing this story I want you to tell me if you think the story is true or false. Raise your hand and vote if you think the story is true. So the rest of you all believe the story is a lie? The story is true and the parents won their law suit because they had gone to the school first with their complaint, tried to get the boys parents' to stop their son from touching their daughter, and they received no help from anyone. These parents thought their daughter could be touched on her body at school by any boy in her class and no one would intervene or say anything.

The young boy had committed a crime and it is called sexual harassment and sexual harassment cannot be allowed in the schools. Teachers and others who work in the schools are mandated reporters which mean we don't have a choice and we have to report or receive consequences. We can lose our teaching certificates, be fined, and maybe even go to jail if we see sexual harassment and don't report it. Now it is your turn to talk. Did the little boy know what he was doing was wrong? Should the parents have reacted so strongly to their daughters report? What sort of actions by students could be considered sexual harassment in middle school?"

After a short discussion, I informed these kids they were spreading misinformation and I wanted them to stop talking about it because it was embarrassing to Tommy. I asked the students, "If something bad happened to you at school would you want people telling lies about you and teasing you?" The students agreed to not mention the event again because they did not know the details and should not be talking about it. Then, we started class over and began to do the original lesson which was planned for the day. I put our science review video on and we watched and discussed portions until time to go.

As I reached up to turn off the TV above my desk, Darren, the small troll who bought Tommy's situation up for discussion, ran up behind me, made humping motions on my backside, and yelled, "Sexual harassment" as he ran out of my room laughing all the way down the hall and out of the building. I was offended! Also, I was surprised that the staff let him out of the building since he was not with the rest of my class. It was not my practice to let students run solo through the building.

I lined up and dismissed the rest of my class after having students sign a group statement evidencing they saw Darren's behavior toward me. When the students left, I wrote a Darren a referral for sexual harassment and went to conference with the principal. I was not having a good day and the principal made it a whole lot worse because he said, "If that's what really happened," after reading the report. I was too furious for words so I waited until the next day to talk to our female assistant principal who was amazed that my supervisor had not taken me serious. When Darren came back to school he was made to apologize but as soon as the authorities left he tried to deny what happened or make excuses. He said, "It was just a joke and you took it too serious and besides I have a problem with cocaine and it makes me act crazy." I corrected him and told him he needed to stop retracting his apology or he would never be allowed to come into my classroom again. I informed Darren I still had the option of legally charging him with a crime. I was thankful I did not have to deal with this student very long because he transferred from our school within a week of the incident. His transgression at school had nothing to do with his move from our district but I can say I wasn't sad to see him go.

Also, Steve came back to school after a three day suspension. On his very first day back, students reported Steve had begun his old routine in the lunchroom of eating food in a sexualized manner while looking at certain boys. So I was not surprised on Steve's second day back when he came into my room sporting a black eye and I thought I probably knew the student who did the damage. However, the injury was not sustained on school property so I rationalized, "What is that saying about letting children handle their own disputes and adults need to stay out of the mix?" Personally, I felt the students were more successful in extinguishing Steve's undesired behavior than school staff had been.

I did inform the lunchroom staff that students were reporting Steve's disgusting behavior to classroom teachers. I reminded them that gays are often the victims of hate crimes and Steve's lunchroom behavior could justify violence in some students' minds. They got the message loud and clear when they saw Steve's black eye.

Discussion

We all know that modeling and teaching tolerance is the best way to eliminate violence in public schools and preventing hate crimes against homosexual students should become a top priority for school staff. However, in this story straight students were ignored when they complained about sexual harassment by a gay student in the lunchroom. The lack of action taken by school staff and Steve's resulting black eye, both evidenced that we all should probably put our brakes while speeding to rescue some gay students. Offending gay actions, like offending straight actions, cannot be tolerated. Let me be clear, this is not a gay student problem only; it is a middle school student problem. Most children this age are socially inept at expressing interest in their love matches and they may often be disrespectful or offend a person to whom they are attracted. However, students might not become violent toward each other if school staff responded appropriately to complaints of sexual harassment. **When the lunch staff was notified that Steve was simulating sexual behaviors with his food while looking at and calling the names of certain boys in his class, what should they have done?**

Before Steve came back from his school suspension, I contacted our school counselor and informed her Steve needed to understand how his actions in the lunchroom could lead to personal violence directed toward him. I asked her to specifically address this concern with Steve on his first day back at school and I know she talked to him on that same day. However, Steve initiated a disturbance that very day in the lunchroom anyway and he was injured that same afternoon on his way home from school. **Why do you think**

Steve continued his inappropriate actions in the lunchroom after being warned?

Personally, I believe Steve should have apologized to both LuAnn and Tommy and the three should have attended a counseling session together to resolve issues and restore normal relationships between the three students. I have a feeling that Steve may never accept responsibility for his actions, he may go through life feeling like a martyr, and he may make excuses for his wrong doings by claiming he is a victim of gay intolerance. It is sad to think Steve may really become a victim of a hate crime simply because he may not learn how to express interest in someone without offending them. However, without Tommy receiving counseling for his victimization, he forever might believe gays are obscene and not worthy of his friendship. Poor LuAnn may never extend friendship to someone like Steve again because he betrayed her trust. All of these students could have benefitted from counseling services. **Do school personnel have the time or the expertise to do this type of counseling with students? Is this type of counseling within the scope of a school counselor's job?**

Topics for Research

What percentage of the United States' student population is gay? What should you say to a student or your child who discloses they are gay? What other groups within our population have been victims of hate crimes?

Things to Do

If you are a teacher, you must report sexual harassment between students and any sexual harassment directed toward you. It is unpleasant for teachers to report student directed sexualized behavior toward them. However, if you don't report it then you could be accused of encouraging that behavior. Teaches should avoid being alone with a student unless the class room door is open and both you and the student can be seen clearly from the hall. Be aware, some students may lie about teachers to get them in trouble if the teacher rejects the student's attention. The sooner you report unusual student behavior directed toward you the better. Make notes on student inappropriate behaviors for reference and be prepared to produce those if you are questioned.

Seek counseling for students who initiate incidents of sexual harassment with other students. Often, these children may just need educated about interacting appropriately with their love interest, their actions may be disrespectful due to their lack of experience, and their actions may not be intentionally malevolent. However, teachers must be aware there will be some students who seek attention through purposely causing conflict whether it is committing incidents of sexual harassment or through other actions. These students have mental health issues and certainly they need identified so they can be referred for help.

Parents of gay students should talk to their children about interacting with other students to whom they are attracted in a respectful way. Unfortunately, gay students' sexual expressions of interest may be considered offensive to straight students and may result in violence more often than heterosexuals' inappropriate sexual advances. So, parents of these students may have a greater responsibility to educate their children to keep them safe. However, all middle school students need this kind of guidance and parents in general need to educate their own children about behaviors which may violate sexual harassment laws or result in assault charges.

22. Single Sex Education

In the previous story, the whole middle school was affected by the drama involving three students in one classroom. I would think most middle school teachers could relate similar stories that evidence the detrimental effects relationship gossip and the accompanying emotional upsets have on middle school environments. The emotional distress displayed about love matches can be quite maddening and it may cause disruptions in learning when students initiate conflicts. Teachers may feel forced to address issues just to clear the air and help students adjust their emotional states so learning can resume. Proponents of single sex education (SSE) claim this kind of drama is easily eliminated when girls and boys are separated from each other at school and there is some evidence which shows academic performance is enhanced in both female and male students when students attend either class rooms or programs where they are separated from each other.

One Cincinnati high school only had a forty percent passing rate on the Ohio state proficiency exam before implementing single sex education in 2002 and they improved their performance to a ninety percentile passing rate when SSE was implemented(Cincinnati, enquirer.com). The astounding rate of improvement was manifested in just two short years proving single sex educational reform initiatives are worth exploring. In addition, Cincinnati parents have accepted the switch from traditional gender mixed classes to same sex education and extol its merits saying SSE has "A multitude of advantages." Parents, who were interviewed for this article, cited the freedom young women received to be who they really were and to not hide their intelligence was one benefit they had noticed. Girl students said they no longer felt they had to dumb themselves down to be attractive to boys while boys reported they no longer had to impress the ladies (Cincinnati Parent). One middle school principal, Sharon Johnson, testified she saw fewer distractions and grades improved at her middle school when single sex education was implemented. Other school districts, which implemented SSE, reported the school experienced fewer discipline problems, students' self esteem increased, and students' attitudes about school improved because students were relieved of some social pressure (Cincinnati, enquirer.com).

Current research shows that gender difference should be considered when constructing academic environments. Boys tend to disrupt learning more; for this reason, they may need a highly structured learning environment which limits their time to socialize compared to girls, who need peer, social engagement to learn (Wik.ed.unic.edu/). This view may be confirmed by one associated press article that reported girl students said one of the things they liked about SSE was "Not worrying about boys causing disruptions" (msnbc.com). Boys disrupt class more often and boys are disciplined more often than girls. In addition, boys tend to need motivated to become better students and they may get a larger share of attention from their classroom teachers for this reason (A Study in Contrast).

From a female point of view, some people worry about inequities developing in same sex education programs; they may fear a return of days when females were left behind academically in subjects like math and science. Research has shown the achievement gap between male and female students in United States is one of the smallest in the world and the number of girls enrolling in advanced placement and honors classes grew at a faster rate than boys starting in 1998. This same source stated there was a larger disparity between white and black students. Other sources say the disparity is greater among lower socioeconomic groups when compared to all students and that SSE could correct that difference. Regardless of female concerns about daughters getting the same educational opportunities as their sons, the truth is that poor students still fair worse and racial differences may still predict lower education outcomes than gender differences (Viadero). National statistics indicate that female students in the United States have a ten percent point advantage in literacy and international statistics show females perform better academically than males across all subject areas in thirty-two countries (Program for International Assessment).

In fact there was concern voiced in one country, UK, that single sex education might give girls more of a benefit, continue widening the gender gap, and for this reason, SSE would give females an unfair advantage.

From this research we can conclude that same sex education works for girls. But… does it work for boys? There is an educational myth that boys do better in class when girls are around because girls set a good example for them. But Graham Able, of Dulwich College in London, studied the performance of students in thirty coeducational schools and discovered that boys received the greater advantage from SSE. Mr. Able went on to say that, "Both boys and girls are academically disadvantaged in co-educational schools, but the disadvantage is greater for boys." Two reasons have been identified why single sex education works for boys; teachers can focus on teaching styles that research shows works best for male students and boys show better social adjustment in SSE schools. Boys attending single sex schools evidence more maturity. Their increased social development may reflect they no longer feel the need for "Macho over-reaction" when girls are not present and the absence of the need for testosterone displays of dominance could lead boys to problem solve rather than physically react (singlesexschools.org/). Boys do benefit socially from single sex education and they benefit academically because they focus more on school and less on females.

Cornelius Riordon, educational researcher and faculty member at Providence College, summarized research regarding single sex education and reported that traditionally disadvantaged students, minorities, working class, and females (non-affluent) do better academically in single sex schools. He stated that there were dramatic positive impacts evidenced for African-American, Hispanic, male and female students when single sex education is used (brighterchoice.org/). Since inner city schools may have higher populations of minority and economically disadvantaged students, targeting single sex education as a reform issue makes sense.

Of course after teaching middle school, I think limiting contact with the opposite sex in this group of students would be a good thing. Most of my students at the alternative school were male and I noticed when a female was assigned to one of my classes then boys' academic performances and their classroom participation declined. In addition, there tended to be more chest bumping, smack talking, and sexual harassment issues when girls were present. Even in the previous story, I believe the outcome would have been different if Steve had been assigned to an all male class. I don't think he would have been so bold without LuAnn's encouragement. From the stories in this book, readers can tell I had to deal a lot with students' sexual distractions in middle school. From an experienced teacher's point of view, middle school students do not have the emotional, social, or cognitive development to successfully deal with their physical urges and they need to be separated so they can focus on learning and not each others' bodies. Some might argue that students will not gain socialization skills with the opposite sex if they are not allowed to interact and some schools have thought about that and developed a quasi-SSE program. These schools have constructed a balance by keeping SSE classes in the same building, using the same teachers, and offering the same classes to the separate gender groups. However, coeducation opportunities are offered in non-core subjects. There are different models of SSE and what it looks like in each district can vary while still improving academic performance of all our students.

There are some objections to single sex education and two groups, the American Association of University Women along with the American Civil Liberties Union's Women's Rights Project, have been outspoken while asserting that single sex education is not a 'silver bullet' for our country's educational woes. They purpose lower class size and sufficient funding as the proven solutions (msnbc.msn.com/). These groups are advocating for women's' rights; they are not representing the entire school population and I dare say, they probably have not had experience teaching coeducational classes at the middle school level. As a woman I have appreciated their interest in female education rights but as a teacher I am concerned their agendas may be more political than geared toward education reform. We cannot throw money at our failing education model or limit class sizes in our current financial state. For this reason, their advice is useless. In addition, girls appear to fare better in single sex education classes anyway so the above groups are wrong about the effectiveness of SSE for their purposes.

We can improve our students' academic accomplishments and make better use of school funding by adopting a single sex education model. We can use our existing classrooms and our current teachers to accomplish this one reform without spending more money. It is certainly worth trying and research does backs up SSE's effectiveness. We have an opportunity to change the lives of many socioeconomic disadvantaged and minority students' by implementing this sort of a reform. This one reform would be easy to make because there are currently several schools around the country that could serve as models.

At one time, only economically privileged individuals could afford to send their children to single sex education schools which were privately owned (123HelpMe.com). In 2002, President Bush signed into law, as part of the "No Child Left Behind" legislation, the reauthorization of the Elementary and Secondary Education Act, which allows local school districts to offer single sex classes and schools (Department of Education). Due to this, there is no longer a legal issue to resolve about separate but equal. Even our Supreme Court justices have given credibility to single sex education. In 1996 the justices involved in the VMI decision all agreed that single sex education offers positive educational benefits and William Rehnquist, Chief Justice, stated there was considerable evidence "That single sex education is pedagogically beneficial for some students... (brighterchoice. org/).

Local school districts have the right to create programs and schools which are single sexed. Many school districts have already done this with the greatest success being recorded in large school districts that have resources to support the switch and it is the larger school districts with higher percentages of lower socio-economic and minority students that need this kind of reform. According to the research shared here, inner city students could benefit the most from single sex education opportunities. Although SSE is beneficial at elementary and high school levels, it is middle school where this type of reform could be critically important. Due to the hormonal changes middle school students' experience, these students can think of little else but the opposite sex. Relationship issues are a huge distraction to the learning process and this is one thing we can do to help students focus on their education. When you consider this type of education reform could be accomplished without hurting budgets in large city schools there is no reason to maintain the status quo.

References and Resources

"Single-sex class results mixed, One problem: Boys will be boys, Karen Gutierrez and The Cincinnati Enquirer; enquirer.com/editions/2004/04/29/loc_kygender.html

"The Benefits of same-Sex education," Beth Burwinkel and Cincinnati Parent; cincinnatiparent.com/Articles-i-2004-08-0194491.112112_The_Benefits_of...

"Gender Inequities in the Classroom," Retrieved from WikEd 25 August 2010 from Wik.ed.unic.edu/index.php/Gender_Inequities_in_the_Classroom).

"More schools trying same-sex classrooms," Associated Press; msnbc.msn.com/id/16817616/

"Advantages for Boys," National Association For Single Sex Public Education, singlesexschools.org/advantages-forboys.htm).

"Single-Sex Classes," Brighter Choice Charter Schools; brighterchoice.org/index.php?id=29

"Education, Teaching, and public Schools-Benefits of Single Sex Education: The Benefits of Single Sex Education," 123helpme.com/view.asp?id=18682

Department of Education, Office for Civil Rights; "Single Sex Classes and Schools: Guidelines on Title IX Requirements," 4000-01-U; 2.ed.gov/about/offices/list/ocr/t9-guidelines-ss.html

"Public Schools Attempt Same-Sex Education," abc, Good Morning America; abcnews.go.com/gma/story?id=2604683

23. Hungry Joe

On the first day of class, I asked her, "What is your name, Sweetie?" I was greeted with angry eyes and a shaking head so I played off the mistake and corrected my tone as quick as possible. However, I was not the only teacher who thought Joe was a girl when he first arrived at our school. Joe had beautiful skin; his face was accentuated on each cheek by a deep dimple and he appeared soft and fleshy like a girl. Adding to his illusion, which caused my mistaken identity of this student, was an exceptionally long, curly pony tail. However, in contrast to Joe's appearance, his behavior witnessed he was all boy. Joe was twelve years old, in the seventh grade, and I would describe him as bothersome but pleasant. Joe did require a lot of individualized instruction and his behavior had to be monitored very closely. He was a special education student who had an aide that sat next to him in every class at his home school. Since we did not have aides in our alternative program Joe was thrown into the mix. There were two exceptions; Joe did not take English or math with our traditional teachers and he went to the special education room for those. Only the social studies teacher and science teacher had Joe in a core class without an aide to help. His behavior was awful some days and this student, more than any others I taught, forced me to learn classroom management techniques which worked with emotionally disturbed and behaviorally disordered students.

Eventually Joe adapted to our alternative program and began to have success; when this happened, Joe did not want to return to his home school. The first time he completed a thirty-day stay at our school he went home and begged his grandmother to call the principal and ask if he could stay with us for the rest of the year. The grandmother pleaded but our program was not designed to keep students long term. Joe had to go back to the school of his origin where he would get in trouble again... so he could be sent back to our alternative program. There were complaints made to our principal that our staff was creating a problem for home school teachers because Joe liked our school too much, wanted to stay at the alternative school, and came back to his regular assigned teachers demonstrating worse behavior than what he had shown before his placement with us. In all, Joe spent two years in each grade level of our middle school and he had multiple thirty day placements with us in each year he attended. I believe Joe may have developed a pattern of misbehavior at his home school just so he could attend our alternative program.

I was sure Joe needed the intense structure of the alternative school to help him manage his own behavior and there were too many kids and too much chaos in his home school for Joe to be successful. However, our program was not a perfect match for Joe's disabilities and in spite of Joe liking the alternative school he still needed a daily attention fix from our teachers or he would demand we notice him through his intentional misbehaviors. Some days were worse than others and on those days it seemed as if Joe had an open pit in his soul which could never be filled with enough attention; he was a classic seeker who was shrieking "Notice me" by misbehaving.

Joe appeared starved for positive interaction with adults and he could often be seen talking to the principal, police officer, or any one of his teachers in a hall. Over time and with positive reinforcement Joe learned he could gain the attention he craved by having good behavior and by being a classroom helper. Joe bonded to our school and personnel when he was allowed to help teachers in their classrooms with simple chores. Because our school was small Joe was able to get to know his teachers, became friendly with the staff, and I believe he felt like he belonged when we gave him small jobs and some responsibility for keeping classrooms running smoothly. Joe did seem happy most of the time he spent at our school but he still had days where he evidenced a lot of personal emotional tension.

Over the four years I taught Joe, he lost his soft, girl-like appearance and he matured to be a six foot-three, 200 plus pounds, muscular young man…with a long, curly ponytail. His drastic physical development was mirrored by his personality evolution which went from bothersome but pleasant to intimidating and disturbing. During Joe's second time in the eighth grade, his last year in middle school, and during his third, thirty day assignment in that same year, Joe was sliding backwards, not making any academic progress, and his behavior frightened our staff at times. I relied on the teacher–student relationship I had built with Joe over the previous three years to manage his behavior and I may have been the only teacher in the school who was not physically afraid of him. Regardless of his threatening dark looks and his physical attempts at proximity control to gain dominance, I would not walk away or back down from this student. I knew Joe needed me to assert my control in our classroom environment and he responded by regaining his self-control when I did this. It was almost like Joe was telling me he was afraid to be left up to his own devices and he needed additional help to control his own behavior.

I struggled to understand the behavioral changes I witnessed taking place in one of my favorite students and I took time to remember and contrast the drastic changes I had already observed in this young man. When he first started in that repeat, eighth grade year, Joe not only appeared different because he had grown a good five inches in height over the summer but he appeared more confident like he knew he was suddenly smarter. I was sure Joe's brain had been given him a formal thinking gift over the summer and he was right on target with his cognitive development. Joe was smarter and he was making better choices that were evidenced by his perfect attendance and his appropriate participation in class. I remembered that I was surprised to see Joe in my class at the very beginning of the year because he had not been on a left over list from the previous school year and he hardly had enough time to get into trouble or sent to us from his home school. When Joe walked into my classroom, the first week of school, I said, "Hello, son. What are you doing here?"

The other students immediately thought Joe was my biological son and asked, "You're her son?"

Joe grinned from ear to ear as I replied, "No but Joe has been at our school enough that I have decided to adopt him and I have his adoption papers in my desk drawer!" All the children laughed and Joe beamed. Joe looked around the room and noticed a young lady in class whom he knew and he requested a seat next to her. Normally, I would not have let a student on their first day pick their own seat but Joe was an exception due to his size. I gave Joe permission to sit at the back of the room next to his friend with the understanding that I would move the seating arrangement if they talked and disturbed class. I ended by saying, "Joe, you may sit at the back of the room because you are tall and you will need to sit at a desk that has a separate seat to be comfortable. But… please manage your behavior.

Don't make me break off both your legs so you can fit in a small desk up front!"

Joe rewarded my comment with, "Yes, Miss OG. I'll be good. You won't have to go gangster on me." The rest of the class laughed at my joke and at Joe's response. Joe adapted to my classroom structure in short time with the help of his friend, Rhonda. His classroom etiquette remained impeccable in that first seating placement and I did not have to rearrange the room to accommodate this one very large young man. However, I knew Joe's unusual good behavior may have been motivated as much by his desire to impress his friend, Rhonda, as it was due to his sudden mental maturity.

Rhonda was a very bright and lovely young lady who dressed like a boy, walked like a boy, and could have easily passed for a male if it had not been for her beautiful female eyes. When I first saw Rhonda, her all over physical appearance looked familiar to me and she reminded me of another student, a male, I had taught two years earlier. I checked her last name on the list and sure enough she had a brother and he was her twin. Rhonda's brother had been a gifted science student and I had enjoyed having him in class. I was hoping for the same things from Rhonda and she did not disappoint me; she turned out to be an awesome student and she was even better at science than her brother.

Putting Rhonda and Joe together in class turned out to be a good decision because Joe excelled in clinical labs which required physical processing skills and Rhonda was insightful and excelled in theory. They made a great team and Joe's attention seeking became less pronounced while Rhonda was in the class. They both were doing above average work that eventually evolved into a friendly competition. That first thirty day stay in the eighth grade that year for Joe was like a dream and all the academic potential I knew was locked inside of him spilled out revealing a real critical thinker! I could not have been happier for Joe because he now realized his own potential and he began to get attention for being a good student. While trying to contend with and outdo his friend, Joe stretched to reach his highest academic levels of achievement. When the first science benchmark scores came back Joe had scored a ninety-four percent and had only missed one question. Actually, he had outdone his friend, Rhonda, but she did not mind and she let him boast without complaining. I was beginning to wonder why Joe was classified as learning disabled because he certainly did not manifest any disabilities in my classroom. I was beginning to think Joe's deficits were strictly related to his family life.

As his academic performance increased in all subject areas, Joe received the attention he craved by being named middle school student of the week. He was excited when he came into my room and asked me if I had heard the announcement on the speaker, "Mrs. G., did you hear? I won student of the week and I am going to get an award, some certificate, and coupons I can spend like money."

I bubbled back, "Yes, Joe I was so excited last Friday when we voted to give you the award that I had a hard time not telling you... but I wanted you to be surprised."

Joe enjoyed his fame and continued his newly established top student attitude until Rhonda transferred back to her home school. Then Joe became almost melancholy in his behaviors and just seemed to drag his carcass around the building. He still complied with teachers' request and he still volunteered to help in my room but Joe was not himself. One day, Joe hung around after school for just five minutes in a pretense of helping me straighten the room. First, he began talking to me about his friend Rhonda and his voice became extremely tender, "Mrs. Gifford, do you know Rhonda fights like a boy and she carries a pistol! Her twin brother was a gang leader until he got sent to jail and now Rhonda belongs to the gang. I have known Rhonda since the second grade and she wasn't like this before...do you know why Rhonda looks and acts like a boy?"

I replied, "I was sorry to hear that Rhonda's brother, Rex, went to jail because he had a lot of potential. However, after teaching Rhonda's brother, I expected she might have a gang affiliation because it sounded like Rex was pressured into joining a gang by his own family members. Maybe Rhonda was expected to do the same... and Joe, I do have an idea why girls sometimes act like boys and I am sorry if I am right."

Joe recognized what I was saying about Rhonda, "I use to like Rhonda as a girlfriend and she wasn't always like this. She used to like guys for boyfriends... then she got raped. Now she won't go out with guys and says she likes girls instead. That just sucks! I still like Rhonda, Mrs. Gifford, but I know she will never be my girlfriend. So, I am going to be the best friend she could ever have and I am going to protect her."

I complimented Joe, "I'm sure Rhonda appreciates your friendship and she cares for you as a friend, Joe. I am glad you told me about Rhonda and I do understand better why she projects herself as a male but her behavior never made me feel negative toward her. Rhonda is a beautiful and smart young lady who just happens to dress and act… like a boy. I can't tell you that what you want to happen between the two of you will ever happen but I can tell you that friendship is a good place to start. Just be careful and don't get suckered into joining a gang with Rhonda. You don't need that trouble because you could end up spending your life in jail. Besides, in this area, I know the only way out of a gang is death. Once you are in the gang it is a lifetime commitment and that is a long time to give up control of your life to someone else." Joe just shrugged his shoulders and looked down at the floor.

I changed the subject because I did not want my student to think I was lecturing him about his choices and I knew if I came across that way then he would do the opposite of what I recommended. So I said, "Let me guess why you stayed after school today. You want to know how many good days you have earned, right? You want me to tell you how soon you might be able to transfer back to your home school and how soon you could see … Rhonda during the school day?"

I showed Joe the number of good days he had earned and left him with a departing word, "Be careful, Joe. Sometimes it only takes one bad choice to change our lives forever. Rhonda may need your friendship but I don't think she needs your protection. I've got a feeling Rhonda can take care of herself since she has a pistol and is surrounded by gangland soldiers."

After I sent Joe on his way, I thought, "I hope she doesn't break his heart because Joe is seriously interested in this young lady." Joe was fifteen and I knew students that age sometimes really believed they were in love and it was a forever love, the kind of love that makes young people think their lives are over if it ends. I was afraid Joe had a bad case of the forever love and the person he idolized had the potential to destroy him because he was fragile. Joe's delicate emotional state was born in rejection; his father deserted him, his mother died of a drug overdose, and he was living with a grandmother who did not want the responsibility of his care. I knew Joe was vulnerable because he was deprived of the love a child needs to become emotionally stable and if Rhonda rejected him then I knew Joe's emotional instability could cause his behavior to spiral out of control.

I knew a lot about Joe's home life because he had shared openly in class his situation. Although I never encouraged students to tell personal information, sometimes my students would just blurt out the contents of their souls while trying to make sense of their lives. I remembered that Joe had started sharing the day another student attempted "Yo momma joke" on him. When Joe didn't issue a prompt comeback, a different student asked Joe if he was going to let the boy talk about his momma that way. Joe responded, "I don't care. My momma was a crack ho and she died of an overdose. Say what you want… because I didn't know my momma and I don't care."

Needless to say, the atmosphere in the room tensed up and the other student felt sorry he had initiated what he thought was going to be a friendly exchange of jokes. Then a girl in class put a new spin on Joe's unexpected outburst, "Man, even if she was what you say, she is still your momma and you should respect her cause she brought you life. She did a good thing in bringing you into the world, she didn't have to, and she could have got rid of you." Joe's eyes widened as the girl spoke and I could tell he was listening intently. Then other students who were sensitive to Joe's feelings sought to comfort him by sharing their personal histories with their drug addicted parents. When this happened, I gently assumed the role of a confidant and only intervened to make sure the children did not make fun of each other or injure each other's tender spirits. These students were healing each others' hurts best they could by sharing their own.

That day I learned why many of my students desperately tried to gain an adult's recognition and why they were manifesting attention seeking behaviors in the classroom. Many of my students were hungry for the attention only a caring adult could supply. Joe learned something too that day. When Joe realized he was not alone and other students had similar experiences with absent or addicted parents, everything that was bothering him tumbled out of his mouth so quickly that I felt the need to caution the whole class. I reminded them of our privacy agreement before we left the room. We had instituted a policy that we would not gossip or share things with other students that were discussed in our PSR class… if it was personal information. Since three-fourths of my students had shared the negative things they had experienced due to their parent' substance abuse, they all nodded in agreement. The students did not break Joe's confidence or gossip about each other after that class period. They were a good bunch of kids and became loyal to each other.

That day Joe shared he lived with his grandmother and older sister, the seventeen year old sister was going down the path of their dead mother and was using drugs, and the grandmother said she didn't want any of the trouble her grandchildren caused her. The whole class got the impression Joe's grandmother did not want him or his sister living with her and the grandmother had made it a point to tell Joe that fact very often. Joe implied his older sister prostituted to make money for her drug habit. He said he did not like what sister did, but he loved her because she was his only close family member. In addition, Joe said he did not know who his father was, other than he was Mexican and Joe evidenced his hatred of a father he never met, with vehement emotion in his voice, while talking about him.

Joe reported he respected and loved his grandmother for taking care of him but it sounded like this grandmother was not affectionate and that she was wrapped up in her own health concerns. I could have guessed as much due to my limited experience with this caregiver. In the beginning our staff had contacted Joe's grandmother because we wanted to keep her informed about Joe's progress but the grandmother told us she wasn't interested and we didn't have to call unless there was a problem. The grandmother let us know we didn't have to call if there was a problem because she could not do anything about it. The older woman told us she had the children forced on her by the state and she really did not want the stress and responsibility of taking care of them. After talking to the grandmother, we concluded she probably wanted and needed the money the state paid her for keeping the children in relative foster care. The words she used to describe her situation were, "It's not fair to me because I raised my children. I don't have the strength to chase these kids around. If you think Joe's bad you should see his sister. I got both these kids and I don't want none." When I suggested she turn the children back into the state if she really did not want to be responsible for their care, she informed me, "Why, I can't do that. How would I buy my medicine?"

I could not tell if this grandmother had any true affection for the children in her care but I could tell Joe had been hurt by her lack of supervision. When Joe first came to us in his seventh grade year, he had been heavily using drugs and I suspected it was an upper like cocaine. I had spent a lot of time teaching about substance abuse issues during that first year because many of my students evidenced aggressive and hyper behaviors that were indicative of someone using uppers. I tried to get these students to rethink their choices and I knew Joe had been influenced when one day in our elective class Joe concluded, "My mother would probably be alive today if she would not have used drugs."

I asked Joe, "If your mother was alive today and could talk to you about drug use, do you think she would want you to use drugs?" Joe said he didn't know so I asked him, "Do you think mothers in general want their children to use drugs?" Joe answered no to this question and I simply responded, "Well, then?" Recognition was reflected in Joe's eyes and he proclaimed, "I hate drugs and I'm never going to use them again!" Joe's behavior had improved after that and I believe Joe stayed clean for about two and one-half years, until now, his second time in the eighth grade, and until he got a crush on Rhonda.

While processing my history with this student, I identified the source of Joe's morphing and I realized that Joe began to change for the worse when he started trying to gain Rhonda's affection! Then, I learned Joe had been hiding from his teachers a house arrest monitor that was strapped to his leg. I concluded that Joe probably was already in Rhonda's gang and his assignment to our school came through the juvenile justice system for some type of summer gang activity. That's when I realized, Joe's presence in our program was not generated by a school referral as his previous assignments had been. Joe now had legal problems.

I felt dumb after considering the clues Joe gave me. He knew too much about Rhonda's after school activities to be naïve about her gang affiliation and I was sure that Joe could have joined Rhonda's posse just to please her. I trembled when a vision crossed my mind of both Rhonda and Joe carrying pistols while high on drugs. Joe didn't appear to be under the influence in the classroom now but I was afraid he would give into the temptation if Rhonda wanted him to use with her. He was so vulnerable that I imagined Joe would do anything anyone asked him if they would accept him and show him attention. Joe's need for love and acceptance would pull him into a pseudo family relationship with other troubled inner city kids. I feared whatever progress our staff had made with this student would soon disappear in front of our eyes and I wished we could have kept Joe from going back to his home school environment where he would have daily contact with his new flame.

Rhonda had left our school and I doubted she would be back; Rhonda did not have a history causing discipline problems at school. So unless, she got in trouble with the law again this year, she would not be back. I was aware that Rhonda had been wearing an ankle monitor because she had talked about the time she had left wearing the contraption; it was soon to be taken off. Her release was at the beginning of our second semester and I had learned Joe was due to have his ankle strap removed about the same time. After that, both Joe and Rhonda could be on the streets together. I reasoned, "If we could just limit Joe's contact with Rhonda and her gang during the school day we might be able to keep Joe from crossing over into a life of crime." Equal influence time was my prayer-plea for Joe. I was sure Joe respected the alternative program teachers enough that we could have a positive influence on him if we gained equal time.

However, Joe earned his way back to Rhonda in record time. When he was notified of his impending release he said he was happy to go back to his home school and I knew his joy was initiated by his anticipation of seeing Rhonda during the school day. However, I was counting on Joe's past history at his home school to initiate his quick return to our program. I didn't think his new motivation to stay in that placement could make up for the negative pattern of interaction he had already established with former teachers. He was bound to get sent back to the alternative program because his former teachers did not like Joe being there.

When Joe cycled back to us, just about one month later, he told me the reason he was sent back was that a male teacher had "Got up in my face about something stupid." Apparently, Joe had threatened the teacher and told him to back off or he would hit him. Since Joe had assaulted a teacher in the past his threats were taken seriously and he was sent back to our program. I had been right about Joe's reputation causing him to cycle back. He was on an unofficial list of students whose behavior posed threats to staff safety and his home school had established a zero tolerance for his behavior. Over time and with repeated threats of violence or actual acts of violence committed by Joe against staff, teachers were careful not to take his threats lightly.

I did acknowledge to Joe that he may have been correct about this last incident; the teacher may have purposely got up in Joe's face about something stupid just to trigger Joe's threatening behavior in order to send him back to us, I let Joe know his past transgressions merited the assignment.

After talking to Joe, he acknowledged he should not have responded the way he did to the teacher and he said, "The whole thing was just stupid and I should not have fallen into the trap. If I get to go back then it won't happen again." I was astonished at Joe's maturity and his thinking process which allowed him to understand how his behavior in the past set him up for his current situation. Joe's vow to change his response to adults in conflict situations impressed me and I felt Joe had learned something about social skills. In addition, his academic performance with us that year showed Joe was becoming wiser. Joe fell right back into our program as though he had never left and even without Rhonda's friendly competition for grades, Joe's grades and behavior were amazing. For that reason, I did not immediately see the negative changes taking place in Joe.

However, the change had begun. Now when I look back, I realize Joe was exceptionally quiet, he did display more hyperactivity than before, and he had a brooding manner about him. I assumed he was a little melancholy over his second separation form Rhonda and that he was just trying to hold everything together so he could earn his way back to his friend. Therefore, I did not analyze his mood differences or even consider Joe might be using drugs again. He was still polite and respectful to me and he was still being an excellent class helper. His grades were impeccable in science and he had the highest score in my eighth grade science class. He was a top student!

The only thing different Joe did this second tour, which was the least bit bothersome, was to request frequent conferences with both our principal and resource officer. Since, our program did allow our school administrator to give students credit for one extra good day for each five days of good behavior, Joe was bent on earning those days. However, he wanted to check his total with the office daily. Joe earned his return in record time because he was in tune with our program, had perfect attendance, and he worked the system to his advantage. In fact, Joe came and left so quickly that second time in his last eighth grade year, we hardly knew he had been there.

Then our school's early release for good behavior policy inspired complaints from Joe's home school teachers; they did not like Joe being returned so quickly. Within a week of Joe's departure to his home school he was sent back to our care and he was not happy! We were exactly in the middle of the school year and starting the second semester when Joe returned. This was his final assignment to our middle school program and it was decided that Joe would stay with us for the remainder of his middle school education. My prayers were answered and Joe would be separated from Rhonda's influence during the school day; she would be in one building and he would be in another. However, Joe would not be able to earn his way back to Rhonda for the rest of the school and he began to rage about his situation.

Joe became a very different kid reminiscent of the seventh grader all our teachers complained about. He was very loud, non-compliant, and he started intimidating some of our staff! I thought Joe just needed to rage for a while to get the anger out of his system and that he would calm down in a week or so. A week became weeks and our staff became exhausted dealing with Joe's emotional outburst and his classroom disruption episodes. Everyone was patient with Joe, maybe too patient, but this was a student who had brought pride to our hearts and tears to our eyes over his accomplishments and we were not yet willing to write him off. I never dreamed Joe would completely reverse the behavior our staff worked so hard to help him develop over three and one-half years in such a short time. Now most of our teachers, like his home school staff, just wanted Joe gone!

Although I often heard Joe being non-compliant and talking back to other teachers in the hall, he was still not causing disruptions in my classroom or being disrespectful to me. Matter of fact, he was not coming to my class… because he was usually in trouble by the third period in the morning and he was either sent to the ISS room or sent home before I saw him. I had been taking work to the ISS room to him and he was making a minimal attempt to complete it. I wanted to keep Joe after school and try to talk to him about the changes I had seen but I could not mandate he attend tutoring and I did not want to issue a detention for failure to complete his work. I felt a detention would insert a negative into our relationship and he was already was already receiving enough of those. I was thinking what to do and how to gain individual time with Joe when Mrs. Lincoln floated into my room off the hall.

My favorite substitute teacher was a joy to be around and I treasured her appearance that day because she always had a kind word to say to all the staff and our kids. Although, I couldn't see the magic carpet she was riding on, I was sure it was there because of the ethereal, lighter than air quality of her appearance. The magic was further evidenced by her smile that reflected light across her entire face. Her hair was short, neat, and pulled back from her face to reveal a pair of the kindest eyes I have ever seen. That day she wore colors I could never have successfully worn together; the blended pink, orange, and red of her accessories and dress complemented her light caramel complexion. She was always beautifully dressed, as only elder church ladies know how to dress, with matching jewelry and other accessories. If I closed my eyes then I could imagine Mrs. Lincoln wearing an extravagant church hat while waving a laced praise-kerchief in service and it brought fond memories to my mind of former church ladies I knew that could correct the direction of their minister with their rallying "Amen's" or their corrective "taint sos." I smiled at that thought then looked down while reflecting on my own usual casual dress that morning which was safe and familiar attire for science teachers, durable slacks and a washable top. My unruly hair was held in place with a headband. "What an unlikely friendship pair," I thought. Then I remembered the common bond I shared with Mrs. Lincoln that was based on three principles, we both were women of faith, we both cared immensely for the children we taught at the alternative school, and we were both praying grandmothers.

Mrs. Lincoln chirped, "Good morning, Mrs. Gifford, I just wanted to come by and say hi. How is your school year going?"

"I would say, I have had a good year and I really do like our new administrators. There is only one thing wrong." In my best teasing voice I added, "The students accused me of acting like you the other day so I thought I better tell you about it."

"Why, Mrs. Gifford, what did you do?" she asked.

"Well, the children have been popping up out of their seats walking around the class and not able to tell me where they were going. I had to go put my hands on their shoulders and lead them back to their seats. I could hardly finish a sentence or give complete instructions because of this annoying new behavior. If I would not have intercepted them then they would have traveled out in the hall. They are using some kind of new drug that's causing the behavior and I was frustrated because I had not discovered it. I rolled up some paper and started swatting those students like I was killing flies on the backside of their heads when they popped up. I was tired of chasing them! That's when one of the students said, 'Why are you acting like Mrs. Lincoln? She be getting after us like that too.' I thought you would understand my actions."

With the most sober expression I had ever seen on her face she commented, "What's wrong with that Mrs. Gifford? The students need discipline and you were just waking them up."

"Well, I just wanted you to know that I thanked the students for the analogy and told them I took their comparison to you as a compliment," I replied. We both laughed heartily after I related my story and Mrs. Lincoln told me of her new job assignment at our school.

We pleasantly conversed briefly during my planning period and I found out Mrs. Lincoln would be teaching reading improvement to our kids for the rest of the school year. I knew she would only have two or three students at one time in her room and Joe would be one of them. That's when I said, "Mrs. Lincoln do you remember Joe? Well, I was hoping you could talk to him. There have been some disturbing changes in his behavior and he would rather stay in the ISS room than be present in class. He scored a ninety-four on his first benchmark in science then failed the benchmark we just completed last week.

The most puzzling thing is that he has become hostile acting and has been intimidating staff members. Even though he has a history of assaulting teachers at his home school none of our staff have ever felt threatened by him until now. Joe's changing and it might be a renewed drug use but somehow... I think it is more than that. In addition, one of the other students told me, 'Joe can sneak stuff into school because no one up front would dare search him too close because they are afraid of him.' I don't know that it has gone that far but the other students are convinced our staff is afraid of Joe. If the rest of our students start thinking we are afraid of them then they might try to get physical with us and we can't have that happening. If Joe continues to intimidate adults in front of other students and is non-compliant to our rules then he will influence the rest of our kids. Since you will have individualized time with Joe while teaching reading, do you think you could find out what is wrong with our boy?"

Mrs. Lincoln returned later that week to my room and in confidence told me Joe was involved in criminal activity. She appeared quite concerned as she reported, "Joe is making money by beating up people. His sister acts as a prostitute and leads guys down an alley where Joe and his friend jumps them, beats them up, and takes their money. When I talked to Joe about what this kind of activity does to his soul, he laughed and said he was only beating up Mexicans because they always carry cash." Now I knew and it made sense that Joe would target and feel no remorse about beating up Mexican males; Joe's absent father was Mexican… and I was pretty sure the friend helping commit the crimes was Rhonda. Rhonda would have no remorse about attacking males who were taking advantage of a girl with a drug problem.

Before Mrs. Lincoln left my room, I thanked her and I agreed with her that when a person physically hurts other people it deadens their soul and they may lose self-esteem. I always thought that self-hate was the true root of violence and I knew Joe did not like himself. How could he when his own parents and grandmother did not love him enough to stay with him or care for him? Now, I was sure the acts of violence were changing Joe and as he became more violent outside of school the staff had more to fear at school when Joe was present. Understanding the urgency of my mission, I left my room to find Joe.

As I walked down the hall, I could hear a former mental health colleague of mine say in her perky little voice, "Let's find out what's wrong with these people so we can fix them!" She used to say this at the start of every day and it always made me smile. I wanted to smile now because I knew what was wrong with Joe and maybe I could find a way to help him. I prayed silently as I left my room and headed down the hall. I had only progressed one third of the way down, when the special education teacher approached me. She had walked ahead of her student who stopped and slumped up against the wall at the opposite end of the hall. It was Joe and he promptly looked down at his feet when he saw me coming. I nodded politely at the special education teacher and I headed toward Joe with my colleague in close pursuit at my heels. Once I stopped and was standing directly in front of our common student I demanded, "What's wrong with my son, Joe?"

Mrs. Crew, behind my rear shoulder, answered for Joe, "We were just on our way to find you, Mrs. Gifford. Joe doesn't want to come to my class today and said he would rather stay in the ISS room and do nothing."

I began, "Joe, can you tell me why you are no longer interested in getting an education? Mrs. Crew has always been one of your favorite teachers and you know she wants to help you."

Joe continued averting his gaze and replied, "It don't matter. I'm turning sixteen and I'll go on to the ninth grade."

I inquired, "Is that true Mrs. Crew? Will Joe be passed on? I don't know how Joe could be certain, since we still have several weeks of school left this year."

Choosing her words carefully, Mrs. Crew answered, "Joe and I had a meeting with the head of services yesterday and he was told that he would be passed to the ninth grade."

I was perturbed that the higher-ups administering special education services would set up the teachers on the front line that way but I stuffed my personal feelings and focused on Joe. "Alright, that explains your desire not to do any work because you know you are going to be passed on. However, it does not explain your hostile attitude and the intimidation tactics you have been directing toward our staff. You were coming to get me to help you talk Joe into coming into your class room right?" I said as I whirled from looking at Joe to gaze at the special education teacher. Mrs. Crew rewarded me with a nod. I continued and whirled back to face Joe, "I've never known Mrs. Crew to need my help getting a student into her class before. I have had to talk students out of her room because they wanted to stay and generally liked it there. Joe, what has changed?"

For the first time in weeks, Joe looked up at me directly in the eyes and said, "I fell off the wagon."

I clarified, "You are using drugs?"

He replied, "Yip, I just fell off the wagon… but I'm going to get back on the wagon."

"I believe you, Joe, and I know you will try to do better but you are going to need help. You know everyone at our school has your best interest in mind and you could choose to talk to anyone of us from the police officer on down to the janitor. Someone will listen to you and will help you without judging. What can we do to help you? "

Joe answered, "I've been doing stuff I'm not proud of and I need to stop."

I chose my words carefully, "You know from being in my class I expect my students to be problem solvers and not become victims of their own drama. So, Joe we are not going to focus on what you have done because people often do stuff they are not proud of when they get involved in drug use. It does not mean they are bad people but they do bad things because they have to feed their addiction. If you are doing bad stuff to get drugs then you might have a serious problem. Joe, do you think you might be addicted?"

"Yes, Miss O.G. I think I need help because I want to stop doing bad things." Joe's voice began to shake a little as he continued, "At first, I thought it was fun, like a game. Then, I began to feel bad inside and I got mad thinking about what I done. I told Ms. Lincoln and she told me she would pray for me."

"Ms. Lincoln is a good friend and you have other friends at our school too. Do you want me to find some help for you today?" Joe said yes and he would appreciate any help he could get. So, Joe went to class with Mrs. Crew and I continued down the hall to the office. There, I met with the counselor and I told her about Joe asking for help and without telling her any details, I informed her that Joe was using crime to support his drug habit. Then, I told her that Joe requested help because he said the drugs and crime were making him feel bad inside. Mrs. Lopez jumped into action to provide intervention for our student. After conferencing with Joe, she researched his family and arranged for him to go and live with an estranged uncle who could provide closer supervision and who would be supportive while Joe received treatment.

After a week passed in Joe's new living environment, he told me that he liked living with his uncle but he sometimes missed seeing his sister because he was worried about her. I told Joe that people have to want help to be successful overcoming addiction and maybe when he was clean and sober he could show his sister it was possible to beat addiction and she would want help too. I cautioned Joe to take care of himself first because he could not help anyone until he helped himself. I cautioned Joe, "Sometimes even when we try to help people they won't accept it. Remember, that I told you this...if your sister won't accept help to overcome her addiction then you can't give up your treatment and join her! If you stay straight she will have a good example and when she is finally ready she will know she can overcome addition because you did! Promise me Joe that you won't give up just because other people you know are still using drugs. You are better than that. Don't throw yourself away!"

Joe told me not to worry that he would not give up and he was going to save his sister by saving himself first. Joe, the rescuer, wanted to save the females in his life from destroying themselves. Joe kept his word; he began attending a youth treatment program after school and his uncle made sure he kept his appointments. However, Joe had no interest in attending classes because he knew he was being promoted to the ninth grade. When Joe was told in advance that he was receiving a social promotion, that notification sapped his former motivation. I never saw Joe in my class more than twice a week and whenever I saw Joe at school, he would demand my attention by causing minor discipline problems.

He would laugh or say something loud in the hall just to get me to pay attention to him. I thought Joe wanted me to stop the student line and look into his eyes so I could see he was drug free. He would gaze upward in a teasing manner and turn his head to the opposite side where I could not readily see his eyes. Then, I would walk up to Joe, grab his shirt collar with both my hands and pull his head down to my eye level to gaze directly at him and say, "You want me to snatch you up outta here?"

Joe would reply. "No Miss OG, I'll be good." The other students were impressed I could manage such a large student and as we restarted our walk down the hall, Joe would give me a wink when they weren't looking. When Joe did this, I believe he attempted to make up for the previous bad example he had set for other students. He purposely gave me an opportunity to discipline him and he respectfully accepted the correction for my benefit. In his own way, Joe tried to right the chaos he had caused earlier.

Joe was a good kid living in a very bad circumstance. He never was disrespectful to me and I never felt threatened by his attitude, physical size, or his past history of assaulting teachers. In the four years I had spent teaching Joe, I had seen him improve from a failing, non-compliant student to become a middle school, award-winning super star. At one point in Joe's education, all the middle school staff was ready to burst the buttons off their shirts due to the pride they felt in his accomplishments. However, Joe had many things in his personal live that were against him and his renewed drug use and the crime spree he committed to support his need for drugs, almost destroyed him. This student was hungry for love and attention and he was willing to do anything to gain what he was missing in his life including joining a gang, using drugs and committing crime to impress his friend, Rhonda.

Discussion:

The emotional development of a human being is a complex thing and children like Joe who have been deprived of a parent's love and attention, may not learn well in school when their lives are emotionally unfulfilled. They may fear rejection and disappointment when they seek attention of adults and yet they may initiate discipline problems to see if they can precipitate the rejection. These students are testing us to see if we can be trusted with their fragile emotional states. While seeking attention through misbehavior, these students wait for rejection and once rejection is confirmed, emotionally deprived children may decide to self-destruct or lash out to harm others who withhold their emotional support. When working with these students, educators have an awesome task; teachers must help emotionally disturbed students bond with the school environment and school personnel. The emotional support has to be there first for these kids to overcome their cycle of misbehavior and negative attention seeking. Educators have to expect emotionally disturbed students to try their patience. The attention students gain for their negative behaviors may serve as a crutch and they are not readily able to give up that source of comfort; they can always get attention by misbehaving. Changes in these types of student behaviors may not take place over a grading period, a few months, and maybe not even in a school year and it may only take one new rejection to bring the emotionally disturbed student back to the initial state of upset. This story testifies to the sacred role teachers may play in some students' lives because teachers could be the only adults that show concern for a single child. Those classroom seekers who gain attention through negative actions, like Hungry Joe, and those children who are wall flowers and fade into the background while asking nothing of us, both may need our recognition. These kids need to know they are valued by someone. **How can we avoid dealing with constant discipline problems in the classroom from attention seekers like Hungry Joe? What can we do to keep students from fading into the background?**

Joe fit the profile of a certain type of criminal; he was born into poverty, experienced rejection from his parents and society, he had feelings of low self worth and deprivation, he was born with learning disabilities, he had experienced long-time failure in school, he witnessed violence in his community, he participated in violent acts against others, he abused alcohol and drugs, and he was a good kid! **What things evidenced Joe's true spirit in the story?**

Topics for Research:

What percentages of criminals in jail today were diagnosed with emotional problems as children? What percentages of criminals in jail today had biological parents who were absent when they were growing up? What percentage of criminals in jail today witnessed violence toward someone they loved or were victims of violence themselves? What percentages of criminals have a drug addiction problem?

Things to Do

If you are an educator, think of the welfare of your students as you would think about the welfare of your own sons or daughters. Help them achieve their highest potential by taking time to find out who they are and what they like (smaller classrooms and fewer students may be needed for this to happen). Youth need to bond with caring adults whose feelings are consistent for them. We can't undo what has been done to a child but we can help all of our students see they have worth. Teachers need to understand that children who constantly seek attention are emotionally immature and are expressing an unfulfilled need. We can find ways to help children feel valued in the classroom and help them bond. If adults fail to reach these needy children and help them achieve positive attention for socially acceptable behaviors then gangs will provide a family for our emotional disturbed, inner city students.

Caregivers should find individual time to spend with each of their children every day. It really doesn't take that much time and as little as fifteen minutes reading a bedtime story and laughing together will do wonders to make a child feel valued. Set aside family time and have fun with your children. Praise your children for the good things they do and tell them you love them often. In our busy lives, it is difficult to find individual time with each child in the family but if we don't then our kids may fall prey to gang membership because they promote bonding through spending time together in illegal activities.

24. Person Centered Education

According to person centered education experts, positive student-teacher relationships are built with "empathy, warmth, and genuineness" (Motshinnig-Pitrik, Cornelius-White). Chronic attention seekers who disrupt classroom instruction may be students who need, more than other students, to experience the atmosphere provided in classrooms where person-centered education is being used. Person centered education fosters caring relationships between teachers and their students, students are respected for the autonomy of their person, and teachers show their students' that their academic success, safety, and well-being are all of concern to them (Stuhlman, Hamre, & Pinta, 2002). I believe ensuring academic success of at risk students may depend totally on the positive relationships teachers build with them and research shows this may be especially true for students with multiple risk factors like Hungry Joe.

Often, poorer academically performing students may just be classified as special needs students without a specific category or label. However, students who over a long period of time are not able to learn when their failure to learn cannot be explained by intellect, health, or physical disabilities are often thrown into a special education category called (ED) emotional disturbance (Specialchildren.about.com). In general, students who receive the ED classification have developed a documented history of academic incompetence and inappropriate behaviors in traditional classroom settings. There is a more serious level 4 EBD classification (Emotionally Behavior Disturbed) which mandates a student be assigned to a self-contained classroom with, one on one, instructional assistance for students who are classified this way (BRIGHT HUB).

Joe, from the preceding story, was an adolescent who had multiple risk factors for academic failure and he had an EBD diagnoses because he could be violent; Joe had a history of assaulting teachers and that is why he had an individual aide assigned to him at his home school. Our alternative school did not have individual aides available to help our students and many times our staff could have been at risk for harm while these students were attending our program. Building a caring relationship with middle school students like Joe was critical for staff safety reasons. However, developing a positive relationship with our teachers may have helped many of our students, like Joe, exceed the expectations of their documented disabilities. One authority states that supportive teacher-student relationships can promote the social and emotional health of early adolescents who have learning disabilities (Murray). While another resource, believes that positive student-teacher relationships may help compensate for the missing element which makes some children aggressive (Meehan, B., Hughes, J., & Cavell T.).

Inner city, large school districts will have many students like Joe because there is a direct correlation with students receiving a taxonomy of emotional and behavioral disordered and their family's low income status. According to one source reporting family income relationship, there could be a higher percentage of poor kids identified as ED. Second, there could be a race bias since African American students were diagnosed ED at disproportionately higher rates than other groups (Project IDEAL, Emotional Disturbance). Since race and poverty demographics are often disapportionately higher in large cities, the need for teachers to connect to their students by developing positive student- teacher relationships in these schools could be critical. When students were interviewed in South Los Angeles, Latino and African American students, the interview revealed that students would be open to learning and trying harder if teachers confronted them in a positive manner and these youth stated they thought positive student-teacher relationships had the greatest impact on low income students and students of color (Cervantes).

According to the above students interviewed, teachers need to connect emotionally to their students to help them gain autonomy and self-actualize. The true authorities are our inner city, at risk youth and they have spoken. Young people like the ones in South Los Angeles have stressed the importance a student-teacher positive relationship has to academic success. At this time when academic failure is high among large city students, person centered education is a method that is worth trying. However, I don't think the pedagogy of PCE is something we can teach all educators because I believe concern for students' total being is at the core of a person who feels called to teach verses trained to be a teacher. Students can tell if the concern is faked. The theory itself, person centered education, can be made a subject of training but the ability to implement it successfully in a classroom reveals the spirit of a truly dedicated and concerned teacher. For that reason, urban administrators may need trained to identify individuals who possess the characteristics of teachers that can successfully create a person centered education environment in their classrooms.

Education reform in large city school districts should offer person centered educational training for its teachers but school districts should also attempt to hire and retain teachers who demonstrate this passion in the classroom. Research tells us that students want positive relationships with their teachers and that they will learn better if these connections are developed. In addition, teachers' relationships to students with disabilities and students of various racial groups can prevent students from dropping out of school according to Project Ideal. One of the most interesting conceptualizations of PCE currently exists in public education and it is called Urban Boarding Schools.

Anchor, a non-profit that partners to create boarding programs for underserved, low-income students in Brooklyn, has responded to the charges that schools must do more to help students. According to the executive director, Barbara Welles-Iler, the organization "Grew out of a belief that what happens outside the school setting has a great impact on what happens at school" (Elenor J Bader and The Brooklyn Rail). These unique boarding school options in public education may be a literal life line for students who live in unsafe gang and drug infested neighborhoods. For many of these youth, attending an urban boarding school allows them not to worry about their own physical safety and they can focus more on learning. Classrooms are smaller and school days are longer with additional social skills classes required. Education often extends into the evening hours, students are restricted in their free time, and teachers provide tutoring late into the evening. The school environment promotes students bonding with their teachers and teachers show their concern for the whole student by teaching and discussing social issues the students face. According to Josh Edelman, a principal who served as a principal for four years of the oldest urban boarding school, SEED, nearly three-fourths of the students went on a four year college when they graduated high school

(Public Education Network). Chicago may now be at the front of this type of educational reform since they have hired Mr. Edelman.

When we think about students who are living in highly dysfunctional neighborhoods and in non-supportive families, or homeless families, a boarding school environment may be the only way to compensate for their emotional deficits. Teaching the whole person, person centered education, involves caring enough about our students to give them a safe and supportive environment so they can learn. Classroom teachers can do this for students during the day but some of our students because they are at high risk for both physical harm and academic failure may need to live in boarding school environments. This is another educational reform we should consider for our inner city youth.

References and Resources

Stuhlman, M.W., Hamre,B.,Hamre, & Pinta, Advancing the Teen/Teacher Connection. Education Digest, Nov2002, Vol.68 Issue3, p15, 3p

"In Special Need Children: Emotional behavior disorder," About.com http://specialchildren, about.com/od/mentalhealthissues/a/ED.htm Retrieved September 7th 2010

"Social Maladjustment Disorder vs. Emotional Behavioral Disorder...," Oct 31, 2009. Bright HUB http://www. Brighthub.com/education/special/articles/54549.aspx Retrieved September 7th 2010

"Supportive teacher-student relationships: Promoting the Social and Emotional Health of early Adolescents with High Incident Disabilities. Christopher Murray, Childhood Education 78.5 (2002): 285-290

Meehan, B., Hughes, J., & Cavell T. (2003) Teacher-Student Relationships as Compensatory Resources for Aggressive Children. Child Development.74 (4) p1145-1157.

"Person-Centered Education: A Meta-Analysis of Care in Progress. Journal of Border Educational Research, 3 (1), 81-87. Motshinnig-Pitrik R., Cornelius-White J., Hoey A. & Cornelius-white C. (2004).

"Emotional Disturbance," Project IDEAL. http://projectidealonline.org/emotionalDisturbance.php Retrieved September 7th 2010.

Cervantes, J. (2007) Student-teacher relationship important factor in learning says kids. Learning Power News. http://learningpower.gseis.ucla.edu/aspirations/articles/story3.html Retrieved 2010.

"Urban Boarding Schools Offer Twist on the Elite, "Eleanor J. Bader and The Brooklyn Rail. Http://www.brooklynrail.org/2007/2/local/urban-boarding Retrieved September 6th 2010

"Urban Boarding Schools, Families and communities Key To Success?" Public Education Network Weekly NewsBlast. http;//www.publiceducation.org/newsblast/march08/March21_printable.html Retrieved September 6th 2010

25. Amos the Axe Man

Amos was bald, extremely thin, and had an alien shaped head with eyes that appeared to fit the top half of his face but were conspicuously too large in proportion to the bottom half of his face and his small chin. I began observing Amos as soon as he walked in the door because his eyes started roving the room and at first, I thought Amos was casing the environment for something to steal. However, Amos's eyes did not linger on objects; his eye movements were mechanical and jerky like two robotic independently moving cameras. It appeared that this student was scanning the room while assessing his new environment for threats. Amos did not blink his eyes once while engaged in his discovery activity and when he was finished with his evaluation, his eyes came to rest on our classroom entrance door, the only way in and the only way out. After my other students sat down in their assigned seats Amos looked to me for approval while selecting an empty place, as close to the door as he could get and I nodded my approval. Amos hesitated slightly before he reluctantly perched on the edge of his seat. Then he immediately twisted to the side while attempting to see the other students sitting around him. Amos continued to move non-stop for the first three minutes in my class and I began to get tired observing his nervous mannerisms.

That first morning Amos appeared almost frantic to assess his environment and I wondered if he might be counting objects or be afflicted with some other ritualistic behavior I had previously seen evidenced by students who had OCD (Obsessive Compulsive Disorder). However, when Amos made a half-turn with his face to view the hall door as other classes passed by, I caught a clue to the source of this student's hyper-vigilance. I observed slight skin discolorations on both his cheek bones, the kind of color variations which are hardly noticeable on people who have darker skin. This unusual showing through of darker blues or purples would hardly be noticeable unless a person had received training and knew what they could represent.

As I observed Amos, the face of another child flashed through my mind, a child who was sat under an ultraviolet light by a physician to determine if there was evidence of bruising under his skin. While remembering I must have starred a little too long at my new student because my observations did not go unrecognized by him. When Amos realized I was studying him he smiled brightly at me and revealed a shiny gold incisor. Another student gapped when he saw Amos's tooth, raised his hand for permission to speak, and said, "Man where you get that?"

I nodded at Amos giving him permission to talk and he reported to the class that his mother was a nurse and she had bought him the golden tooth because he had an accident. He had broken his real tooth off and the damage was so bad that only gold could be used to repair it. One student let out a "Whew" and then commented, "I wish I could break off my tooth and get one like that!" Most of Amos's classmates nodded and another said "Yip, me too! I would go home and knock out both my front teeth if my momma would buy me gold ones! I think gold teeth are fly!" The whole class seemed impressed with Amos and his extreme bling. I knew this authentic golden tooth was bound to make Amos popular with his classmates. Teachers at our school had been confronting students for weeks about chewing foil candy bar wrappers in class while forming imitation bling in their mouths; these classmates had been simulating golden teeth.

Amos seemed delighted at the other students' attention. He smiled even wider to show as much of the tooth as possible and he began to evidence his growing comfort in class by pulling his legs up under him while he maneuvered to sit on his feet. I was glad when Amos relaxed a little because his moves could excite some other students who were also hyper. I was ready to move on to the days' work when I noticed Amos had turned the identification badge on his shirt around to hide his picture from view.

"Hey new kid, Amos, turn your badge around and sit down correctly! If you continue to sit on your feet you will cut off the blood supply to your brain and you are going to need your brain in my class!" Amos put his feet down but did not turn his badge around. "Amos, teachers need to see your picture and be able to read your name on your ID at all times. Now, please turn it around this instant. If you do not wear your badge correctly, I will keep you after school for detention. We don't play here; the sooner you follow the rules the sooner you can get back to your friends and your home school."

Amos responded, "I don't like my picture."

I was becoming impatient with my new student's attitude and I snapped, "I did not ask you if you liked your picture and I do not care if you like your picture. I asked you politely to turn your badge around but now I am telling you... do it now or you will be saying after school!" I glared at the boy until he swallowed hard, looked at other students for clues to what might happen, and was rewarded with head nods and finger twist motions indicating that he should do as I said. Now, I was determined to impress upon this student the identification badge etiquette that was required at our alternative school. I began to lecture about not coming to school without an official school ID, replacement fines when the badges were lost or disfigured, and the need to follow our school rules at all times. My current students had just completed this rule review at the first of the week and I could see some eye rolling and feet shuffling going on while I focused on our new student. However, I felt like I needed to immediately indoctrinate this new seventh grader because his assigned group was exceptionally immature and he looked like he was going to fit into the crowd all too well.

After my unfriendly tirade I chastised myself, a little, for being so negative to this student on his first day. Amos really did not seem like a kid who would make trouble on purpose. Instead, his actions reminded me of a small furry animal caught in a trap that was prepared to gnaw off its foot to be free. I had the distinct impression this kid could bolt and run without warning and his hyper eye and body movements were done in preparation for the break. During attendance taking, he continued to fidget in annoying ways which made me fearful for his safety. I could not allow him to rock his desk around; I knew he might fall out of his seat and hit his head on our tiled concrete floor.

Once again, Amos was getting ready to perch on his feet when I smiled at him and nodded my head downward. Amos said "Oh!" as he registered recognition of my meaning and he adjusted himself to a proper seating position. When he did this I had a revelation that Amos seemed to be more in tune with the non-verbal cue I just gave him compared to verbal directions. I made a mental note to try non-verbal discipline cues first with this student. I reminded myself that Amos would be watching my facial expressions closely and that I should take care that my words and actions match. Amos was one of those kids who had learned people's actions are more truthful than their words and he had learned to watch adults instead of listening to them.

While I assessed my new student's attributes, I groaned within because I realized the science activity I had planned for the day was Pollyanna foolishness. My new student along with his equally energetic classmates would run amuck in our middle school hallway if I proceeded with my lab plans. I needed to adjust my processing activity quickly because all my young scientist were showing signs of wanting to break free and run; they were twisting in their seats, absent-mindedly rocking back and forth, and some had begun mouthing words to a rap song while drumming on their desk. When I surveyed the classroom, I just knew they could not handle the extra freedom they would be given in the hall and they would probably disturb other classes.

It was late winter or early spring depending upon a person's perception and I was not personally immune to the cabin fever phenomenon that had recently overtaken our student population. These learners were not the only ones who wanted to leave the confinements of our small classrooms for larger spaces. The math teacher had been marching her students outside the rear entrance and had been allowing them to sit on the concrete steps warmed by the sun while doing their in-class assignments. Earlier in the week, I had allowed eighth grade students to create a model of the solar system with string measurements to help them discover the concept of distance in space.

However, today it was too cold to go outside without coats and the students' outer-wear were all locked away safe until school departure time. It was a school rule that students could not have hoodies or coats in the classrooms because things could be concealed in the linings of this clothing or obscured in hidden pockets. My students had to stay inside because it was too cold to venture out without coats and the cabin fever epidemic would continue. I could not trust these rambunctious youth with the privilege of open hallway spaces and I was disappointed because I too was feeling hemmed in.

When I created the hallway lab alternative I was not expecting a new student to enter into our midst on Tuesday; usually new students attended intake on Tuesdays. For this reason, I had purposely set my lab days for Tuesday and I tried not to do clinicals on days I received new kids. I usually waited a couple of days until I made assessment of the student's propensity for violence before turning them lose with glass and metal weapons. However, I was used to adapting my lesson plans in order to adjust for new student's personalities. I had learned to expect the unexpected at our alternative school and Amos was certainly unexpected!

I spoke to myself, "I need a processing activity that will allow the students to mellow out and it needs to go along with our learning objective. Maybe… drawing will take the edge off their anxious behaviors." I knew most of my students loved to draw, it had a calming effect on them, and diagramming science concepts was a perfect substitute for my group lab that day. First, the lesson… I had to gain the students' attention quickly. So, I began with a story that would help students understand the body's physical response to stress.

"How many of you have ever been to Chicago, Illinois?" I ventured. No one raised their hand so I continued, "How many of you have ever heard of Chicago?" All raised their hands so I knew I had their attention and without delay I jumped into my story. "One time about six years ago, a friend and I traveled to Chicago to attend training. I was working for the public health department and my job was to identify babies who might be at risk for abuse and neglect and my friend's job was to provide education and help parents take care of their babies without hurting them. We both liked our jobs but we did not like the idea of traveling so far from our homes or being away from our families for a whole week. I had been to Chicago many times before and had even driven to Chicago by myself but this time it was different because we would be staying at a hotel in a part of town that could be dangerous after dark.

Now, the location of our hotel was a big problem because it was wintertime and in Chicago it can be dark at four-thirty in the afternoon. Our training did not get out until four and we had to walk back to our hotel after we finished. On the first day, we made a decision just to stop at a sandwich shop we saw along our walking route and take the food back to our hotel room. However, the second night we were better prepared and had used a hotel map to identify a museum in walking distance from our training area and we decided we would visit the museum. Again, we just grabbed a sandwich on the way back.

By the third night we were more comfortable with the city and we decided to walk to an Italian restaurant a little bit farther away because we were starved for a hot meal. After our supper, we ventured back out on the streets to discover several of the lamp posts were out; there were whole sections of the street which were in darkness. We talked about going back inside and about calling a cab but we had limited money and we still had two more days to stay in Chicago. We knew we needed to save our money for a cab ride to the airport on Friday, so we started walking. My friend and I were careful to walk only in the lit part of the street and we criss-crossed back and forth over to the sides of the street where there was the most light. Also, we tried to stay close to other large groups of people.

However, soon the crowd thinned leaving just my friend and me alone on the street and our path suddenly looked black ahead. None of the street lights in the one block area straight ahead of us were turned on. We could see a hotel at the end of the dark trail and it was clearly our hotel because we could read its name in fuzzy appearing lights across its' top. Since we were so close to our destination we made a decision to continue walking toward our goal through the darkness. After all, it was only a block away or so we thought. Once committed to that direction we noticed that we had to walk farther than a block and we had misjudged the distance. We continued with caution because we were the only pedestrians on that part of the street. That's when it happened!

A dark figure of a man peered out from an alley we passed and he began following us. We picked up our speed and his footsteps became louder and more rapid just like ours. When we stopped he stopped and because he did this, we knew he was trying to cover the fact he was following us. We turned to confront the man and said, 'We know you are following us and we are prepared for you.' The figure melted back into the darkness but we knew he was still there. As we pulled our hand bags closer around and to the front of our bodies we walked purposely toward the hotel while taking turns looking over our shoulders to check the progress of our would-be assailant. Our pursuer began running toward us just as we approached the well lit intersection in front of our hotel but he turned off and went another direction when we whirled to face him. We foiled his final attempt at theft because we showed him we were aware of his intent and were prepared to fight him if necessary. We were safe but it took a while for my heart to slow down and my mouth felt dry and fuzzy. I noticed that my muscles were tense, I had begun to perspire, and I felt a little nauseated. When we were standing in the street light before we crossed to our hotel I noticed that the pupils in my friend's eyes were dilated and she was shaking a little."

After finishing my story, I began a discussion, "Do you think it is normal to shake or feel sick at your stomach when you get stressed out or feel scared? Why do think our bodies react that way when we become afraid?" I let the students name common physical reactions to stress they had experienced when they had become afraid and I showed them a large chart of all the different body changes that can take place while explaining the purpose of those physical stress reactions. Then, I had students open their textbooks to view a diagram with their vocabulary terms "Fight or flight "at the top of the picture. While the students diagramed the human body's physical responses to stress I moved around the classroom overseeing their progress and providing needed supplies.

When I came to Amos's desk he said, "Mrs. Gifford I am afraid my heart will burst out of my chest cause I am scared like that all of the time. I have a lot of stress in my life. I carry an axe around the house and try not to go to sleep until my mom comes home from work. She works at night, I know she has to do it, but I am afraid the whole time she is gone. Will my heart explode and will I die if I don't get relief from this stress?"

Amos appeared that he was serious and he was asking for help. It was seldom a child disclosed anything that was personal so quickly to me. Nevertheless, there was something about his manner that made me believe him. I asked, "Doesn't anyone stay with you when you mother goes to work?" I was thinking maybe the mother did not realize how being alone at night worried her son. Amos was probably old enough to stay by himself during daylight hours but he was showing signs of stress from staying home at night by himself. I reasoned to myself that sometimes parents can't afford childcare and finding a night-time childcare provider is rare. Surely, there was a relative or a friend who would take care of Amos if he would just tell his mother.

Amos carefully and slowly answered, "Sometimes I am alone but most times my stepfather is there. He drinks and he tells momma he don't, but he does... when she is gone. When he gets drunk he does stuff and

I hit him in the head with a hammer last time. That's why I am here at this school. My step daddy said he would tell the judge to send me to jail for a long time where I could not see my mamma if I told what he done. He wanted me out the house but mamma said no and she would give me another chance. So my step daddy told the judge he just wanted me to be sent here." Amos looked at me with desperate eyes, "You said you use to help babies so they would not be abused. Well, I'm abused and need help."

I calmly told Amos, "I will do my best to help you, Amos, but I need to know if you want me to call your mother first and tell her what is going on. She doesn't know, right?"

Amos panicked at the thought of calling his mother because he said his stepfather would kill both of them. Apparently, this is what Amos had been told. I kept Amos after class and as the other students went to lunch, I told Amos I was required by law to tell child welfare authorities what he had reported to me. "It may take about three days before anyone from the child welfare system comes out and then there will be an investigation. In the meantime, can you stay all night with a friend or have someone stay all night with you. Your stepfather doesn't bother you when you have someone sleep over does he?"

Amos and I worked out a safety plan during our lunch period and I let him call his mother on my class phone to get permission to sleep over at a friend's house. Amos said his friend knew about the stepfather and the abuse but he had been sworn to secrecy. Amos's friend said he would stay all night with Amos the next night if CPS (Child Protective Services) did not come to investigate. I was praying Amos would be safe for a couple of days due to our safety plan and CPS would respond quickly to the allegations I was getting ready to report.

I dreaded making the report because every time I had made reports in the past, CPS had been slow to respond. After all, Amos did not come out and say he was being sexually abused. He only implied his stepfather did stuff to him when he was drunk. I knew better than to ask too many questions because the investigation could be tainted and I could be accused of putting ideas in Amos's mind. I was careful to use Amos's exact words when I made the report. I found the forms I needed on the agency's website to report Amos's suspected abuse, stopped short of filling them out, and sought a conference with my principal. "Do you have a minute? I have a situation I need to report to child protective services and I wanted to keep you informed."

I went on to explain the context in which the student shared his highly personal information with me. After I exposed the possible abusive situation, my principal advised, "You can't believe these kids. They're apt to say anything just to play you and cause trouble."

I interrupted him before he philosophically dismissed Amos's fears, "I know the kinds of children we serve and I agree with you about their possible motives. However, according to the law it is not our job to determine if children are telling the truth and we are required to report it. If I had ten incidents told to me by children and only one turned out to be true then that would be good enough for me. One child who is being abused is one child too many."

"Alright, but…you will have to wait till the counselor comes back because she handles these kinds of reports. She will be gone till Friday and then you and her can get together the next Monday. I have other things for her to do when she gets back which take priority." I fumed as I left the office, I fumed as I walked back to my room, and I fumed as I filled out the form on the computer and sent it on its way. I purposely disregarded my administrator's instructions because I knew he was wrong!

I puzzled to myself the rest of the day, "Was the conversation I had with my principal birthed out of ignorance or purpose?" I felt he would not be happy to know I had gone against his directives so I waited until he left for the day and placed a note in his box which said, "The form on the CPS website said I am a mandated reporter and I need to report all suspected abuse and neglect within hours not days. The penalties for not reporting include being charged with a felony, being fined, and I could lose my teacher's license if I don't report in a timely manner. Therefore, I made the report myself and here is a copy of the form." The next day, I ran into the principal in the front office and he asked me for the web site address and I told him I could do better than that and I handed him a stapled reference packet about mandate reporting with the web site address. I realized he probably did not know what needed done and had only demonstrated a learning curve when he gave me the faulty advice.

The investigation happened on Friday, the first day the counselor returned. In addition to my report there had been a second report filed by a mental health counselor Amos had been seeing at his former school. I spoke to this counselor when he came to our school to see Amos and he reported Amos had told him about the abuse during his first counseling session. I surmised this student was either playing a game or he was desperate for help. Amos had not known either of his reporters long enough to build a relationship with us when he shared his story. It seemed that Amos did not require trust before asking strangers for help and he was willing to risk his situation. I was puzzled until I considered the clues I gleaned from observing this child's behavior. He was hyper-vigilant and he responded better to my non-verbal cues than to my words. I had seen those characteristics in other abused children. For that reason, I was certain Amos shared out of desperation.

The outcome of Amos's case was not clear and due to confidentiality laws which the child protective agency had adhered to, the only thing I found out was that my report was ruled unfounded. However, I saw Amos meeting with the CPS investigator in our school library due to the second report made by the counselor, I recognized her because she had interviewed me, and this time the outcome was different. The second report filed by the mental health worker must have been more specific because Amos was removed from our school within two weeks of the reported incident and I was told that he was placed in child welfare custody.

Discussion

It may worry some parents when their children report allegations of abuse to strangers before talking to them. Parents can be completely blindsided by their child's accusations and in some cases, parents may truly be unaware of their own child's plight. However, none of us should be surprised because adults who prey on children are masters of manipulation; they know how to intimidate kids to keep them quiet. In some ways the emotional abuse committed by child predators while trying to ensure their anonymity is almost worse than their damaging physical assaults. Here are some of their tricks: (1) your mother or father will be jealous and will not love you anymore if they find out what happened (2) You will be punished and taken away from your family and put into foster care and never see your mom or dad again if you tell (3) I won't hurt your sister or brother if you let me do what I want (4) I will kill your puppy or pet if you tell (5) I will

315

kill you and your family if you tell (6) No one will believe you because you are a child and I am the adult (7) Your mom or dad loves me more than they love you and they won't do anything about it. These are a few of the statements children reported to me that were made by their perpetrators when I worked in foster care. Abusers do manipulate children by making them believe they will receive unfair consequences for telling the truth. So children may after disclosing the truth lie when questioned by authorities. In our story about Amos his stepfather convinced him that he had the power to send Amos away from his mother and to jail for a very long time. Amos had committed a crime when he hit his step-father in the head with a hammer; he had been arrested and tried, and he was sent to our school by the judge hearing the case. Amos was convinced that his stepfather had agreed to the alternative school placement instead of Amos receiving jail time and his stepfather used that deception to get Amos to go along with the abuse. The abuse must have intensified because Amos determined to kill his stepfather with an axe the next time the abuse was attempted. The hammer had not worked as well as he had intended! **Why do children talk to strangers about their life events which cause them pain?**

Being objective is very difficult when a child is exposing their abuse. The best response to give in that situation may be, "I am sorry that happened to you." Don't quiz the child and just let them say what they are going to say because you could taint an investigation by pumping a child for more information. Sometimes children will embellish and make up fantastic details if the person they are exposing their abuse to has a dramatic and emotionally charged reaction. Any concerned person can make a report and everyone who works with children are mandated reporters. If you are not sure you are one, then go to the state site and become informed and search the web for more information on the signs of child abuse. **Under what circumstances would you call the police instead of making a child abuse report?**

There are some children at higher risk than others for abuse. Children who are disabled or developmental delayed may often be targets because they cannot protect themselves and may not be able to communicate their abuse. Very young children who lack cognitive ability and language development to comprehend and explain what has happened to them are also at high risk. Children may often suffer abuse when they are given over to the care of an adult which is not their biological parent and has no bond with them. Today with an increase of blended families and paramour relationships this could be a larger concern than what it once was. However, child abuse occurs in epidemic proportions in certain segments of our populations; there is a high correlation between caregivers who abuse drugs and alcohol and commit child abuse. Remember, Amos indicated his stepfather lied to his mother about drinking alcohol when she was at work? **Use what you have learned about child abuse to create a list of factors that create a high risk situation for children.**

When children are experiencing abuse at home they may manifest signs of always being on edge or have angry outburst. Certainly, many abused children show signs of post traumatic stress disorder and some may initiate conflict to get adrenaline highs. Humans living in a high stress situation may get addicted to the natural stress hormones released by their own bodies and may not feel normal without them. They may hurt other children and be disrespectful to teachers or other adults to initiate conflict and manipulate their own body's chemistry. However, each child will react differently to abuse and some children may just withdraw. One thing is certain, it is harder for these children to learn in school and they may be diagnosed with learning disabilities. **Could we catch child abuse early if families were required to complete a social history when their children are diagnosed with learning disabilities? Should an investigation into family life be required along with a cognitive assessment?**

Topics for Research:

Are males or females more often the target of child sexual abuse? What is the punishment for mandated reporters in your state who fail to report the abuse and neglect of a child? Can you tell by a child's behavior alone that abuse might be occurring? Does your school district offer yearly child abuse identification and report training for school staff? Should schools get involved in teaching parenting skills to students' parents?

Things to Do

Take training and volunteer at a shelter for abused children. Become a licensed foster parent and provide care for abused children. Give an abused child a permanent home by adopting them from foster care. Create support services for foster parents at your church or community organizations. Foster parents need extra food and clothes for children because they are not paid in advance but only reimbursed for expenses they have already incurred while caring for children. In some situations, foster parents may suddenly receive children around the holidays (This is when alcohol/drug use increases along with family violence) and may need Christmas presents for additional children. For more ideas how you can help abused and neglected children, search the web for agency names that provide services to these children. I'm sure they will make suggestions how you can help.

If you are a parent, talk to your kids! Let your children know that you will always love them and you will always listen to them. Tell them if anyone makes them feel uncomfortable by something they say or do, even friends or family members, they should tell you. Always believe your child, especially small children who may be confused about what has happened to them and may not have the vocabulary to describe the situation. Most important watch for behavioral changes in your children which cannot be explained by normal life events they have experienced.

If you are a teacher, don't consider children brats that act out in your classroom. Children have stress in their lives too and you may need to track the child's behavior, figure out what triggers their episodes, and what calms them. Most of all stay calm and become consistent with your own behaviors because some of our abused students live in chaotic and unpredictable environments. They need predictability!

26. Child Abuse

Recently, the issue of child abuse and neglect and how it can relate to a student's academic failure was exposed in a film which was nominated for several academy awards. There is one particular poignant scene in the movie which shows an alternative school teacher trying to help her student learn to read. The teen girl's mind was occupied with reliving the trauma from her abuse and she could not focus well enough to decipher letters or decode words which are essential skills for reading (Precious). I'm sure this one scene may have caused some teachers in the theater audience to relive similar experiences they have had with their own students because it certainly brought up past spectras to my mind. However, most educators today may not make the connection between their students' learning difficulties and their students' possible child abuse or neglect profile.

Instead, students may be labeled as emotionally behavior disturbed, a label which is often assigned to students who cannot learn and who do not have documented disabilities, by school staff when they seek special educational services. The EBD label and the services provided these students do not necessarily guarantee academic success; according to an article in the Journal of Negro Education, "EBD students are more likely to drop out of school than their disabled and non-disabled peers" (Osher, David, Morrison...). For this reason, it appears that education, the great equalizer may not be able to equalize the effects of child abuse and neglect when it is the root of an EBD student classification. The facts show that regardless of our expertise and training, teachers are accomplishing little to prevent EBD students from dropping out of school. Therefore, maybe our current nomenclature is wrong and perhaps we are missing the target by providing services which are too generic to meet this population's needs. Some of our EBD students could be like Precious or like Amos from our preceding story and they could still be living in abusive environments which could negate their abilities to learn. Their emotional and physical healths are at risk due to their living milieus and until their environments change, they may not be able to focus on getting an education.

Family emotional health has an impact on every human being because all of us are raised in some type of a family. According to T. Berry Brazleton, a child development expert, "Every child needs someone to fall madly, crazy, fully out-of-control in love with them." However, the basic emotional, human need for love may be ignored in some families and perverted in others. Families that produce children who clearly demonstrate emotional problems and who echo behavior maladjustments are unhealthy families. As an educator, I have seen patterned academic failure in kids coming from the same family and I have heard other teachers bemoan the prospect of receiving a student in class whose familiar family surname has the distinction of producing low performing, trouble-making, special education students. These families' dysfunctions are well known and documented through the failures of their offspring but official family health assessments may have never been completed or even suggested. Instead, the children bare the brunt of their families' ridicule and teachers may add insult to injury by heaping low-expectations upon these students' heads. These non-specific, special-education students may then perform as their teachers expect due to the Pygmalion effect because "One person's expectations about another person can cause a person to achieve or behave as expected" (Brehm & Kassin, 1996).

These students are doomed to failure because they receive a misnomer, an educational label of emotionally behavior disordered when they are really environmentally at risk. Some youth are failing to get an education because their families and neighborhoods are toxic. The urban boarding schools we learned about in the previous strategy have recognized the plight of inner city youth and some give priority to students who are homeless or living in dysfunctional families. Certainly, a boarding school assignment would have been welcomed by some my students who hid out in abandoned buildings to avoid gang activity or who, like Amos carried around an axe for protection in his own home. These students may in fact be emotionally behavior disturbed but their disturbance is relevant to their family life and neighborhood. When placed in the context of their living situations these students' behaviors may be highly ordered, not disordered, and may serve as communication attempts while these youth seek relief from their unsafe and unpredictable worlds. Evaluating risk factors in the lives of these students and offering services based on those risk factors makes more sense than classifying students as disturbed because they demonstrate aberrant behaviors.

Student risk factors parallel parent risk factors and here are some that have been identified by child abuse authorities. The profile of abusive or neglectful parents is as follows: "Single parents, *who bare*, the sole responsible of care giver to a child. Usually with little or no family or friends to assist them. They are lonely, did not plan their pregnancy, have little or no knowledge of child care and child development, and have unrealistic beliefs of child behavior. Substance abuse is a common finding in families of abused children" (Why Child Abuse Occurs...). In spite of common held beliefs about child abuse, mothers are responsible for 39% of substantiated cases and "African American, Pacific Islander, American Indian, and Alaska Native children had the highest rates of victimization (National Victim Assistance Academy, 2007). The research from the NVAA documents that mothers who are: single parents, are substance abusers, who do not have anyone to share the role of caregiver with, and know little about child development are at the greatest risk for abusing their children. Therefore, because single parenting women are at the greatest risk for abusing their children future generations of students may continue to copy aberrant behavior unless we successfully educate young women and help them overcome their substance abuse issues. One source that interprets census information for urban areas says, "Educated parents are the best path to educated kids" (narpac.org/PERENTS.HTM.) It seems that the predictor this group identified for student success was parents' academic success.

Therefore, it makes sense for public schools to complete family risk assessments and to offer educational services to all family members in the district who wish to improve their living situation. In some cases, the assessments might need to be mandatory when children manifest an emotionally behavior disturbance. Some of these special education students might need placement in urban boarding schools if family assessments prove their environments are toxic. However, the goal of assessments would be to promote family health. Assessing family health could be part of a person-centered education model and it could have many benefits; (1) parents could learn about family emotional health and set goals to improve students' living environments (2) parents could learn parallel discipline methods which might compliment what is being used at their child's school making the student's environment more predictable and eliminating some discipline problems (3) parents could be motivated to complete their own education and set a good academic examples for their kids (4) parents might receive job training and improve their marketing potential and income level thereby reducing stress in family life (5)child abuse might be prevented because parents could be socially supported by their local school's involvement and (6) parents could receive referrals and help for social problems like substance abuse which may be causing a negative home environment and may be at the root of parents' child abuse and neglect issues. Many inner city low income parents have multiple needs for social services, supportive environments, and educational or job training alternatives for themselves. (Where are social services needed the most?) Education might have to become a family affair and schools might need to pare with community social services when family assessments are used.

As a former foster parent for specialized and treatment level foster children who had been abused and neglected, I know that often times the only things a child needs to gain academic success are a safe environment, a structured family life, and emotional support to overcome their traumas. Education alone, even if it is specialized, cannot meet the needs of children who are experiencing life trauma. We need to evaluate family health and target services for our students based on those evaluations. Special education has tried to meet the needs of all students and I admire special education teachers for the work they do. I don't believe it is their fault EBD students drop out of school at a higher rate than other groups. Instead, I believe we have not targeted the services well enough for this one group. Family health assessments and family educational services could be the key to this one group's success.

Appropriate education that fosters academic success can be a strategy for our at risk students because education has the potential to restore, to some degree, a child's feelings of self-worth. Experts have confirmed that higher self esteem is a sign of emotional health, that the school environment plays an important role in building self-esteem in children's lives, and abuse and neglect victims demonstrate a deficit of self-worth. Adolescents with low self-esteem are more often judged depressed and rank lower on psychological and psycho-physiological measures of anxiety, on overt aggression, irritability, and anomie (Margret Francis; Rosenberg in Changing Minds.org). Therefore, education may be the great equalizer for these students but unless, we step back a generation to educate their parents we may not be able to help these students. Public schools providing parent education services make sense for this one unique population of at risk students.

When thinking about targeting a specific group of students for educational reform, this one group, abused and neglected children who may receive a non-specific EBD classification in our special education programs, is a good place to start. Not only could it make a difference in the academic outcome for millions of students, a reform which recognized and used family health as a person centered model could improve the lives of under educated, lower economic, stressed out parents. Therefore, all the people in the family could benefit and maybe the patterned academic failure of siblings could be contradicted.

According to census information, the number of single parents continues to increase about "3.9% a year with one-parent, situations being higher among African Americans than other groups. Single parents accounted for almost two-thirds (65 percent) of all Black groups with children present compared with twenty-five percent among whites" (US Census Bureau, Rawlings). This brings us back to the inner city racial demographics that work against large school districts and lead us to a conclusion that young black women need our help. Once the backbone of their families and respected for their dedication to family values, it appears now that generations of young women have given into social pressure to: use drugs and alcohol, become pregnant as teenagers, join gangs, and live in poverty with their children who they have a propensity to abuse or neglect due to their substance abuse. Substance abuse plays a huge role in the profile change in this one group. Young women in general, all races included, have increased their use of illicit substances and child abuse and neglect correlate highly with that increased use.

Therefore, a previous educational reform we have talked about makes sense for all these young misguided, urban students. One of the most amazing educational reforms to be implemented in recent years is urban boarding schools. Combining educational reforms like single-sex education in boarding school environments and supporting students with family living education may be the straw that breaks the cycle of child abuse and neglect, single-parent poverty, and substance abuse in urban areas. These are the social plagues which produce many of our EBD students and contribute to their academic failure (www.narpac.org/...).

Can we in good conscious continue to label children as trouble making, low-performing, special education students (EBD) when they are hurting and being victimized? Human compassion should inspire us to complete this type of educational reform. When EBD students drop out of school they may experience not just negative but life-altering consequences. Current national survey data reveals that 73% of students classified as EBD will be arrested within three to five years after leave-taking their education. There are a lot of reasons that educational reforms need to target this group of students.

In 1999, the U.S. Department of Education mandated that states had to establish performance indicators to be used to assess progress toward reducing dropout rates of students with disabilities (U.S. Department of Education, 1999). In spite of that edict, special education students still have the highest dropout rates and one segment of that population, EBD students fare worse than the rest. Emotional behavior disordered children are at extreme risk for academic failure and negative life consequences. We need a new approach and mandating a family assessment for emotional health and social risk factors would be a good place to begin. Just saying these students have an undefined educational need is not enough because the services they receive may not be appropriate.

References and Resources

Osher, David, Morrison, Gale, Bailey, Wanda (2003). Journal of Negro Education, "Exploring the relationship between student mobility and dropout among students with emotional and behavioral disorders," http://findarticles.com/p/articles/mi_qa3626/is_200301/ai_n9186102/ Retrieved 9 September 2010

Child welfare Information Gateway, "Child Maltreatment 2007: Summary of key Findings; "Who reported child maltreatment? and Where are social services needed the most?" Year published 2009. http://www.childwelfare.gov/pubs/factsheets/canstats.cfm

"Why Child Abuse Occurs…," Childabuse.com; Prevention Through Education and Awareness. http://www. Childabuse.com/fs19.htm Retrieved 9 Sept. 2010

Steve Rawlings. "Population Profile of the United States," U.S. Census Bureau. Http://www.census.gov/population/www/pop-profile/hhfam.html Retrieved 9 Sept. 2010

Brehm, S.S., & Kassin, S.M. (1996). Social Psychology. Boston: Houghton Mifflin.

Margret Francis. "Self-Esteem," in Changing Minds.org; http://changingminds.org/articles/self_esteem.htm

Single Parents Demographics, narpac.org/PERENTS.HTM.

Resource Manual, National Victim Assistance Academy, 2007. "Child Abuse and Neglect," authored by Mario Gaboury, Ph.D., University of New Haven; and reviewed and edited by Anne Seymour, Justice Solutions, Inc. Washington, D.C. https://www.octtac.gov/navaa2008/documents/resource-cd/Child%20Abuse.pdf Retrieved 9 Sept. 2010

27. Targeted Education Reforms

Now that readers have met some of my students and have had an opportunity to experience vicariously the challenges educators face when teaching inner city youth, we can begin together to reform education. In fact, over the past ten years education reform efforts have been initiated and some are well under way. Both urban boarding schools and single-sex education programs hold promise for at-risk students. According to innovators who have implemented use of these two models, the reforms are successful because they change classroom environments by removing some distractions and they help students feel safe. Safe classrooms have long been an issue for large city educators and students coming from gang and drug infested neighborhoods. Experts referenced earlier in this book have stated that students cannot learn when they feel unsafe. For this reason, school safety should be the primary target of education reforms and the first question reformers might ask themselves when creating initiatives, designing models, or seeking additional funding is, "Does the proposed reform make schools safer?"

Student dress codes and uniforms make schools safer because they help students adjust their focus on school and lessen students' concerns with gang activities. We want students to recognize and respect the neutrality of our learning environments and requiring students to wear school uniforms along with other dress code standards (haircuts, jewelry, and other things) promote gang detachment during the school day. The National Teachers' Association recommended uniform dress as one of its principle interventions to eliminate gang activity in our urban schools. Yet, less than one-fourth of school districts who serve students from gang populated areas require their students to wear uniforms. School safety is compromised when students are allowed to vary their dress to show gang affiliation and violence can result when gang members from different groups try to stake a claim on turf that belongs to taxpayers, our public schools. Requiring students to wear school uniforms can make our schools safer. Therefore, uniform dress is a reform that needs to be revisited by school districts that are struggling with gang populations and gang initiated school violence. This reform will not cost additional state or federal government spending nor will it break school districts' budgets. For zero dollars, we can make our schools safer if we implement this one change.

Students using and selling drugs at school is definitely a safety issue. Youth are placed at risk for harm while in the care of educators if drug use at schools is allowed to continue. Groups of middle school students across the United States have been taken to the hospital in recent years because they became sick and were at risk for dying after using drugs at school. This student safety risk factor can no longer be ignored! All of our dog-sniffing, drug testing, and student arrests have not diminished drug use significantly in our schools and school districts have faced legal consequences while trying to enforce some of their zero tolerance policies. It is time for a new approach and a no refusal policy should replace zero tolerance. Educators should be allowed to refer any student to the office for drug testing based on physical and behavioral indicators. Teachers should be trained to identify these in a scientific manner and document their observations. Under the no refusal policy, parents would have the right to refuse drug testing for their child so individual student rights would be retained because students would be given a choice. However, when a parent refuses on behalf of their child then that student would be declared guilty of using drugs at school. Schools could legally refuse traditional classroom attendance until proof was furnished by the parent that their child was not using drugs or their child had received an evaluation by professional substance abuse experts. Schools could develop stepped consequence procedures to document attempts made by school personnel to identify and refer students for treatment and the parents' cooperation or lack thereof. Educators would be alerting parents to their child's behavior and possible health needs by using a no refusal policy. If the student's drug test was negative then documentation of the student's behavior and physical symptoms could be useful for special education referrals or family doctor evaluations.

Keeping students safe at school is part of every educator's job and we have been given the legal authority to do so under locus parentis rights. Zero tolerance has not worked well for schools for a variety of reasons exposed earlier in this text but a no refusal policy holds potential because it is legal, does not violate a person's right to choose, effective because all students would be subject to drug testing, and could greatly diminish drug use at school. This reform, like the previous one, would not cost taxpayers, governments, or school districts. Parents would pay for testing, treatment, or other expenses associated with their child's drug use through public or private means. In addition, public income assistance, like earned income tax credit, could be withheld from some families to reimburse government programs for drug testing and treatment. This type of a policy would increase parent involvement and motivate parents to seek help for their children's drug use problems.

This one policy change could improve the academic success of all public school students by reducing the incidents of drug induced misbehavior in our classrooms and the drama it causes during the school day, save school districts unnecessary legal fees when parents oppose their child's drug testing, and identify students drug use before addictions develop. This one targeted education reform has the potential to greatly lessen, if not eliminate drugs from our schools. A simple change in school policy and working closer with parents to identify drug use in schools is an easy, inexpensive fix. More important this reform would make schools safer for kids because drug dealing activities and gang turf disputes should lesson in our schools while school liability would decrease.

Student health is another reason why drug testing policies should change. Many of our students are overweight and developing type two diabetes and others may have high-blood pressure. A higher liability for athletic directors and coaches has resulted from the increased medical concerns students are presenting. Exercise, the one thing most children in the United States need more of, may in fact cause sudden death of students participating in physical education classes or sport competitions when these students are using drugs. Comprehensive health education classes should be required in every school across the United States because our students' health and their very lives could be at risk. In addition, students are receiving deadly consequences associated with having unprotected sex. This fact is witnessed by youth between the ages of 13 -24 year showing the highest increase in new HIV positive tests and receiving AIDS diagnoses. Many times drug or alcohol use among teens precipitate students having unprotected sex and teen pregnancies but students have not made that connection. Teen pregnancies cost school districts money because some of these young parents will have poor attendance or drop out of school if special programs are not created to meet their unique needs. For these reasons health education has to undergo reform because school budgets cannot maintain services they already are obliged to offer if student attendance is low and teen parents drop out of school. Health education has to undergo reform to include comprehensive sex education.

Some large city school districts may not incur any opposition from parents when offering comprehensive sex education in health classes. Parents of high-risk students have been asking their school districts to provide this type of education. Concerns about keeping their kids safe, has overturned some parents' moral objections to comprehensive sex education and statistics regarding teen HIV/AIDS rates of infection should cause all parents of teens to reconsider. Requiring every teen to take health education, just a course, should not cost school districts a lot of additional funding. This is a targeted reform aimed at what our nation's youth need and it is in response to their declining health and at their lack of knowledge about health consequences they face based on life choices.

Eliminating gang activity and drug use at school are two targets for reform which are needed in some school districts more than others. However, health education is a national school issue that all districts should consider targeting and the state of children's health in the United States might initiate intervention from the Department of Health and Human Services. Public service messages like the ones being used to target cigarette use which warn citizens about their health risk have been effective to reduce smoking in our nation. Our students need specific targeted public announcements about the health risk they face and the social consequences that result from drug/alcohol use. One of these social consequences is a failure to get an education. Students do not make the connection between their abuse of substances and this outcome. We need equal time to promote our health message to these students because many of their families and neighborhoods advertise 24-7 the normalcy of drug and alcohol use.

Another area of reform we have to address is special education and specific populations within that classification who drop out of school at higher rates that their classmates. These high-risk students often become frustrated with grade retention, curriculum irrelevancy, and forced school attendance. These youth's high level of education dissatisfaction and the demands administrators place on teachers to engage these sometimes angry students can precipitate confrontations and end in teachers being assaulted in their classrooms. Our current factory education model was not designed for special needs students and it promotes student failure. A new model is needed, one that allows for different tracks of education which all lead to high school completion. The key to appropriate education for individual students is a student assessment process which creates one long term education goal per student which takes into account, students' abilities, students' interests, and parents' preference. The progress made toward the goal should be assessed every year and the goal could be changed based on student performance or students could be required to complete remediation services like Saturday school or after school tutoring to keep their goal the same.

Standardized test should only be used to place students in relevant curriculum tracks and assess students' progress toward their goals. Teachers should not be held accountable for students' failures. Administrators should retain or fire teachers based on the teacher's performance not the students 'performance; there are too many things in students' live that educators cannot control to hold them responsible for student failures. Teachers' supervisors need trained better to follow federal employment laws because even unions are powerless to force employment retention when these laws are applied. School districts could fire ineffective teachers if their administrators were more professional in this one area. There is evidence that school administrators may be creating toxic environments that become hostile when state test results are used to determine continuing employment for teachers. Use of these tests for that purpose is inherently wrong because most of the variables that go into a student's education are out of teacher's realm.

Sexual harassment, bullying, and intolerance are concerns that all education partners have identified as posing safety issues in school. Even affluent school districts have experienced episodes of bullying, some through the internet, with tragic consequences. How do we teach students to accept their own frail human attributes and show empathy for their fellow human beings? Once, schools did teach social etiquette in the form of manners or the "Golden rule," which is a global cultural principle now often ignored. Educators and parents might want to revisit the necessity and purpose of social skills classes to emphasize the consequences individuals and society face when humans treat each other inhumanly. Again, social skills instruction is just a course and implementing social skills instruction course requirements for students should not be terribly expensive. Social skills represent another targeted reform which has the potential to make schools safer.

Most of the targeted education reforms mentioned here would cost little additional education funding, some are being requested by parents, and one is necessary to save special education services and prevent students from dropping out. All of the proposed reforms promote safer classroom environments. The one I think could effectively change our student's academic outcomes the most is creating a new model that would individualize instruction for all students and be person centered. We would not let kids fail if we were teaching to the whole person; we would celebrate their accomplishments and individualize instruction to meet their ability levels and interest. We would give them safe environments to learn in and we would allow them to set their own long term education goal. The focus of educators would be their classroom relationship with learners.

At the beginning of this book, I said that the baby gangsters I taught, taught me as much as I taught them and I believe this is true. My students were emissaries of their inner city neighborhoods showing me the reasons why they were at risk for failing school and not getting their education. These students deserve a voice in the reform process and what they are telling us is pretty simple. "Make education relevant to my learning ability and individual education goal; don't discourage me by retaining me in a grade or by separating me from my age appropriate peers, and let me move fast-forward at my own speed if I have that ability. Give me the social support I need to escape dysfunctional family life and unsafe neighborhoods. Educate me about good health practices and help me avoid addiction. Celebrate with me when I achieve academic success at any level and don't make me feel dumb by failing me. After all, I may not have learned it all but I learned something!"

As a post script I would add, large city school educators are the ones taking the most heat for student failure right now and some of their students' shortcomings could strictly be the result of geographical boundaries and population demographics. Whole student populations coming from drug and gang infested neighborhoods are at risk for academic failure. Learning environments have become less than perfect due to student drug use. Our current education model is archaic and promotes students failure. Teachers are stressed, held accountable for things that can't control, and many may be leaving their chosen profession while still owing student loans, in a disillusioned state. Teachers can only work with what we are given and many of us are being given low-performing, special education students affected by multiple social issues which detract from their learning. These students are smart but they may have limited consciousness in our classrooms due to their drug use and their gang activity mindsets. It is counterproductive to blame teachers whether students cast the stones or the general public hurls media boulders. Let's just focus on our students' needs and acknowledge that it is time to reform education in the United States.